MORE RANSOM NOTES: WALK WITH JOY

Kathryn Ransom

Susan Flynn
May your life be
enriched and
blessed as you
read these stories.
Kathryn Ransom

Blauw Shack Media

Copyright © 2024 Kathryn Ransom
All rights reserved. This book may not be reproduced, in whole or in part, in any form, without written permission. Inquiries should be addressed to Blauw Shack Media (www.blauwshackmedia.com).

Blauw Shack Media

ISBN:979-8-9867313-3-9

Cover art by Kirstin Vincent

Unless otherwise noted, all Scripture quotations are from THE HOLY BIBLE, NEW INTERNATIONAL VERSION®, NIV® Copyright © 1973, 1978, 1984, 2011 by Biblica, Inc.® Used by permission. All rights reserved worldwide.

**In Dedication To
Countless Friends
for their many words of encouragement
as we endeavor to share
God's Message of Love for Each of Us**

Praise for More Ransom Notes: Walk with Joy

"Loved, loved loved your latest edition of Ransom Notes! I was so impressed with how you took our 'Fall Cleanup' and turned it into a lesson. So many powerful thoughts in this essay that I have read it several times, each time finding new takeaways." (Connie Lorenz, Springfield, IL)

"Kathy, I absolutely loved your meditation today. To be prepared, in season and out of season, is indeed one of the clarion calls of the Lord. How often do I allow the mundane tasks of the day to take over my thinking and planning? It seems to me that shame is the perpetual state of being for Christians who truly understand and appreciate their relationship with Jesus, because it's too easy, and all too often we tend to leave Him out of our plans and thoughts. Thanks for the reminder." (Lynn Poling, International Missionary)

"I LOVED this Ransom Note issue! I am sure I will be able to use it once I grasp the full depth of insights and revelations included in this creative piece! THANKS!" (Dr. John Castelein, Distinguished Professor, New Testament Studies, Lincoln Christian U., Lincoln, IL)

"As a fellow blogger to seniors—and to others who fear they are getting to that stage of life—I have long enjoyed Kathryn's Ransom Notes. She is a studious observer of the human condition and couples that talent with her love for the word of God. The result is a thoughtful challenge to her readers to look at the world in God' way."(Charles R. "Chuck" Boatman)

"I really appreciated the 'Power of a Smile' essay. I would like to share it for my Sunday devotion. There are lots of great suggestions in this article for those who find it hard to smile." (Dan Thompson, Jacksonville, IL)

"A quick note to say how much I enjoy your reflections and stories … as well as godly encouragement. You are SUCH a wonderful writer/author." (Kent Paris, Pastoral Counselor, Urbana, IL)

"This is a very timely article and obviously required a 'bit' of research. You have skillfully interwoven secular and religious themes and thoughts. God has certainly gifted you in this area." (Marilyn Britton, Springfield, IL)

Table of Contents

For Sale - Baby Shoes, Never Worn	1
Adrift at Sea for 24 Days	3
Talcum Powder or Washing Machine	6
Unused, Yellow Safety Hat	9
Grant Forgiveness = Receive Forgiveness	13
Snow person	16
Overwhelmed and Humbled	19
Loneliness & Solitude	22
Go? No Go?	24
Three Choices	27
Forty-Nine Spuds and Still Chopping	29
Angel in the Laundromat	32
Memories: What Good Are They?	35
Join The Tea Party	38
Lessons from a Blueberry Patch	42
You Have a Choice	45
What's In Your Hand?	48
"Noisy" Stillness	52
Frozen Fowl Fill a Truck	55
Peace & Quiet	58
Bear Country	61
He is There! He is Always There!	64
Abandoned? Missing in Action?	67
V-Day — A Time for Thanksgiving	70
Meaningful Conversation with Teens	72
Making a Joyful Noise	75
July - Delight of Many	77
Banana Peeling Pachyderm	80

Table of Contents (cont)

Are You a Twin? Probably Yes!	83
Job Opportunities…at 84?	86
Stillness - Solitude - Memories - Tears	89
Garden Joys and Tragedies	92
Burning Coals and a Burning Bush	96
A Jar of Frozen Pears…	99
A Trio of 'O' Words	102
Unwrapping the Gift	105
Curmudgeon - Long in the Tooth	108
Soda Jerk	111
The Value of One	114
He Hears	118
Disaster to Delicious…	121
Paul's Final Travelogue	124
A Life Experiencing Transformation	129
How Big is Big?	132
Green Apple Experiment	135
Parasites Plagued Royal Thrones	138
Pineapple Party	141
Sterilized Tomb	143
Alone and/or Lonely? What About You?	145
Invisible…Maybe a 'Hammock' Moment	148
Hurting - Healing Heart	151
He-She: Talking to God	154
Birthday Wish	157
One Bean at a Time…	159
He is Risen…	162
Celebrate New Life	165

Table of Contents (cont)

Dragon Musings…	168
Tired of Waiting?	171
Making Melody in Your Heart	175
Cruise Liner or Battleship	178
Cruise Line or Aircraft Carrier	181
Power of a Song	184
Cluck Cluck and T-Rex	187
Kings T and J	190
Sauerkraut Apple Gravy	192
The Empty Grovery Cart…	195
Tiny Turle and A Mouse	198
The Lonely Road	201
Noah and the Challenges of Life	204
The Boats Keep Coming	207
The Empty Cup	210
Lessons from a Kid	213
Banquet With a Giant	217
Chlorine to the Rescue	221
Are You a Bug?	224
Optic Challenges	227
Are You Unique???	230
Pioneer or Settler: Which Are You?	233
Rescue of the Potbellied Pig	236
Christ Follower + 'ing'	239

Preface

More Ransom Notes: Walk With Joy is the second book under the general title Ransom Notes. Initially the author began her urge to write by creating one page essays which were given out weekly to the class of adults she taught at South Side Christian Church in Springfield, Illinois. These stories were focused on real life experiences and needs of adults desiring to grow and stretch in their spiritual lives.

Working with more mature humans, she began to recognize the need for a bit of light-hearted, yet serious support and dialogue, designed to encourage and support the thirty-plus crowd. Even life-long followers of King Jesus needed to grow in their understanding of the scriptures, especially in making daily applications. Gray hair and umpteen candles lighting the annual birthday cake does not mean the individual is confined to a rocking chair.

Today's seniors are often eager to serve, go, learn, and stretch their gray cells. The Christian community needs many workers in the field, as life seems to get more complicated. Youth and adults require models of people interacting with every day challenges. How do we connect and provide for those needs? Ransom Notes was a tiny answer to that global challenge.

The general title was selected, since the author's last name was Ransom, but even more importantly, Christ paid the ransom for each of us. Each essay was based on an every day event or bit of interesting news, embedded with a spiritual connection. Generally there was a bit of dry humor sprinkled throughout the text. The key focus centered on encouraging self-reflection, action, engagement, and growth in a Christian's life and example to the world.

Eventually the author was encouraged to assemble several of the essays and produce a book, thus the birth of, Ransom Notes: Moments of Reflection, Courage, Engagement, Worship, and Humor. She spent many agonizing hours attempting to learn the art of writing, producing, and marketing a book. With the support of many, in 2019 the dream was realized and thus the adventures began for a published author.

No trip is without bumps along the way, but the fun meeting and sharing her creations with new readers, produced excitement for the eighty-plus year old. Each day she attempted to model that life and excitement does not end when the retirement checks begin. God is good and has a place in His kingdom work force for each person, regardless of their physical or spiritual age.

Each week she continued to produce a weekly Ransom Note, distributing it to several hundred readers at her church, senior living community, and through email. As the readership grew, so did the encouragement to produce book two.

Today the goal remains the same. Invite new and long-time readers to continue reading and sharing Jesus and His love with others. Hopefully More Ransom Notes: Walk With Joy will provide one tool to help you, the reader reach that goal.

CHAPTER ONE
For Sale - Baby Shoes, Never Worn

"For sale: baby shoes, never worn", is a six-word story allegedly written by Ernest Hemingway many years ago. As I read the words, my heart immediately cried out as I envisioned a mother weeping at the loss of her baby. Whether a piece of short fiction created by a great writer, or just an unsubstantiated anecdote credited to Hemingway, we will never know.

One person was overheard mumbling, "Won't need these anymore", as she tossed a pair of brand-new baby shoes into the Goodwill box. The observer noted she was holding back tears as she swallowed hard.

The grieving parents, at least, are symbolic of events in the lives of countless people. For nine months this family must have anticipated the joy (and challenges) of loving and caring for a squealing bundle of wiggles and joy. The nursery was prepared. The grandparents were anticipating sharing the wee one for a few hours at a time, only then to return the infant to the parents. No more midnight alerts for rocking, walking, or caring for a child these days. Let the parents have *their* sleep disturbed.

The delivery date arrives. Whether the baby is stillborn or dies shortly after birth, we leave it to your imagination. Nevertheless, the anticipated mountaintop experience becomes a time of despair and grief. Perhaps the grieving couple sits in the darkness near the now unneeded crib, holding hands, and wondering how they will move forward. The emptiness has canceled their joy. Dreams and plans have been shattered. Memories will exist forever in the minds of the parents.

Paul, the apostle, takes a few moments to chastise the Christians in Corinth for forgetting. In fact, he has a pair of six-word stories. In 1 Corinthians 11:17 his first message is, "I have no praise for you." What have those followers done to have a spiritual leader make such a startling statement? How would you react if told, "I have no praise for you?" Would you flinch, scream, and stomp out of the meeting, or quickly ask for forgiveness and better understanding? Few of us genuinely enjoy receiving strong criticism.

Word apparently had reached Paul that there were divisions in the church when members gathered. He acknowledges that people will have differences, but he reminds them that partaking in the Lord's Supper is not a time for discord, or even for eating your own lunch goodies. To make matters even more repugnant, word reached Paul that the rich had dinner, while others went hungry, and some got drunk. He verbally "spanks" them.

Paul continues in the rest of chapter eleven with a bit of history, relating the purpose of the Lord's Supper. He reminded the Corinthians that just before His betrayal, Christ gave thanks and broke bread. Christ said the bread represented His body, which would be broken for them, for us, and for all who follow.

And then the next six-word sermon."Do this in remembrance of me" (I Corinthians 11:24). Remembrance is the key word. The parents' memories of death and grief will be part of their burden to bear for all time. Our remembrance of Christ not only includes painful memories BUT also memories to celebrate. We think of the trauma He suffered from the trial until His burial. But we also must remember to celebrate the memories of His resurrection from the stone enclosure.

To make those memories even more joyful, we must acknowledge that His death was a sacrifice for all. He paid the penalty for us, and now, by His grace, we look forward to the fulfillment of His stupendous promise. Paul opens the curtain for all people, yes for everyone who is a follower, to take time to remember. But verse thirty-three gives the divisive group of Corinthian followers one last reminder. Eat your pancakes or eggs at home. Come, all of you, to celebrate Christ and partake of His memory celebration as you break the memorial bread and juice together. Yes, rich and poor, people of every race, age, and nationality, may participate in this joyful memory.

Remember and Honor
Christ's Death and Sacrifice for You.
Maybe Even Shed a Tear.

CHAPTER TWO
Adrift at Sea for 24 Days

It was six-thirty on a rainy Saturday morning, and as my eyes blinked open, I searched the news on my iPhone. Suddenly I was drawn to a headline, "Man Survives Nearly a Month on Ketchup and Seasonings." How could a guy do that? It certainly was not a balanced diet. And then I read on…

Elvis Francois, 47, living in the Caribbean, had just been rescued by Colombian military, after he became lost while working on his boat. His story was fascinating…so perfect for comparison with the lives of each of us as we travel through life.

Elvis, an experienced sailor since he was fifteen, was making repairs on his sailboat. The boat was not tethered or anchored while near the shore. In fact, he didn't even have an anchor, so he had nothing to hold the boat in place.

Two other men had been helping Elvis with repairs prior to his adventure. Just before the boat started moving, however, the two men had gone ashore. Elvis continued working. He was already a quarter mile from shore before he noticed the drifting taking place. The engine on the boat was not working and his cellphone reception was ineffective. He was in trouble.

Now switch to our lives as Christians. Perhaps you can remember a time when your own life was not running smoothly. Fatigue, pressures from work and family, or health issues were consuming your being. Grumpy, frazzled, weary, overwhelmed, or exhausted, you suddenly realized you were in trouble. Your life was afloat. Worship and Christian fellowship were missing. Tears and depression were sneaking into your mind and heart. Perhaps even your loyal Christian support team had stepped aside. You were alone and adrift. Your anchor in God was missing.

Realizing his perilous situation, our sailor said survival mode kicked in, and he focused on food and being rescued. He tried eating seaweed, but it was too strong, so he rummaged around in his boat.

Guess what he found? Somewhere on board was a full bottle of ketchup, garlic powder and Maggi Seasoning - packaged bouillon cubes, designed to add flavor to soups, stews, and other dishes. According to my research, each cube not only adds flavor, but contains vitamins and minerals. They may be high in nutrition, but they don't make for an exciting menu on a twenty-four-day floating experience. Even a fast-food burger, or an occasional orange would have brightened his food intake. Incidentally, the ketchup lasted only fifteen days.

I immediately thought of the Prodigal Son eating with the pigs, which probably was about as unhealthy and unappetizing as the seaweed Elvis tried first. At least the Prodigal fellow started for home. Our sailor just drifted aimlessly for almost a month. (Luke 15)

When Christians realize their spiritual life is adrift, they should also kick into survival mode. Maybe the spiritual equivalent of ketchup and garlic might be an occasional attempt to share our challenges with a friend for a few moments. Perhaps crying with total frustration, "Now I lay me down to sleep…" would help somewhat like ketchup, but it is certainly not a diet allowing for total restoration. Even sprinkled with a bit of "garlic" seasoning from a helpful friend will leave one spiritually hungry.

Francois used everything at hand to attempt to be rescued. He used a mirror to flash at airplanes flying over. He used a marker on the boat to spell out "help" and even tried sparking a fire to send a distress signal.

Eventually the mirror's reflection proved successful, and an airplane began to circle around his location. The pilot contacted a Coast Guard ship. It took teamwork - the combined efforts of the airplane crew, the Coast Guard, and our focused sailor - to make the rescue happen.

As part of the Christian family, we need to be observant, ever-vigilant for signs indicating that friends or family might be in distress or in need of a helping hand. Who is missing from class or worship service? Does a friend suddenly disappear from the eager group helping pack gifts for missionaries or working in the nursery? Is a regular attender at the men's coffee either absent or withdrawn and quiet? Quietly check in and see if a bit of support would rescue a hurting follower of God.

Obviously, there was much rejoicing with the return of the drifting sailor. But even more exciting, the Heinz company heard the story and immediately set out to locate the rescued sailor using social media. The title of their Instagram page was, #FindtheKetchupBoatGuy. 4.8 million people received the message and 4,000 "liked" the story.

In Luke 15, Jesus teaches a great parable about lost sheep. I have heard, according to one scholar, that when a sheep discovers that it has become lost, it simply sits down and bleats. Once the shepherd picks up the sound of the traumatized sheep, he follows the sound until the sheep is found. Another sheep expert said that sometimes the sheep won't make a noise at all, for fear of being found by predators instead of the shepherd. Regardless, the shepherd comes to the rescue.

So, we are the sheep of His pasture. Some of us will bleat loudly as we face traumatic experiences. Others will withdraw into quiet solitude. We must reach out and help, as we are God's servants here on terra firma. Then we will hear the Prodigal son's father say to his older, complaining offspring, "My son, you are always with me, and everything I have is yours. But we had to celebrate and be glad, because this brother of yours was dead and is alive again; he was lost and is found" (Luke 15:31-32).

This is not the end of the tale for our drifting sailor. He was given a clean bill of health, having just lost a bit of weight. But the great news: the Heinz company decided to provide Elvis with a new boat to replace the one he lost, equipped with solar panels for unlimited power and with security cameras.

Our Captain, Christ, is eager to find His lost or drifting followers. He is eager to reach out and assist in rescuing us, but He also waits patiently to welcome us home to our final dwelling with him.

Watch -- Be Ready to Call for Help When Needed
or
Reach Out to Help Others When the Call Comes

CHAPTER THREE
Talcum Powder or Washing Machine

Strange memories pop into my head as I reflect on 1953—the year of my high school graduation. The emotions of this seventeen-year-old were a mess. I strongly remember the following feelings:

- Excitement, as I anticipated receiving a diploma, thus qualifying me to enroll in a college of my choice.
- Fear, because college meant leaving the security of home, parents, and the local church family.
- Uncertainty regarding my ability to survive without words of encouragement from a loving mother.
- Pride about a summer job selling shoes in my home town, Rolla, Missouri.
- Joy of opening graduation gifts, including a set of plaid bath towels (which I still have) from a favorite aunt.
- Anticipation as I embarked upon a life with a clean slate, able to determine my own direction for the future.

One other memory, however, still stares at me each morning as I hop out of bed. Sitting on the corner of my dresser is a small box, a miniature cedar chest. Thanks to the local Null & Sons Furniture Store, each female graduate was given a mini Lane cedar chest in which to store jewelry or other trinkets or memories. Lane made over twelve million of these wooden boxes between 1912-1987. Probably the company hoped each grad would purchase a full-sized cedar creation in which to store woolen items. Why would I buy one? The oil in cedar wood repels moths, thus avoiding ugly holes in woolen items.

In researching the origin of these chests, an incredible piece of information surfaced. Evening gowns in 1910-12 for wealthy, upper-class ladies were made from fabrics light and airy (chiffon, silk, lace) and decorated with fine details (beading, embroidery, lace, crochet).

Puffy sleeves, wide-scoop necks, and skirts which hung down in columns, often more than one layer, provided beauty but also a problem. How does the owner keep them clean until the next wedding or party?

Victorian women were just as likely as ladies today to find wine, grass stains, or mud on the surface of these flowing garments. Using soap and very hot water was not a helpful option. Throwing the silk garments into the washing machine or sending them off to a dry cleaners was not available for their ladies in waiting, following an evening of partying by "her majesty." What was the solution?

They cleansed the gowns by sprinkling talcum powder over the surface and then vigorously brushing the powder off again. This brushing removed body order and some dirt and brushed in the smell of the talc. Probably beet juice or wine stains remained as constant reminder of a "careless" evening.

Following the talc bath, the garments went into a cedar lined closet or cedar trunk. The petticoats, hoop-skirts, or crinolines could be washed by hand in strong soap and water and stored in an ordinary dresser drawer. Apparently, the aroma of the oils in the cedar repels moths. If, however, someone left the items in the cedar chamber too long, the oils would dry, and the protective powers vanish.

As I read this information online, my thoughts went to people, rather than clothing. Humans become soiled with sin. None of us is perfect, "for all have sinned and fallen short of the glory of God" (Romans 3:23). Throwing humans into a washing machine filled with hot water or shipping them off to the local dry cleaners is not God's option for how we are to become cleansed from our sins. Neither is the option of rubbing us down with talcum powder a soul-saving solution.

David asks God, in Psalm 51:2, to "Wash away all my iniquity and cleanse me from my sin." David even invited God to "Cleanse me with hyssop, and I will be clean; wash me, and I will be whiter than snow" (Psalm 51:7). Maybe the talcum powder for Victorian dresses was a substitute for a brush down with hyssop.

Paul reminds Titus that under the new law of Christ, cleansing is available for humans. This is because the Son of God "gave himself for us to redeem (cleanse) us from all wickedness and to purify for himself a people that are his very own, eager to do what is good" (Titus 2:14).

We must confess our guilt and sin and acknowledge His saving power. Then we can be washed clean by the blood of the Lamb through baptism. I, for one, am delighted that I do not have to be literally thrown into a washing machine or even covered with talcum powder and brushed down in order to be cleansed and become one of God's children.

Returning to our dress analogy. Here is another little tidbit that was discovered. If the dresses hung too long, the garments might need to be hung upside down in order to smooth out any wrinkles. How do we get rid of our sinful wrinkles in our lives? No, we do not have to hang upside down, but we do have a challenge to stay "unwrinkled."

There is a phrase at the end of Paul's words to Titus that made me think of the upside-down gowns. Following cleansing, we are to be "eager to do what is good." We have a greater responsibility than just attending weekly worship services. We are to become part of the body of Christ and do good, or as Peter tells us in 1 Peter 1:22, "Now that you have purified yourselves by obeying the truth so that you have sincere love for each other, love one another deeply, from the heart."

In Ephesians 5:25b-27, Paul helps me close out this epistle. "Christ loved the church and gave himself up for her to make her holy, cleansing her by the washing with water through the word, and to present her to himself as a radiant church, without stain or wrinkle or any other blemish, but holy and blameless." Make certain you are a part of that radiant church.

Talcum Powder or Washing Machines? Neither.
Let's each be washed through the blood of Christ.

CHAPTER FOUR
Unused, Yellow Safety Hat

The afternoon was cloudy, with a hint of storms, as we entered the church. In anticipation of rain drops, my hand gripped a small umbrella. Heart and mind, however, anticipated a delightful experience. Talented musicians, from Westminster Presbyterian Church, were scheduled to create melodies to cheer and delight the audience, a perfect plan for a windy, spring afternoon.

Dale Rogers, the organist, struck the opening chords, and voices from the rear balcony broke into song. The words of "Bless This House" filled my head, as my mind mentally hummed along. What a great opening number. Today's program was designed to introduce Westminster's new outreach effort. As part of their outreach, they are working with volunteers from Habitat for Humanity, building small homes near the church for use by people in need. Their most recent home will soon be occupied by a family of six.

Imagine the joy as families, needing some help, move into new homes, in a comfortable community, and supported by friendly church neighbors. Then think about the promises in Revelation, about the heavenly home, prepared for Christ followers. John also shares a promise from Jesus in John 14:2. "My Father's house has many rooms; if that were not so, would I have not told you that I am going there to prepare a place for you?" Paul, in 2 Corinthians 5:1, also expands on this glorious promise. "For we know that if the earthly tent we live in is destroyed, we have a building from God, an eternal house in heaven, not built by human hands."

Personally, although I have no desire to exit this world in the immediate future, I must admit that my inborn curiosity is eager to explore this promised new housing development. Human hands did a great job with the house near the church, but it was built by people flawed by sin. My imagination anticipates an even more glorious future dwelling place built by our perfect Creator. What do you anticipate?

As about seventy-five people listened eagerly, we heard the choir sing the heart-thumping words, "O Divine Redeemer." I mentally hummed Charles Gounod's thoughts expressed in the lyrics. Gounod pleads to the Lord to not turn away from us, even though we are unworthy. He wants the Lord to hear our cries of distress as He sits on His throne. His final plea encourages God to please reply swiftly.

Needy families must express similar thoughts. If I were wanting a home for my family, I am certain I would cry out, "Oh, friends of Westminster, hear my plea. A home for sheltering my loved ones - where we can gather around the table as a family to share a meal along with our daily joys and worries; where we can tuck our children safely under the covers - is so needed. Count me worthy, God, of your love."

Praise the Lord, as we are confident that He listens to the needs and pleas of his earthly families. The words of John Stainer's, "I Am Alpha and Omega," also floated down from the balcony, that Sunday afternoon. Embedded into the lyrics, we heard John's words in Revelation 21:4. "He will wipe every tear from their eyes. There will be no more death or mourning or crying or pain, for the old order of things has passed away."

Midway through the concert, our musicians moved downstairs, away from the organ, which Rogers played with such skill. The storm outside made its presence known. Thunder, wind, and rain drops rattled the stained-glass windows.

Auditorium lights blinked. A women's trio continued singing Mozart's beautiful "Ave Verum Corpus," as Dale accompanied them on the piano.

Then it happened!

The blinking stopped. Total blackness filled the auditorium. The music halted. No longer was light available for our musicians. The audience sat motionless. Then, just as suddenly as light was extinguished, brightness returned. Chuckles were heard as voices finished the lyrics of timeless words beseeching Jesus to have mercy on us sinners.

Light is so essential for our lives, for our homes, for our very existence. What an enlightening promise Jesus made, found in John 8:12. "I am the light of the world. Whoever follows me will never walk in darkness, but will have the light of life." Guess I won't need to pack a camping lantern in my bag for use following my death. Heavenly dwellers will not worry about temporary blackouts.

As the choir returned to center stage, we blinked twice. On top of each head sat a yellow, plastic, safety hat. How fitting, as May H. Brahe's song "Bless This House" became part of my memory that day. I expected at any moment to see the singers raise their hands, holding hammers or saws. But then, building lives for the Lord does not require earthly, carpenters' tools.

The musicians that eventful afternoon included professionals and amateurs. They were a team. Likewise in our churches today there is a need for trained scholarly leadership, but the ranks must be filled with every-day followers who love to contribute to the building of the Body of Christ. Volunteers are essential.

The final line from George Cook's "Heavenly Sunlight" was so appropriate. We were reminded to shout "Hallelujah", to rejoice and sing, and remember that Jesus is ours. Yes, He is your friend and mine. With that comes a mix of taking responsibility for helping the team and for rejoicing.

Then, as the yellow hat singers stood before the audience, I spotted one lone, unused hat by the stage. I immediately wondered if a performer was ill, or if that singer had just failed to show up. Could the storm have deterred some fragile soul, or was there just an empty position waiting to be filled? Who was missing in action?

Who, in our Christian family, might represent the unused, yellow hat? Could it be an overworked parent? Did a youthful athlete take adoring parents away from a service opportunity at camp? Perhaps a timid adult skipped a public helping opportunity, but also failed to recognize the need for a quiet, caring person to write notes to a lonely soul, or to help in the church office. There are service opportunities for every last follower — every single day. We must keep our eyes open and leap at the opportunities for wearing the yellow "Service" helmet.

For a home to be fully functioning, each family member must lift up his or her arms and accept some responsibilities. Everyone needs to don a yellow safety hat and join the work force. What a blessed promise will then await us, as described in James 1:12. "Blessed is the one who perseveres under trial because, having stood the test, that person will receive the crown of life that the Lord has promised to those who love him."

As we left the sanctuary, I smiled. The music was a mixture of choir, small group, and solo works. We experienced "Dry Bones" to "Prelude opus 23, no.4" by Rachmaninoff. Selections were joyful and exhibited beautiful harmony, with thoughtful lyrics. Other times the melodies seemed to almost match the quiet storm happening outside that afternoon.

Life is similar. We have joyful moments mixed with the storm clouds of life. I'm just glad the choir was directed by an extraordinary leader. His name is Dale. Likewise, we are under the direction of the perfect leader for bringing music, peace, and calm into our lives. His name is Jesus. He brings us "Deep Peace" as shared in the music of Elaine Hagenberg.

Join in the heavenly choir of "Yellow Hats"
Maybe a Chuckle Will Also Be a Part of Your Day

CHAPTER FIVE
Grant Forgiveness = Receive Forgiveness

The headlines read, "Child pulled from car and killed as parents were made to watch." What would you do if standing in the shoes of those parents?

Oh, it is no problem to forgive someone for stepping on your toes or bumping into you, especially when in a crowded situation. But . . . forgiving an individual who has publicly and intentionally told a lie about you or a family member, run a stop light and thus severely injured your grandchild, or perhaps even missed during target practice on a rifle range, resulting in the death of your father . . . how in the world can we forgive?

Stephen, a first century Christ follower and church leader, provides a wonderful example of forgiveness. Many Hellenistic Jews were complaining their widows were being overlooked. Stephen began to perform great wonders and signs, but opposition arose from some of the Jews. This group secretly plotted against Steve, and ultimately, he was seized, arrested, and had to stand before the high priest and members of the Sanhedrin. Following false testimony against him, the high priest asked Stephen if the charges were true.

Wow! The door was opened for an opportunity to speak, and Stephen took advantage. With his face shining like that of an angel, he gave the courts a history lesson. I have no idea how long his sermon/speech would have lasted, but it takes fifty-one verses in Acts 7 to record the message. Thank goodness the Spirit provided him with wisdom as he spoke, as there was no time allowed for a quick Internet search to refresh his memory. It is especially interesting to read his closing comments in Acts 7:51 - 53. He does not hold back his pointed comments about the negative behavior of his persecutors.

He finished speaking and the Sanhedrin was furious, gnashing their teeth at his words. I'm not quite certain how a person really gnashes their teeth, but I don't think it was the equivalent of "love and kisses." Now pause for a moment. Think about what You would do at this moment. You have been taken to court because of the wonders and signs you had performed. You've given a long speech, reminding your accusers of their negative actions in the past, including the fact they were not always truthful in their accusations against you.

I would want to scream, holler, and yell. Not Stephen. Instead, his accusers screamed at the top of their voices. They rushed at him, dragged him out of the city, and began to pepper him with stones. Stephen started praying, "Lord Jesus, receive my spirit." Then he fell down. Perhaps another large stone slammed against his knees, or maybe even hit his ear or temple, yet he continued talking with God. This is the sentence I know I would have found almost impossible to say. "Lord, do not hold this sin against them" (Acts 7:59-60). He wanted God to forgive those stone throwers.

As he finished those words, the Bible says he "fell asleep" - or as we would say - he died. Those words would be foreign to my natural reactions. Stephen forgave negative actions toward himself and against the Lord, an almost unbelievable behavior.

Of course, the most incredible act of forgiveness was spoken by none other than the King of Kings, as he hung on the cross. Some of Christ's final words were, "Father, forgive them, for they do not know what they are doing" (Luke 23: 34). Imagine experiencing excruciating pain, your mouth so dry that shortly the soldiers will wash your lips with wine vinegar, and yet you speak the following, "Father, forgive." My voice would have been screaming, "Lord, chop off their ears!"

Forgiving others is commanded. The Lord's prayer includes asking God to "forgive us our debts, as we also have forgiven our debtors" (Matthew 6:12). If we want the Lord to forgive us, we must practice that behavior in our own life. My mind focuses on the multiple public shootings in the first third of 2023. How do we help grieving humans forgive the individual responsible for the death of their loved one? Vengeance must not be a part of a Christian's thought patterns. Is there someone you need to pray with or comfort as they attempt to forgive, or maybe even you need to be the recipient of a prayer partner?

A tough scripture for me is found in Romans 8:28. "And we know that in all things God works for the good of those who love him, who have been called according to his purpose." I am thankful for Paul's reminder of this glorious promise!

When tragedy strikes, hurting individuals often try and identify the "good" that God can do through their circumstance. But God's ways are so much greater than our ways. Our job is to trust Him - to take Him at His word and know that He will work for our good - even when we don't see it or feel it. That takes an incredible amount of faith and courage. But consider Joseph, the son of Jacob, forgave his brothers who sold him to Ishmaelite merchants, who in turn took him to Egypt and sold him into slavery. (Genesis 37). Forgiveness takes a giant heart and, I'm certain, often brings tears.

Vengeance never settles situations, even though our human side believes differently and desires revenge. Love must prevail. Paul reminds us, "Therefore, as God's chosen people, holy and dearly loved, clothe yourselves with compassion, kindness, humility, gentleness, and patience. Bear with each other and FORGIVE ONE ANOTHER if any of you have a grievance against someone. Forgive as the Lord forgave you" (Colossians 3:12-13). But it doesn't end there. Look back at the title of this chapter. The joyful part of forgiving others is the promise from God, written as the RF factor of the equation in the title of this chapter: Receive Forgiveness.

Let us attempt to glorify Christ as we become more forgiving of others.

Will you take the challenge?

CHAPTER SIX
Snowperson

Snow is beautiful. Crystals of frozen moisture cover the imperfections of the world, leaving a pure, white blanket of fluffy powder. Energetic youth and adults wait eagerly for the covering to increase sufficiently for snowball fights, sled rides, snowmobiling, and leaving footprints embedded in the snowy fairyland. Yes, snow creates a sparkling winter playground.

But snow is also dangerous. Freezing Arctic crystals coat tree limbs and sidewalks. Icy particles cling to power lines and roofs, which could result in damage and frantic calls to insurance agents. Blizzards create ice rinks from roads and bridges, oftentimes resulting in screeching emergency sirens, as crash victims are rushed to care centers. Broken arms and hips result in the added expenses of braces, crutches, and even a wheelchair or two. You guessed it. Snow, sleet, and high winds deserve serious respect and cautious behavior.

Snow also represents forgiveness. Isaiah, the prophet, reminded the nation of Israel of their rebellious behavior toward God. The people would experience destruction, a result of their evil ways and straying from Jehovah God. Their country had become desolate, like a city under siege. But, God's amazing command, spoken to the nation through the mouth of Isaiah, is recorded in Isaiah 1:16-18. In summary God tells the people to wash and make themselves clean. "Take your evil deeds out of my sight. STOP DOING WRONG. Learn to do right. Seek justice…Though your sins are like scarlet, they shall be as white as snow, though they are red as crimson, they shall be like wool." (Format into all-caps emphasis by the author) The analogy to snow is clear and beautiful.

What a wonderful promise Jehovah God made. He would forgive their sins, but there was a catch. They had to stop doing wrong; to change direction; to seek forgiveness in order to collect on the "insurance promise" of cleansing from their sins and wrongdoings. Their sins would appear as "white as snow" IF they acknowledged their error and sought reconciliation with our Creator.

David sought God's mercy after having committed adultery with Bathsheba. He confessed his sin and pleaded to God for mercy; to blot out his transgressions. "Cleanse me with hyssop, and I will be clean; wash me, and I will be whiter than snow" (Psalm 51:7). Snow and forgiveness are each beautiful concepts.

This year we had almost no snow in Illinois. For some reason, however, this gray-haired writer had a funny little urge. I wanted to play in the snow, to make a snowperson. I don't know why, but I remembered the joy of taking a small snowball and pushing it around the ground until it grew the size of a giant beach ball. This exercise was then followed by rolling two additional, but smaller spheres of snow and stacking them into a weird creature. Of course, facial features were added, and maybe even a scarf.

My imagination was going crazy. I wanted to have at least one final snow experience, but snow eluded Springfield, IL. I drove people crazy with my repeated references to the desire to create a snowperson. Then it happened. Snow began to fall one day in early March. Joy, oh, joy! I anticipated getting my mittens and boots and trudging out to create a snowperson. I was so happy with the prospect of multiple feet of snow.

Dreams sometimes come crashing down. The Lord delivered a very thin layer of fluffy white. As I drove into the garage later in the day, however, I saw that the snowplow had scraped the thin layer, mounding it up on the edge of the drive. Could it work? I dashed upstairs, grabbed gloves and a few items from the refrigerator, and returned to the mini mound of snow. Carefully, I tried to collect the packed snow into some type of rounded shape. Actually, I kicked it loose from the road, smashed bits together, and managed to make three extremely rough imitations of snow spheres. I added a couple of tiny arms and a few twigs on the head.

From the plastic sack, I retrieved the items from the fridge. A tiny carrot was tenderly tucked into the icy blob for a nose, followed by two black olives for eyes. In one arm, that continued to fall off the body, I tucked a small, decorative snowman which normally sat in my bedroom window. The entire creation was about two feet tall. Grabbing my phone camera, I recorded the image to share with family and friends and returned to my apartment in a happy mood. I had made my "Snowperson."

Joy sometimes is short lived. About three hours later, a friend reported that my creation was no more. My joy had melted into a pile of nothingness. Reflecting back on the day's adventure, however, disappointment was not part of my memory. For a senior citizen to be able to get down on her knees and create a funny, icy cold, somewhat artistic object, was happiness personified. The fun of chatting with friends and sharing an essay based on the experience was reward sufficient to create a smiling memory in my heart.

Shaleg, in the Hebrew, is a simple word meaning snow, the content of my snowperson. Snow is also used as a metaphor by God to describe purity. God can make us white as snow. His desire is to give us pure hearts. Just as snow covers up the dead grass, twigs, and rocks, so God's grace can cover our goofs, hard hearts, pain, suffering, and troubles. We need to get on our knees, seeking his grace, and He will cover us with arms of love and forgiveness until we, figuratively speaking, also become white as snow.

**Join me, as we become snowpersons
in God's lawn of life.**

CHAPTER SEVEN
Overwhelmed and Humbled

Three Times in Thirty-Four Hours

Sitting in a pew recently, listening to an organ concert at the Cathedral, I suddenly realized tears were oozing from the corners of my eyes. Adam Chelbek, a Polish American from Chicago, was playing Allegro from Symphony No. 6 in G minor by Widor. A camera in the balcony enabled us to view the master organist at work. A giant screen projected his hands and feet as they moved at the speed of hummingbirds' wings while snatching nectar from a rose.

Those magical moments, filling the auditorium that Friday evening, still remain in my memory. At one point Chelbek's creation demanded volume like the roar of Niagara Falls; seconds later we could have heard the wings of a hundred and one monarch butterflies during their long-distance migration season.

I held my breath. I shut my eyes and let the experience engulf me. I was overwhelmed with sound, talent, and emotion. This tall, slender moving dynamo, an Eastman School of Music grad, brought a hush to the auditorium, followed by appreciative applause.

The second instance of mastery of skills was on a Thursday. The ladies 10:00 a.m. discussion group at my retirement community had gathered for their weekly program. A guest was sharing her talent. In the center of the meeting room was placed a pair of beds covered with a mound of quilts. Our guest speaker, Carol Wesolik, gently began to uncover her creations. As she lifted each quilt, the ohs! and ahs! increased as we viewed the intricate, multi-colored patterns. The skill of blending shades, snipping out tiny pieces of cloth, and then arranging them in intricate patterns, was breathtaking. Never had I experienced such delicate work. I was overwhelmed.

I'd like to share one other event in my life that occurred during this thirty-four-hour period of time. Waking up Friday morning, I realized the apartment felt a bit warm. Glancing at the thermometer, I saw that it read 87 degrees. Ugh! Thinking perhaps we had accidentally set the temperature too high, I grabbed a flashlight and peered at the monitor. No, it was set at 75, perfect for these two gray/white haired ladies. What could be wrong?

Grabbing the phone, we took advantage of one of the perks of living in the senior living center. We left a message that life was a bit uncomfortable upstairs. Hardly after we put the phone down, a knock was heard at the door. Yes, you guessed correctly. The staff member who knows "everything about everything" was waiting to demonstrate his diagnostic skills.

As he began testing the equipment, I slipped away to attend a meeting, hoping that a miracle might occur in my absence. Returning about an hour and a half later, coolness overwhelmed me as I entered the room. Sure enough, the miracle man had accomplished a resolution. A piece of paper folded into a fan would have been my solution for the heat issue. Once again, I was overwhelmed with the talent and skill of another human.

Although for years my parents paid for piano lessons, the world stage will never find me attempting to entertain nor overwhelm an audience with my keyboard knowledge. Perhaps, however, having agonized over preparing for a simple recital piece, I was more appreciative and humbled by Chelbek's organ talents.

Occasionally, years ago, I would join my mother at church to help the ladies prepare very simple quilts for missionaries somewhere in the world. My stitches were few and uneven. Our quilts would never be hung on a wall, calling attention to our simplistic patterns. Perhaps, though, my childhood stitchery sessions allowed me to be appropriately appreciative of our quilter's talent that day.

In a mere thirty-four hours, three individuals shared their skill and talents in amazing ways. I appreciated their efforts and was blessed. But I pause as I write this paragraph. Have I forgotten to be overwhelmed with the Creator's skill? When was the last time I spoke to the Lord and expressed my awe at the beauty of a sunset, or the colorful feathers of the birds that cause me to grab a camera to make a permanent record?

Am I grateful for the promises that He will be with me, and comfort me, even when life has caused stress in my daily health or activities? I am overwhelmed when astronomers say there could be approximately 200 billion trillion stars in the sky, or some would say,

200 sextillion. David, in Psalm 147:4-5 proclaims, "He [the Lord] determines the number of stars and calls them each by name." I can't remember the names of twenty to fifty people at a party. David continues, "Great is our Lord and mighty in power; his understanding has no limit."

Yes, the abilities of three adults overwhelmed me with their talents. I thanked each of them personally. Today, I need to take a moment and thank the Creator personally for the beauty and awesomeness of His world.

Please Join Me in a Prayer Thanking God for His Wonderful and Beautiful Creation.

CHAPTER EIGHT
Loneliness & Solitude

Perhaps today you are alone. The day is overcast in Illinois. The temperature is in the 30's. Some of us were shorted about 60 minutes of "shut-eye" as we entered daylight saving time recently. It's too early to really plant the garden, but too late to anticipate great piles of snow, at least in most of the USA. Today is just plain March, the windy one. Today, I felt alone. But I don't think I was lonely.

I recently read something by the world-renowned thinker Paul Tillich that hit me like a two-by-four right between my eyes. Mr. Tillich believed that there is a difference between "being alone" and being "in solitude".

How are your spirits? Paul Tillich approaches the concept of "being alone" in a couple of ways. He talks about the pain of being alone physically, which we usually define as loneliness. This is one side of the coin. You cry out for the ears of another to hear and share your esoteric or idiotic thoughts of the moment. Oh! To have a friend or companion with whom to share some microwave popcorn. Maybe you even wish for a partner for a game of Scrabble or Old Maid. Regardless, your heart cries out for a friend.

On the flip side, Mr. Tillich refers to being alone as a moment of solitude. You are still the Lone Ranger in the room, but you are rejoicing. The quiet encapsulates your entire soul and body. Thoughts of peace, contentment, or maybe even ideas of creativity filter through your brain. Suddenly your eyes sparkle as you breathe calmly and rejoice for a time just to reflect and create. Solitude is a time for daydreaming, growing in peace with God, or taking inventory of your life. (Well, maybe for a prisoner in solitary confinement that might not be a joyful moment.)

Look at those moments of silence and isolation as an opportunity to meditate and communicate with the Master of solitude and aloneness. Yes, our Savior went to the garden to pray alone to His father. He recharged His battery, thus enabling Him to return to the hustle and bustle of the crowds eager to hear Him speak. He needed quiet and conversation with God, the Father. Rest helped Him tackle Course #2 in the "post grad" teaching program for His twelve closest followers.

Even twenty-first century Christians need "alone time." Of course, we need conversation, connections, and interaction with others. God gave us the ability to talk, listen, and encourage others. BUT celebrate the time in your "prayer closet," alone with God. I've penned the following poem to remind myself and you dear reader of the need for alone time. What do you think?

> "Quiet
> expresses the
> joy of
> preparing for
> togetherness"
>
> or
>
> "Isolation and Silence
> express the
> opportunity for
> meditation and growth
> while being
> alone."

Author: Kathryn Ransom

We are never really alone, however, as God is always present. We just need to acknowledge His presence. "Be strong and courageous. Do not be afraid or terrified because of them, for the Lord your God goes with you; he will never leave you nor forsake you" (Deuteronomy 31:6).

Have an interactive week with God.

CHAPTER NINE
Go? No Go?

Decisions, decisions! Departure is eminent. My bag lay open on the bed. What should I include for a two-week jaunt to the land of my Scottish ancestors? Questions swirled in my mind.

The weather would vary, as we planned to travel to London's Heathrow Airport and then north as far as the Orkney Islands. Weight, especially that of my carry-on, was an essential consideration. I would be required to shove it into the overhead bin. But then, I also needed emergency items — meds, a few snacks, and a set of extra clothes in the event my checked luggage should find its way to Spain or Hong Kong. How much could I possibly cram in, and yet still tote it around the airport? My heart raced as I pondered my options — Go? No Go?

Thoughts hopped around in my brain. First, should I take my leopard-colored carry-on or the larger black bag with tiny wheels? The leopard won, as it would sling over my shoulder and even sit on the floor in front of my feet.

A rescued pair of tennis shoes from the giveaway day at my retirement community would be perfect for trail walking, but my rubber water shoes would be more appropriate if we were directed to hop out of the boat and walk a few steps in the water. Tennis shoes won out, even though they would take up three times the space. But then, what shoes should accompany the tennis shoes? Maybe going barefoot would be the best decision.

Slacks: should I choose light weight and slightly wrinkle-proof, or a pair made of dressier material? Light weight is now ready for stuffing into the bag. But, what about shirts, sweaters, or a blouse? "Go or no go" became the words of the day. A very worn shirt was included with the thought of ditching it at the end of the trip, thus leaving room for a tiny souvenir.

Some of these options culminated in a go — no go decision. My mind drifted to my life. As a follower of the Lord, His will must be considered. Shall I enter a quiet space for reflection and prayer, or dash off to buy lettuce and sardines for lunch? Christ certainly valued moments of quiet as part of His routine. Matthew 11:28-30 finds Jesus encouraging His followers to do the same. "Come to me, all you who are weary and burdened, and I will give you rest. Take my yoke upon you and learn from me, for I am gentle and humble in heart, and you will find rest for your souls. For my yoke is easy and my burden is light." Yes, I'd better pack a moment for prayer and reflection in my day's schedule.

Daily medicine mandated space in the bag, as I wanted to remain healthy. David's Psalm 107:20 reminds us that God's word heals when we seek healing from our rebellious ways. "He sent out his word and healed them; he rescued them from the grave." The challenge is remembering to take both our physical meds as well as allowing God's healing to bring peace in our lives. "Praise the Lord, my soul, and forget not all his benefits—who forgives all your sins and heals all your diseases . . ." (Psalm 103:2-3).

Added options resulted in at least one additional white hair on my head. Trip information indicated that weather in May could be rainy, windy, and not appropriate for bathing in the sun. Now, should I leave my swimsuit in Illinois and stuff in rain wear, mittens, and boots? The swimsuit will remain home, and earmuffs will have to wait for another trip. Undoubtedly a jacket with a hood that will cover my shoulders will keep me warm and dry as I am out and about.

Likewise in the Christian life, we must remain ready when life gets stormy. Remember the day Jesus and His disciples boarded a boat following a long day of preaching and teaching. Jesus was taking a nap on a cushion in the back of the boat, when suddenly a furious squall came up. The rocking of the boat was so severe that those seasoned fishermen feared for their lives. The disciples woke Him. "Teacher, don't you care if we drown?" (Mark 4:38) We remember that He woke up and ordered the Sea of Galilee to be quiet and still. Then, however, the Healer asked the men why they were so afraid. "Do you still have no faith?"

These men had brought with them the saving medicine, Jesus, but forgot to trust in the healing/saving power of His Word. Yes, we too sometimes forget we have in our spiritual bag the hope of healing and calming of our soul even when we are in distress. The disciples grew afraid, but they did remember to call on the passenger in the boat, the one able to calm the storms of life. He is our life jacket. Don't forget to wear it.

Remember as we grab the bags of our life, made not of leather but of burdens, to go prepared, not leaving behind our "bags of faith." Waves of distress may engulf us. Your house just sold, and your next nesting spot is not available. You have a new job, with many more responsibilities, and you are worried about meeting the demands. Word just arrived of the death of a dear friend or family member, or perhaps a phone call confirmed the news — your tumor is malignant. Can you trust the great healer? The Lord does care. We must apply the dose of faith and trust.

With the Lord at Your Side, Go For It!

CHAPTER TEN
Three Choices

Swim, Sleep, or Tough It Out
vs
Pray, Believe, & Look Forward

When winter arrives and temperatures drop, animals have three choices in order to survive: they can escape to a warmer climate, sleep until spring arrives, or just stay and tough it out. God has programmed all of the creatures in the animal kingdom to instinctively follow one of these options in order to survive.

The little lemur, for example, climbs a tree and lives off the "fat in its tail for seven months a year." Perhaps in human terms, we would amend that statement to say, "Some people live off the fat of the land." Or perhaps, the lesson for me is, "Go climb a tree and live off the fat of your body when worries, sadness, or pain fills your soul." Take time for moments of prayer and isolation. (By the way, wouldn't it be great to be slim by spring? Maybe I'll find a comfy tree and snooze.)

Our friend the alligator, using the senses God provided him, knows to pop his nostrils above the water, when it is about to freeze, in order to breathe. Humans probably should consider taking a "deep breath" and remain calm during moments of severe stress. When we are inclined to speak out with anger, impoliteness, or denial of God, remember Ally the Alligator and count to ten backwards. Trust the Holy Spirit to aid you with your vocal responses during those tense moments. God will be pleased.

The giant humpback whale has the perfect solution. When winter storms approach, he takes a trip. Imagine swimming up to 3000 miles to a warmer climate. Well, that's not too different from many humans. Off we zip to Texas, Arizona, or balmy Florida for a few weeks or months. What about people in the Bible? Jonah left town in a hurry after God commanded him to warn the people of Nineveh of their impending destruction if they didn't repent. Our prophet took an unexpected, underwater trip inside of one of God's largest creatures and ended spit out on the shore. Guess what? He had a change of mind and heart and decided to listen to God's orders.

Could it be true that Christ followers try to disappear when our load appears too heavy? Do we zip off into isolation because we are tired of serving? Are we in denial when asked to perform a task for the Kingdom that seems to be ill-suited for our skills or personality? Do we vanish from our Christian family when commitment interferes with our own desires and wishes? Time to re-evaluate!

The whale takes a three-thousand-mile swim, leaving the cold waters behind, but continues to live a normal life. Perhaps the lesson for us today is tough. We may need to request an adjustment of our service for the Lord. An alternative might be to re-evaluate our daily agenda. Too many golf games may sneak in as a priority, thus frustrating my schedule when a visit to a shut-in is God's whisper in my ear. Do I need a new $25,000 van to reach Miami for a swim in the ocean or is the call for clothes for the needy at a mission my priority? Alternatively, maybe we really need a new van, but a swim in the ocean may need to be replaced with a mission service project in southern California. While helping with an outreach program, it could include a dip in the warm Pacific.

Finally, let's consider the little chickadee. This one is tough to imagine. Just think! This feathery creature can expand its brain 30%, thus increasing her memory in order to remember where to find food. Oh! That some seniors today could emulate the chickadee and replace the effects of Alzheimer's with the joys of remembering their past.

I continue to be amazed at our Creator. For each breathing creature He created variations in their abilities. We, also, are each different. I cannot repair the church bus, but perhaps that mechanic does not feel competent to teach a class of squirming toddlers. Pray for wisdom to understand your unique job skills. Believe that God will direct you.

Look forward to His coming. Learn to use your unique skills to further the Kingdom, but still have a wonderful life on earth in anticipation of a future with the Creator himself.

CHAPTER ELEVEN
Forty-Nine Spuds and Still Chopping

The alarm sounded. Rubbing my eyes, I rolled out of bed to begin an interesting, engaging day. I was going to camp. Yes, this eighty-seven-year-old was off to church camp. Before you become too concerned, understand this would be only a three-to-four-hour experience. I planned to have fun.

After I swallowed my morning pill, grabbed a hot shower, and selected just the right outfit, breakfast became the focus point for the moment. Of course, time was needed to read the non-newsy newspaper and work a couple of puzzles, before adding a special item to my attire. Hidden in the closet behind my blouses was a denim-colored shirt with an appropriate logo: Lake Springfield Christian Assembly. My outfit complete, I was ready for church camp.

Grabbing a hat loaded with travel pins, I scurried to the garage and zipped out to Lake Springfield. Thus began the day I had been anticipating: a day of engagement, of completing simple tasks, and ultimately, of tired feet. I was headed to be a volunteer in the kitchen. A young couple from our church also stood eagerly waiting at the kitchen door to begin our work experience. (Well, it was not really "our" church, but the Lord's church. We are just a part of the church family.)

My mind danced with eagerness as I anticipated what culinary challenges might be assigned. Perhaps, since it was a church camp, angel food cakes would be appropriate, and I knew I could whip egg whites like a pro. I hoped, however, that devil food cake was not the alternative. Raw, baby octopus or French Boeuf Bourguignon seemed unlikely menu items for ninth graders, which was fine with me. I had raw octopus once in Italy, and that was sufficient. No more tiny, slimy morsels, with eight, itty-bitty curly legs for this lady.

About midway through my thought process, the chief chef finished popping two large pans into the oven, and introduced herself. Coleen is an eager, organized, helpful, unassuming leader. Her smile quickly makes you feel welcome. After introducing ourselves, two options were given: slice four watermelons or make Snickerdoodles for about a hundred hungry mouths. Thankfully the other woman volunteered to be the baker, and her husband and I grabbed the knives, chopping block, and a melon each and began to transform the green melon into small, personal sized portions.

Whoops! I almost forgot. We were instructed to wash our hands and don a pair of gorgeous, royal blue, clingy, plastic gloves. In fact, prior to working with a different food product, off came the old blue, on came new blues. My mind wondered how many hundreds of gorgeous blues were consumed each camp season? Perhaps I need a chat with my broker, suggesting we invest in gorgeous blues. My online search had me read James 4:8 where it suggested we "cleanse our hands, ye sinners." I didn't realize the Illinois Department of Public Health really cared if I was a sinner, but I was not about to argue. As I thoroughly washed my hands, I remembered the old-time (but still true) kitchen cliche that just as Jesus is found everywhere, so are germs.

Back to the watermelon challenge. After a few quick directions, the slicing and dicing began. Before you knew it, four gorgeous green melons were reduced to a hundred or so small, hand-sized pieces of juicy, red fruit for hungry teens. Thank goodness there was a leader directing us. Coleen's actions reminded me that as followers of the Lord, we should so rejoice that He leads us, and provides us with guidance and direction as we read His manual, the Bible. Psalm 32:8 expresses that thought: "I will instruct you and teach you in the way you should go; I will counsel you with my loving eye on you."

On to challenge number two: reduce a mound of red potatoes and carrots to small cubes, suitable for cooking over the campfire in a stew of who knows what else, designed to feed a bunch of youth sleeping in tents on a lower level of the campgrounds. New blues were selected, clean cutting board and sharp knives grabbed, and I began to dissect a mound of forty-nine or more round, red spuds. Whack, whack, slice, and dice, too small, too large, and finally just right, thousands of bits of potatoes were ready for cooking in the evening, stored in the cooler.

A funny scripture came to mind, while chopping the vegetables. Proverbs 15:17 says, "Better a small serving of vegetables with love than a fattened calf with hatred." Hopefully the youth consuming the vegetables around the fire will be exhibiting love and kindness for each other, and maybe they will even say thanks to the trio chopping up their stew that day. They could be exhibiting love for us.

Well, our day was almost over. The pork loin needed pulling. I thought immediately of a tug of war or a tug of pork as I yanked little pieces of cooked pig into a pan. Whatever, we shredded a huge mound of delicious pork, part of which had been baked in apple juice and spices that morning.

We even had an opportunity to taste it, as following cleanup the volunteers were encouraged to join the campers in the luncheon feast. As the pork was piled on taco chips, covered with melted cheese, and provided with sour cream and BBQ sauce, we three found our plates. We added some salad items, sampled our juicy, red slices of fruit, and began to appreciate what the Lord and generous Christians provided for each person present.

A dining room of teens does not hear an army of mice dancing in a corner. Teens are exuberant. Singing, visiting, and inviting fellow campers to perform funny actions, makes a kaleidoscope of sounds. Even as these energetic humans cleared and cleaned their tables, the atmosphere was full of joy. The Lord, in Psalm 98:4 seems to encourage this exuberant behavior, as he says, "Shout for joy to the Lord, all the earth, [including teens], burst into jubilant song with music." It is a wonder no guitars or drums were a part of our joyful meal that noon.

Climbing into my car and exiting the campgrounds, my feet said, "Hurry home," but my heart sang the words the old, but beautiful, hymn "Count Your Blessings" while my brain started naming all of the many blessings that day. Maybe I'll even check to see if help is needed another day this week.

Volunteering is sometimes work, sometimes hard, but always rewarding. Won't you consider volunteering today?

CHAPTER TWELVE
Angel in the Laundromat

Quiet, Unsung Witness of Love

Angels - what mental image appears when the word "angel" is mentioned? Perhaps you envision a human-like form in white, flowing robes, fluttering around with massive wings, and maybe even a golden halo floating over the head. Others may catch a glimpse of a sweet cherubim, the size of a plump child, with halo and tiny wings, strumming a wee harp. Most of our understanding and mental pictures come from painters and sculptors in the Renaissance. Did their ideas come from the Bible or from a weird dream?

Occasionally the idea of Satan, as an angel, also appears in our thoughts. White robes become a tight-fitting, red outfit. With horns on his head and a pitchfork clutched tightly in one hand. We think of a cruel, evil being called "Lucifer." Actually, Paul reminds the Christians in 2 Corinthians 11:14 that "Satan himself masquerades as an angel of light."

The Bible lifts the curtain a bit, providing a tiny glimpse of these creatures of God. Genesis 2:1 implies that angels were created prior to day seven. The Word says, at the end of day six, "Thus the heavens and the earth were completed in all their vast array." Hebrews 1:13-14 further says that angels are ministering spirits sent to serve those who will inherit salvation. Occasionally, however, angels took on a bodily form and appeared to various people in Scripture. For example, remember the angel who spoke to the women at the tomb, when they came to visit that early morning?

Although artists tend to depict angels as female, the scriptures name only two. If you pause in your reading, perhaps you will remember their names. Yes, "Michael" (Jude 9) and "Gabriel" (Luke 1:19) are the only two names provided, and we generally associate those names with males.

There are many other hints in the scripture that offer a glimpse of these heavenly beings. Today, however, I want to extend the concept of "angel" to a human. The word "angel" has expanded in meaning and undoubtedly each of you will quickly recall from your memory bank a friend or acquaintance, or even a stranger who suddenly assumed the role of a "human" angel.

A friend shared an experience she recently had, as she cared for her husband. It was a difficult day. An extensive mess needed to be cleaned up, including the washing of much bulky bedding. To find a machine with sufficient capacity to accommodate the wash, she went down the hall to a washer available to all residents of the complex. As she struggled with the heavy load, and how to stuff it into the washer, another resident appeared. My friend related, "I don't know why she was there, but I know she became my wingless angel. She could tell I was distressed and calmly suggested that the size of the load probably required a commercial laundromat."

Even knowing that was the wise thing to do, she commented to the "angel" that she had never been to a laundromat and did not even know a location of one nearby. Of course, she was quickly provided with an address and was assisted in lugging all the bedding to the car, and off she drove for a new experience.

Frustrated and discouraged, but focused on cleaning everything, she quickly met her second angel of the morning. As she drove up, the young, male attendant recognized our friend was distressed and asked if he could help. After providing instructions on how to use the machines, he also indicated that quarters were necessary, helped her buy some, and acquired some necessary soap.

As she thanked her second wingless angel of the day, my friend expressed to him how much she appreciated his help. She then shared a bit more of her previous several hours, including her efforts to help her husband, who is facing dementia challenges.

The young man gave her a hug, said he understood, and that he was there to help. This angel in disguise continued to support our friend through the drying process and the loading of the wash back into her car.

Of course, these two helpers were just ordinary humans, not angels, but exhibited angelic characteristics. They were observant and recognized stress. They each stepped up to the plate and lent a helping hand and heart. Kindness and concern for another human motivated each to offer support. Perhaps Proverbs 17:17 says it all. "A friend loves at all times, and a brother is born for a time of adversity." I like to also think that Psalm 34:7 supports the idea that angels are with us, or are at least examples for us. "The angel of the Lord encamps around those who fear (respect) him (God), and he delivers them."

The storms of life are no match for angels disguised as caring friends. Perhaps Each of Us Should Keep Our Eyes Open and Become a "Temporary" Angel!

CHAPTER THIRTEEN
Memories: What Good Are They?

"Alzheimer's" is a word that terrifies me. Each of us has encountered loved ones who no longer recognize us. There are many and varied manifestations of Alzheimer's disease. None are pleasant. Watching friends exhibit signs of memory loss causes me distress. To forget where you placed your phone five minutes ago, or to be unable to locate your own room at a care center is just plain sad. My own memory generally fails me when attempting to remember the name of a friend, spell a word of three or more syllables, or even recall many childhood adventures with my family. Memory is a precious part of our being.

My question, then, is, "What good are memories?" As I wander around our apartment, I am surrounded by memories. Personalized wall hangings from a trip to Africa take my mind back to a safari where my camera was in constant use, snapping pictures of cougars, lions, elephants, and zebras. Family pictures remind me of a most unusual childhood filled with constant travel but included loving parents. Thank goodness my younger brother was patient and fun to be with, as extensive travel reduced childhood friends to almost zero in the first nine years of my life. Filling my shelves, there are memories from a professional life focused on books while working as a reading consultant across our country. Then there is a very special memory which sits on my dresser. It is a tiny, well-worn bear, given to me by my Uncle Justin on the day I was born in Portland, Oregon.

Crazy as it may seem, I still have a colorful bath towel, given to me in 1953 for a high school graduation present. It is not the towel itself that is special, but the memory of the giver of the gift. My Aunt Kay, after whom I was named, shipped it from Portland, Oregon to Rolla, Missouri. I don't really know why I saved it, but each time my eyes glance at it, Aunt Kay comes to mind. I remember the thoughtful, adult-type conversations I could have with her, as we sat on her couch overlooking Lake Oswego. Sometimes a growing teenager needs an additional set of adult ears beyond her parents with whom to share queries about life. Aunt Kay played that role so well. Memory is a wonderful ability the Lord provided us.

The apostle Paul expresses it well in a letter to his friends at Philippi around A.D. 50: "I thank my God every time I remember you. In all my prayers for all of you, I always pray with joy because of your partnership in the gospel from the first day until now, being confident of this, that he who began a good work in you will carry it on to completion until the day of Christ Jesus" (Philippians 1:3-6).

During one of his missionary journeys, Paul traveled to Philippi, a Roman colony. One Sabbath, during his visit, he sought a place of prayer by the river. Then, to the surprise of no one, he began to speak to the women who were present. One woman named Lydia, a dealer in purple cloth and a worshiper of God, listened carefully and then responded to Paul's message. She and other members of her family/household were baptized.

Then a somewhat unexpected event happened. Lydia invited Paul and his friends to come to her home. My brain immediately wonders what she might have served her new friends that morning. Perhaps sardine sandwiches or maybe honey, spread liberally on some homemade loaves of bread, were offered to the guests. I suppose it could have been locusts. Ancient records indicate that there were 800 different kinds of edible locust. Probably a toasted locust would be no weirder than frog legs or snails enjoyed by twenty-first century gourmets. At least sweet and salty locusts are highly nutritious, and often are "crunchy and crispy."

Regardless, the family had a wonderful visit. This hostess shared the gospel with her friends and the church grew. The group was so responsive and encouraging that they began financially supporting Paul's ministry. No wonder Paul thanked them and remembered their kindness as he wrote his letter to the church from a jail cell.

Paul faced all types of persecution because of his boldness in preaching. Imagine spending time in a cold prison cell, with little food except what friends would bring. I'm certain no king-sized, Sealy Posturepedic mattress rested on the floor of his cell. At times he was beaten or chained. He did not dwell on sad or unpleasant memories, however. Instead he shared his heart and positive memories of Philippi with the "home folk." Think how encouraging his letters must have been to these new Christians.

Today, we too, need to follow Paul's example. Reconstruct positive memories in your life. Let those memories bring you joy. Include times when you blessed and cared for another or when you were the recipient of kindness and a sharing of God's love for you. Yes, it's time to pass the message of God's love to a new generation, but relish memories. Those happy moments will translate into peace and smiles as you survive today's challenges.

Please take a moment and read the entire first chapter of Philippians. Then share great moments of love with others.

PS — If interested in eating a locust, boil the insect for one minute, rinse in cold water, and drain.

CHAPTER FOURTEEN
Join The Tea Party

Memories of December 1773

The stage was set in Boston that evening on December 16, 1773. American patriots, frustrated and angry about "taxation without representation," decided to defy their British rulers and hopefully grab the attention of King George and the British Parliament.

What stimulated this raucous, grassroots group, the Sons of Liberty, to board the Dartmouth that wintry day? Low prices? Lousy teatime? Lack of excitement? Tea shortage? Anger at the government? Perhaps, we might say, a bit of each of those elements.

Despite what some think, the protesters, who caffeinated Boston Harbor, were not protesting a tax hike, but a corporate tax break. The British government enacted the Tea Act in the spring of 1773. Although this seems a bit complicated to this non-historian author, apparently the British had reduced the tax on tea sold in America by the East India Company. This Tea Act would have allowed colonists to purchase tea at half the price paid by British tea lovers back in England. Incidentally, the tea was Chinese green tea.

The problem, however, was that the Tea Act left in place the HATED British three-pence-per-pound duty enacted by the Townshend Revenue Act in 1767. This irked colonists as another example of taxation legislation without representation. In fact, this principle so offended the colonists that several other port cities refused to sell the now inexpensive tea from the East India Company.

It is interesting that rebellion by humans has existed since the Garden of Eden. Adam and Eve listened to the crafty serpent who encouraged their snacking of the forbidden fruit. This was not a tax problem, but in a way, this couple was upset they could not make their own laws for snack time.

God the Father was telling this first pair in His world what they could eat or not eat. We humans seem to love being in charge. I'm confident that at times people even think, for example, they know what speed limit is more appropriate than the highway patrol.

The Tea Act was a government bailout for the struggling East India Company, which was on the brink of financial collapse. Our readers today might remember our own twenty-first century government extending a financial helping hand to some large cooperations experiencing a meltdown. The difference is that the colonists had no representation in England as the decision was made.

The British lawmakers gave the East India Company a virtual monopoly on the American tea trade, thus bypassing the colonial merchants. In fact, they even undercut the price of smuggled Dutch tea, which was the primary source for the colonists' teatime beverage. Boston's wealthy merchants and area smugglers, including John Hancock and Samuel Adams, were struggling with these new financial challenges. They helped stimulate the disturbance within the colonies.

The Tea Act helped bail out the financially struggling tea businesses. What God has done His share of bailing out His children. Elijah helped provide for the widow in Zarephath who needed food for her son and herself. I Kings 17:7-16 tells the story: she shared her last few bites of bread with Elijah. He, with the Lord's help, provided food for mother and son until the drought was over.

The Good Samaritan, as related in Luke 10:30-36, extended God's care to the man beaten by robbers. He transported him to a "care center" and paid the bill. Thank goodness these two acts of kindness, on behalf of hurting individuals, did not result in struggles or war.

The most famous act of disobedience by the Sons of Liberty was the destroying of an estimated 92,000 pounds of British tea in the Boston Harbor on December 16. That would have been sufficient tea to fill 18.5 million teabags. The present-day value has been estimated at around one million dollars. The tea was in 342 huge crates, which the Bostonians chopped open with axes and then dumped the loose-leaf, not brick, tea overboard.

I chuckle as I think of the tea being tossed into the sea. Then I think of how one evening in Egypt, God, in a sense, tossed an army into the sea. Remember? The Children of Israel were fleeing Egypt and the Pharaoh after their forty years of slavery. As the group, estimated to be six hundred thousand men on foot, besides women and children, reached the Red Sea, God opened the waters, allowing His children to cross on dry land. Then the fun began.

Pharaoh's army reached the edge of the water. The winds, holding back the water to produce a dry route for the Children of Israel to cross, ceased to blow. Bingo, the water began to cover the dry ground, and chariot wheels got mired in the mud. In fact, Exodus 15:4-5 says it so well: "Pharaoh's chariots and his army he has hurled into the sea. The best of Pharaoh's officers are drowned in the Red Sea. The deep waters have covered them; they sank to the depths like a stone." Reminds me of the rebels hurling tea into Boston harbor. Bye-bye soldiers. Bye-bye tea. No more cheap tea. No more advancing army.

Probably the destruction of the tea was not the original goal of the leaders. Their first preference would have been to send the tea back to England. But when the merchants (consignees), ship captains, and the governor were unwilling to send ships back or to bend the rules, the off-loading of boxes of tea into the harbor took place. Customers would have been unable to resist the now very cheap, British East India Company tea. They would pay the three-pence-per-pound duty and thus drive the smugglers and local merchants out of business.

Reflecting on the evening "splash party," the Sons' defiance of the British probably helped spur the onset of the Revolutionary War. Some historians believe this action was the first unofficial act by the colonists as they demanded their independence from England. Actually, the more direct cause of war was Britain's passing of a series of laws called "The Intolerable Acts" in 1774. It certainly, though, fostered an American tradition of grassroots activism.

Today, we too may need to be prepared to take a stand as we face challenges to our Christian beliefs in an ever-changing society. In Philippians 4:6-7 we find a promise. "Do not be anxious about anything, but in every situation, by prayer and petition, with thanksgiving, present your requests to God. And the peace of God, which transcends all understanding, will guard your hearts and your minds in Christ Jesus."

Stand Up for Jesus.
He Stands Before God for You.

Note #1: Be assured, this author was NOT present that evening in 1776. Maybe I was too timid, or maybe only men felt the need to exercise their right to complain. Perhaps women were to stay home and have the tea ready following the dumping experience. You can decide why I was absent.

Note #2: The immediate major consequence of the evening was the closing of the Boston harbor until all of the value of the tea lost by the British East India Company was paid back.

Note #3: The event on December 16 was not referred to as the 'Boston Tea Party' until about a half-century later.

CHAPTER FIFTEEN
Lessons From a Blueberry Patch

Glancing at my watch, I groaned. Six-thirty AM and my alarm shattered my dream. I have no idea the content, as memory fails me every time. I think, however, it would be fun to continue some of my dreamland adventures in 3-D and real life.

Leaping out of bed, I quickly showered, dressed, and grabbed a bite of breakfast. Saturday morning and we were off to Jefferies Orchard and their blueberry patch. A trio of ladies popped into the car and drove the several miles to the edge of Springfield, north of our airport and then down a long, three and one-half mile dead-end road to join the other blueberry lovers.

Although it was barely after eight AM., the line of cars parked along the edge of the narrow county road was surprisingly long. As we approached the entrance, I remembered an old saying an uncle of my friend said: "When parking may be limited, never stop at the first empty spot. Undoubtedly if you continue, you will find a more convenient place." Today that motto held true, and we saved many steps by advancing down the road.

Grabbing sunglasses and hat, and picking up the bucket for our berries, we started searching for the most heavily laden bushes. Fortunately, many plants were covered in shade from a huge tree located at the edge of the patch of berries. And so, the fun began.

Selecting a bush that appeared to have many ripe berries, I quickly got the rhythm of look, find the blue hidden among the tiny, green bits, pick, and drop into the small bucket on my left arm. Look, pick, drop. Look, pick, drop.

As the rhythm became automatic, my hands continued to work, but my mind took a major detour. I became aware of the world around me, and thus ideas popped into my writer's little brain.

Humans of all ages, shapes, and varied dress were present. One group was speaking an unfamiliar language but seemed to be very focused in the attack on the berries. Some were chattering away, and others were totally focused on the "Look, Pick, Drop" plan. A tiny two-year-old was grabbing berries and changing the plan. He popped the berries into his mouth, not the bucket. Yes, my first observation was, "Berry Pickers Can Include All People."

As I identified my first lesson, I realized I was translating that to followers of Christ. God is calling out to everyone and has a place for them. Tall, short, chunky, teens, lean or lank, white hair or no hair, all are welcome. We just need to acknowledge that we each attack the job in different ways. I guess we need to encourage everyday people to know they can be an engaged follower.

Lessons two and three appeared while closely viewing the blueberry branch. The berries are clustered together. They actually touched. As one ripens, it enlarges and becomes easier to identify and pluck. People assist the departure from the branch, and the berry becomes supper for someone. Perhaps we need to remember this with people. A community of believers associate closely with others, perhaps not actually touching, but cluster for conversation, help in time of need, encouragement, and actually support each other.

Then, as the Christian matures, the individual moves out of the tight cluster, leaving room for others to grow and mature in service and understanding. I was reminded of this lesson the other day while commenting to a friend, that at eighty-eight, I probably needed to begin to think about giving up my class of adults I teach each Sunday.

Her response was, "Well, then perhaps you need to train or help someone grow into the task of providing spiritual food each week for mature adults." Now whenever my thoughts go to retiring from Sunday class instructor, I will probably remember the blueberry lessons. Green, Grow, Go. Begin as a greenhorn, ripen, grow, and then leave to allow others to grow and repeat the cycle.

My two companions that morning indicated it was time to move on. Grabbing a final few berries, popping them into my mouth, and picking up my bucket, I glanced into the container. Lesson four appeared in my head. My hand was shuffling around in the berries, snatching out the few twigs, an occasional small leaf, and several tiny, green berries. Yes, yes, I did not want to pay for or take home anything but the pure blueberries.

I was sorting out the "chaff" from the "grain." In Matthew 3:12, John the Baptist illustrates this lesson by saying about Jesus, "His winnowing fork is in his hand, and he will clear his threshing floor, gathering his wheat into the barn and burning up the chaff with unquenchable fire." As Christians we must live worthy lives, or, figuratively speaking, risk becoming trash, dropped on the blueberry field, and stomped on.

The next blueberry patch lesson was the tough one. We had to **pay the price** for our goodies. So, too, in life. Now, however, we are the blueberry and Christ had to pay the price for us. He gave His life's blood that we might have life.

One more blueberry lesson came to view, as we returned home. Several friends are unable to walk, bend, and pluck berries on a warm day, located on uneven ground, several miles from their home. Fresh blueberries are for sharing, so off we went with several offerings of blueberries for others. It is good to share, both your hand-picked berries and your love of the Lord. Saturday was a wonderful, fun-filled day of learning.

As you go about today, remember the Six Lessons from the Blueberry Patch. Which lessons need your time and attention?

CHAPTER SIXTEEN
You Have a Choice

Mature, senior citizen, long in the tooth,
antique, coffin dodger, or just plain "old!"

Which title(s) drive you crazy?
Which terms best describes your current
physical and mental ability?
What word(s) do you hope your friends don't associate
with you, as they introduce you to a new friend?

Answering my own question, this white-haired, senior citizen with eighty-eight years of experience, cringes when called "antique" or even "old". Never have I been called "coffin dodger." Maybe the best idea is to just call me names related to my birth name. Kathryn, Kathryn Ann, Kathy, Katie, or K.A. work just fine. Chatty Kathy is probably accurate, but maybe a bit too truthful.

A friend of mine recently shared one of his poems related to the topic of "Aging." He referred to aging as a mixed blessing. As my eyes initially focused on the message, two words caught my attention — "distressing" and "scared." They reflected the negative side of adding a sixty-first or eighty-eighth candle to the party cake when friends gather to sing the birthday song.

Perhaps "distressing" or "scared" have been a part of your waking moments in the middle of the night. Our poet takes these two words and flips them over. You, however, cannot imagine how "scared" or "afraid" could ever cause cheering in your nightly thoughts. Well, Richard caused me to stop and think. Yes, even seniors can still activate their cognitive skills. Just remember to not let them get too rusty.

Take a moment now and think, relate, and create, as you read the thoughts expressed in these carefully selected words.

Mixed Blessing

I've found that getting old's distressing.
But then again, it's a mixed blessing.
It's good to know that you survive
And feel assured you're still alive!

It's sad to see how friends have fared
So many ills, it leaves you scared.
But as your friendship circle wanes,
It spurs you on to seek for gains.

New friends are out there — young and old.
New friendships are like mining gold.
It gives your ageing life a spark,
Refreshing like a singing lark!

So don't let ageing get you down.
Keep thinking "young" and "go to town."
You'll find that spark to be your blessing,
And getting old not so distressing!

Author — Richard Bilinsky
Concordia Village, Springfield. IL

Ideas tumbled out of the print. I have had distressing moments as gray hairs replaced the vibrant hair of my youth. Hearing the words, "Your osteoporosis has now advanced to osteomyelitis," shook me up. Running, leaping over tall buildings, or eliminating all medicine from my cupboard is impossible.

Then, the curtain opened. Stop! I thought of what a blessing that I have survived for eighty-eight years. Restoration from a pair of knee replacements and three years of recovery from a triple bypass and aortic value replacements make me leap with joy. I'm mobile, able to wander around New Salem State Park, or even write a weekly Ransom Note for over six hundred contacts. I can still "go to town."

Ecclesiastes 7:10 tells us to not say, "Why were the old days better than these?" The author reminds us it is not wise to ask such questions. We must consider new opportunities for service, use our experience and wisdom to help others, and recognize the joys of still breathing and celebrating our Lord each day.

I choose the words, "Mature" and "Still Kicking." What are your words of hope?

CHAPTER SEVENTEEN
What's In Your Hand?

I asked myself the question, "What's in my hand?" At the moment it was a bucket of strawberries. My mind, however, began to hum, "He's Got the Whole World In His Hands." Memories of church camp surfaced. Campers were sitting around the dining table or campfire, enjoying fellowship, and someone began singing. Perhaps you remember the lyrics.

Beginning with the whole world and moving on to the wind and rain, we know that God cares about our world and the environment. The following verses, however, hit closer to home. He holds the baby, you, and me, and finally He holds everybody in his hands. What a glorious promise! "The earth is the Lord's, and everything in it, the world, and all who live in it" (Psalm 24:1). Even you and I are under His wing, in His hand, and being watched over. That is a super promise.

Today, however, let's shift our focus from God's hands to our hands. What do you personally hold in your hands? God once asked

Moses that question. Moses was hesitating to take command of the Israelites and lead them out of slavery and into the Promised Land. Actually, Moses was reluctant to even approach the elders, let alone the king of Egypt, and present the request for the Children of Israel to take a three-day journey into the wilderness to offer sacrifices.

Reluctant Moses responded to God's directions with a question: "What if the elders don't believe me, and in fact, what if they don't even believe that you, the Lord, even appeared to me?"

The Lord then asked Moses, "What is in your hand" (Exodus 4:2).

Our timid leader responded, "I-I-It's my shepherd's staff."

"Throw it on the ground."

Following orders, the staff was thrown down and immediately became a snake. In fact, the viper was so real, Moses ran from it. If that wasn't enough direction, Moses was then commanded to pick up the snake. Now, I must admit, I would probably have been willing to chat with the elders and even visited the Pharaoh, but picking up a snake — No Way.

Reaching down, however, Moses got the snake by the tail, but it was now a staff. God demonstrated how His power could work through his servant, Moses, in a couple of additional examples that day. Of course, Moses eventually realized God was going to be with him, and he might as well get with the plan and begin ultimately to move the people away from their slavery situation and toward the Red Sea. Moses even used his rod to bring water from a rock during those dry, desert days. Many years later, as promised, the descendants of this huge group walked into the Promised Land.

Moses originally lacked trust in God. He failed to realize that if God gave him difficult directions to follow, He would also provide appropriate support and guidance to accomplish the task. God worked through Moses, the human. God could have accomplished the task of freeing His children from the control of the Pharaoh without Moses. But no, God wanted, and still wants, to work through everyday people. As Moses stumbled along, expressing excuse after excuse, God just patiently continued to challenge him to go forth and do. Ultimately Moses became an incredible leader and worker for the Lord.

I repeat the question to you. What is in your hand? What skills, talents, interests, or resources do you possess that can be used for the

Lord and for Kingdom work? Perhaps your hands and brains understand the complications of modern-day technology. These skills are so needed by "umpteen" churches and faith groups to complete their mission in the local church, the community, and the world.

Do you have a lawn mower? Fishing pole? Guitar? Needle and thread? Mechanical skills? Law degree? What's in your hand? How can it be used to support the needs of hurting or overburdened church leaders, single parents, youth lacking mentors, or families worldwide lacking knowledge of the Lord?

Have you thought, "I am just too busy to volunteer?" Maybe your timid personality whispers in your ear, "You're not good enough or you're too old, too young, or too afraid to help?" Child workers, singers, listening ears, card writers, friendly smiles, kitchen help at camps, or transportation drivers and chaperones are needed throughout our world as we spread God's love to the unloved, hurting, needy, tired, lonely, busy, overburdened humans. Perhaps your hands work well with restoring and painting a widow's home? Could you take over the cleaning or lawn upkeep for a faith-based organization?

The ultimate volunteer for God's cause, Moses had to be buffeted a bit to realize his untapped leadership skills. Ultimately, though, he got the message. Even his brother, Aaron, became part of the team. Families may find ways to share in service tasks, and in the process find their own family relationships are strengthened. Remember, God can do marvelous tasks through ordinary people. It is our job to open our eyes to the needs and calls for help from those around us. Then we need to move to serve, trusting that God will provide His helping hand through us.

You might help by finding that strawberry patch. Fill your bucket with lush berries. Make a few pies, jars of jelly, and/or fresh fruit salads. Then round up your family and friends, ages three to ninety-three, and find special homes for your products. Leave a smile and an invitation for each recipient to come celebrate the Lord of our lives at the next worship service. Be present to greet, welcome, and chat a bit with a new friend that Sunday.

You are now an official "Kingdom Worker." Moses had a few tough challenges along the way as the Children of Israel complained, got bored with their desert diet, and wanted to return and worship a golden calf. But despite these challenges, the trio of Moses, Aaron, and God accomplished their goal of leading the Israelite family to the Promised Land.

So don't get discouraged. Don't give up. Identify your "rod," your talents, natural abilities, or skills. Pick up that talent "snake" by the tail. Then keep on keeping on, even as you reach the ripe old age of twenty-five, fifty-five, or eighty-five. God never gives up on you. Moses was asked to throw down a very important item for a shepherd. The rod was how this shepherd made his living, beating off wild animals, rescuing stranded sheep, or perhaps even supporting himself as he walked along the dusty paths of Egypt. God commanded him to put that rod in his hand and put his skills to work.

Moses ultimately used his rod, as noted in Exodus, to...
- Confront Egyptian soothsayers - 7:12
- Turn waters of Egypt to blood - 7:17-20
- Bring forth the plagues preceding the actual exodus from Egypt - chapters 8, 9, 10, 14, and 17
- Part the Red Sea - 14:16
- Bring water from a rock in the desert - 17:5

Make your list of actions your hands can perform. Then follow through, as a faithful servant of God.

Note: Read Psalm 105 and 106 for a wonderful review of the Israelites and their exodus from Egypt, travels through the desert, and their entrance into the Promised Land, just as God had promised.

CHAPTER EIGHTEEN
"Noisy" Stillness

A warm, June afternoon and no scheduled appointments. Wow! What a joyful thought! Hard to think that nothing demanded immediate attention. A bit of fatigue, following nine holes of golf and an early brunch with the senior golf gang, engulfed me. Appointments, committee meetings, and other responsibilities earlier in the week seemed to have drained my energy.

Choices faced me. Re-shingle the roof on our apartment building, dash around the park across the street and set a world record for an eighty-plus female, or maybe slip out to the church camp and help prepare food for the campers' evening meal. Somehow none of those choices appealed to my weary body and mind that day.

Our apartment was quiet. No scheduled events stared at me from my phone calendar. Then a brilliant idea flashed across my brain. Go! Go grab a book. Go out to your third-floor balcony area and finish the P.D. James mystery you've been reading for at least three weeks. And so began an interesting hour or so, quietly resting and reading, with my feet up on a small table by my chair. Well, maybe not much reading.

The temperature was warm and the air a bit heavy with smoke floating down from Canadian forest fires. I checked my phone messages and then grabbed my book. Before completing more than a dozen pages, you know what happened. The eyelids slipped closed, and a brief nap happened, including, I do believe, some dreaming experience. I never remember what I dream, but as I woke up, total quiet seemed to encompass me.

My eyes began to scan the yard area below, letting the environment intrude into my privacy. Scanning the seventeen small balconies and porches within my sight, I was amazed at the variety of objects displayed. A beautiful potted plant of petunias sat at my feet. A thermometer registered about 74, but the dangling hummingbird feeder had no visitors.

Other balconies sported chairs of various descriptions, but all minus human bodies, except for this writer. Plants and flowers of a wide variety brightened my day. Hanging on two railings were American flags, waving in the light breeze. It was an unusual day as no geese were sitting on the railings, depositing spots on the floor and I really missed their smiling goose bills grinning at me. A few sparrows were ok, and I know God had them all counted, but I prefer the majestic elegance of the goose to the flitting sparrow's wings.

The world around me was wonderfully silent, or was it? Relaxing, eyes closed, the silence began to disappear. A few cars zipped by on the nearby road or slammed on their brakes as they approached the turn circle at the corner. In the distance, the racing of a motorcycle's engine was heard.

And then, as my ears became more sensitive, I realized the stillness was broken as the chimes hanging from our porch made soft, tinkling sounds. When really tuned in, the gentle buzz of a chorus of crickets was heard. Mixed in were some gentle bird tweets. Even the slight breeze added another voice to this magnificent array of sounds. Nature's "noise" shouted out, as I moved my focus from P.D. James' story to Creator God's handiwork.

Psalm 46:10 reminded me, "Be still, and know that I am God; I will be exalted among the nations, I will be exalted in the earth." Sitting quietly, just listening, I was reminded of God's greatness. I was overwhelmed for a moment with the sounds and noise hidden in God's stillness. David reminded me, in Psalm 100:3, to "Know that the Lord is God. It is he who made us, and we are his people, the sheep of his pasture." Somehow, these moments of quiet and noisy reflections caused my weariness to evaporate.

Friends, take some moments in your hectic schedule to seek "stillness" hidden in the day-to-day "noise" of life. Perhaps, for others, life is too quiet, even boring. May I encourage each of you to find a little balcony, a quiet spot in a forest reserve or park, or a fishing pole at your familiar watering hole? Go and sit. Turn off your worries, challenges, or daily distractions. Maybe even snooze for ten minutes.

Then, ever so gently, open your eyes and turn on your ears. Be sensitive to God's creation. If you're very, very quiet and focused, you may hear God whisper to you, "I made this world for you. Enjoy and celebrate my creation."

As my mind began to wander a bit, the front door opened. My friend was back, and her voice broke the spell. "How was your golf game today?" Reality returned, but for a few moments, God and I had a noisy, quiet time. My battery was recharged, and off I went to accomplish some other responsibilities.

Hear God's Silence.

CHAPTER NINETEEN
Frozen Fowl Fill a Truck

A normal day begins at Inner City Mission in Springfield. Jerry hustles around tending to the needs of the families located at the mission. And then, a soft voice is heard. "I would like a chicken salad sandwich," and Jerry's world is turned upside down. Crystal's sad, pleading eyes focus on this gentle man. His mind clicks into gear, as he plots how to fulfill this simple "gourmet" request.

He suggests she check the freezer and cabinet. Returning, he hears the words, "We do not have any bread. We don't have any chicken, either." Disappointed eyes turn toward Jerry, who smiles and replies, "Well, we will pray," and so a prayer for bread and chicken is lifted heavenward. One wonders what is going through Crystal's mind as she closes her eyes and listens to Jerry's prayer for a chicken salad sandwich.

As the prayer concludes, Jerry notices a Taurus Ford station wagon pulling into the parking area. He recognizes the driver from a local food bank. Unable to use all the food items, they come bearing gifts for other hungry folk. Guess what the van is crammed with—over thirty cases of food (a very special type) - bread. Yes, bread, loaves and loaves of bread, ready to eat. In fact, there is probably sufficient bread for sandwiches to feed a local hospital or high school of teenage guys. Is this an accident or . . .?

The slices of comfort food are barely unloaded when the phone rings. Our leader of the day grabs the ringing machine and listens. His expression changes from politeness to unbelief and wonder. The caller is informing him that the cooling unit on a semi has broken down and their load of food needs to be refrigerated in the next three hours, or all will need to be thrown away. The speaker explained that the truck is loaded with frozen, you guessed it, chickens. Could the mission use any of them? Imagine for yourself the thought running through Jerry's head as he shares this information with our "sandwich hungry" twenty-year-old.

Grabbing his keys, he hops into his pick-up and dashes to the source of frozen hens. Quickly cramming the pick-up to the top, he races back before the deadline for throwing the birds away. The freezer is stuffed with a truckload of featherless, frozen chicken, enough for hundreds of sandwiches.

And then, a quiet voice whispers, "But Jerry, we still have a problem. We need three more items for my mother's favorite chicken salad recipe. We do not have any mayo, mustard, or pickle relish." With a sigh, Jerry's discouragement engulfs him. Then another voice enters the scene. A visiting friend pipes up. "Let me see what I can do," and disappears. Shortly, and you can predict what's coming, he returns, handing Crystal a large sack. Yes, in the sack are jars of mayo, mustard, and relish.

Crystal has her sandwich wish fulfilled, but just imagine what the adults are thinking. In fact, that evening the entire group of folks staying at the mission munch on mayo and chicken. God surely was involved with this narrative. Specific, focused, unselfish, God-related prayers have answers, often with very visible results. The arrival of loaves of bread, mounds of chicken, with a few jars of mayo, mustard, and pickles thrown in could not be "just an accident."

As I am hearing this story, two young people from church are standing beside me, their eyes focusing on Jerry as he relates the story. They hear every word without comment, but I am confident that these young folk will long remember this ever so powerful, specific answer to prayer.

Returning home, my mind reviews the answered prayer. The memory then takes a quick detour to the story of Jesus' teaching-picnic by the sea. Over five thousand folks have just heard Jesus speak. The children began to get restless. Tummies were hungry. Perhaps a murmur was heard by the disciples. They approached the Master, requesting that He send the folk back to town for food, maybe for a sardine sandwich. Jesus, however, took over. Giving thanks, He handed the small boy's five loaves and a pair of fish to the disciples, who in turn distributed the food, feeding 5,000 guys plus their families. All ate and were satisfied. (Matthew 14:13-21)

That is answered prayer. Don't you wonder if the twelve disciples were as amazed as the two youth who were listening to Jerry share his story?

Let us, however, remember today that we must constantly "hunger" after the "bread of life." When life seems impossible, to whom should we turn? The disciples immediately approached the Master for help. Jerry quickly bowed his head and made a request of that same Master. Crystal undoubtedly also said a word of thanks to the Lord. Hopefully I, too, can remember to do likewise.

Life is Hard. Remember that God is on your side, ready and willing to assist your daily walk.

CHAPTER TWENTY
Peace & Quiet

Rub-A-Dub-Dub
Three Days in a Tub! Peace...

"Peace I leave with you; my peace I give you.
I do not give to you as the world gives.
Do not let your hearts be troubled
and do not be afraid" (John 14:27).

"Rejoice in the Lord always.
I will say it again: Rejoice!
Let your gentleness be evident to all.
The Lord is near. Do not be anxious about anything,
but in every situation, by prayer and petition,
with thanksgiving, present your requests to God.
And the peace of God, which transcends all understanding,
will guard your hearts and your minds in Christ Jesus"
(Philippians 4:4-8).

Anxiety, fear, uneasiness, inner turmoil, secret worries, burdens on the heart—which of us has not experienced moments of one or more of these descriptors? Personal peace seems to vanish in our world of business, technology, financial stress, or physical challenges and pain. Difficulties, perceived or actual, crowd out thoughts of God's promise of peace. Scurry, hurry, and worry, a trio of action words, tear our lives apart. We forget to "rejoice in the Lord always".

As born-again believers we focus on inner frustrations, rather than remembering Romans 5:1. "Therefore, since we have been justified through faith, we have peace with God through our Lord Jesus Christ."

When we take a quiet moment of meditation, do we really know the joy and peace promised in Romans 15:13? "May the God of hope fill you with all joy and peace as you trust in him, so that you may overflow with hope by the power of the Holy Spirit." It is not just us, however; the quest for peace is timeless and global. Take for example the definition of peace for the Quechua Indians in Ecuador and Bolivia literally translates, "To sit down in one's heart." It means to rest rather than running around amid constant anxieties. Biblical peace is not the absence of trouble. It is a feeling of goodness in life, even in the midst of great trials. Paul demonstrated peace and contentment even while in jail at Philippi! (Acts 16)

Recently a friend demonstrated perfect, God-trusting peace during an extremely frightening situation. Shall we call her Angie? Angie attends a Sunday class for senior adults, of which this author is a part. She enjoys chatting with friends on the phone, thus filling moments of loneliness or boredom.

One week, a friend, (we'll call her Jenny), had received no calls from Angie for a couple of days. She wondered a bit why the phone had not rung. By the third day, Jenny was worried and drove by Angie's apartment. The car was parked outside so Jenny knocked several times on the door, but no one answered. She became even more worried, and since the door was locked, she attempted to locate a key. She checked with folk across the hall. They did not have a key but said they would call the landlord.

As Jenny waited, she thought she heard faint sounds from the apartment. Finally, the landlord arrived, and the door was unlocked, only to discover that there was a chain lock in place. Standing back a bit, our "key" man slammed the door, breaking the chain, and the pair entered the apartment.

Jenny called out and heard a weak voice responding from the area of the bathroom. Jenny approached the room, and there she found Angie, fully dressed but lying prone in the bathtub, feet extended under the faucet area. She looked weak and worn. Jenny swiftly got some water, encouraging Angie to drink only a small amount and then share what happened. With a trembling voice, the story became clear.

Apparently three days earlier Angie had felt weak and attempted to sit down on the toilet to rest, but instead, tumbled into the tub and was unable to extract herself from the temporary "tomb." For about seventy hours she had remained stretched out on this hard surface with no phone, water, or food. Her only companion was the Lord, to whom she prayed over and over for help. In fact, she had been praying specifically for Angie to miss her and to seek her out OR that the Lord would take her to Him. God heard and answered her petitions.

9-1-1 was called and our prayer-believing follower was taken to the hospital, and later to a care center for some rehabilitation. She is now home, regaining her strength, hoping to soon be resuming her normal activities. Through all of this, she praises the Lord for the peace she had during her ordeal. This peace helped her remain calm throughout the storm. What amazing faith!

As I reflected on her story, I was reminded of Jonah and his three days in the belly of the large fish. I wonder what he was praying as he was confined in a rather tight-fitting situation. The smells alone would have made peace impossible for this scribe.

"Therefore we do not lose heart.
Though outwardly we are wasting away,
yet inwardly we are being renewed day by day"
(2 Corinthians 4:16).

CHAPTER TWENTY-ONE
Bear Country

Bears have been a part of my life since day one in 1935. A gift bear still remains on my dresser that Uncle Justin brought to the hospital in Portland, Oregon on 9-8-1935. Collections of bears are scattered throughout our home, including umpteen in a trunk belonging to my father. Big bears, wee ones, new, used (one given to me with only one eye) and a pair of clever bear bookends fill my apartment. Although I have never been chased nor eaten by a bear, it is great fun to watch them lumber across a wooded area, nibbling berries.

Bears wander into the scriptures several times, as we take our journey from Genesis to Revelation. Of course God created them, along with camels, hippos, grasshoppers, and you and me. David reminds Saul that bears came and carried off his sheep (1 Samuel 17:34). In Revelation 13:2, John saw in his vision a beast coming out of the sea with feet like a bear, along with many other features.

A bloodier encounter with these four-legged, hungry beasts appears in 2 Kings 2:23-24. Elisha was jeered by some young males from town who called, "Get out of here, baldy!" This brave man of God, turned around, looked them in the eyes, and called down a curse in the name of the Lord. Guess what! Two bears appeared and mauled forty-two of these young men.

More importantly, however, "bear" appears as an action word. A few examples include, "bear witness" (Job 16:8), "bear good news" (2 Samuel 18:25), or "no good tree bears bad fruit" (Luke 6:43).

The most vivid example of "bearing up" reminds me of Moses and the Israelites as they faced the Amalekites (Exodus 17:8-13). Moses goes to the top of the mountain and holds up his staff to encourage Joshua and the fighters. When he grows weary and brings his arms down, his team begins to lose the battle. Arms up, winning; arms down losing. Aaron and Hur decide to help. They seat Moses on a rock and then, one on each side, "bear up" or hold his arms until sunset, allowing the Israelites to overcome and win the battle.

Now, you might ask, why bring up this "bear" topic. When reading Galatians 6:2, these fuzzy carnivores pop into my mind. "Bear one another's burdens, and so fulfill the law of Christ" (RSV). What does Paul mean when chiding the Galatian Christians to bear burdens? How does one "bear" another person's burden? Should one immediately locate a person struggling to carry a mattress up three flights of stairs by herself, and offer to tote it for her? Would Paul be suggesting that a "burden" is something other than a heavy object needing to be moved? Of course he does. So, what are our responsibilities?

Paul gives us a tough order. "Brothers and sisters, if someone is caught in sin, you who live by the Spirit should restore that person gently. But watch yourselves, or you also may be tempted" (Galatians 6:1). He then follows it with the bearing or carrying-the-burden-for-others command. What a charge! This two-fold command makes me tremble. Restoration of a fellow human being implies a tremendous responsibility. A person trapped in sin may not be receptive of a helping hand. Knowing that none of us is perfect increases the challenge. It would be helpful if God would send an e-mail to those He knows are living as the Spirit desires. We know "The fruit of the Spirit is love, joy, peace, forbearance, kindness, goodness, faithfulness, gentleness and self-control" (Galatians 5:22). But how much love or joy qualifies you to reach out to restore another? This question brings fear and trembling to this author.

The challenge increases in difficulty. We must also carry each other's burden. This is a partnership. You help me as I help you. We don't have an exact roadmap for accomplishing this task. Could we perhaps think that we need to care about others? We must hand-hold in times of distress. Giant listening ears, accompanied by a spirit of love, but minus a judgmental attitude, seem to be required. Building relationships, vs. living in isolation, increases the opportunities to both recognize Christians in need of a helping friend and bear their burden.

As I pen these words tonight, I scan my brain for situations in which reaching out and burden-carrying would be helpful, yet still within my ability to carry them out. Then I figuratively SLAP my hands. I am not alone. God and the Spirit are with me in this endeavor. They are not just watching, cheering, and waving flags.

We are partners. My mind is open to instruction and guidance from the Holy Spirit. Today it may be our (God's and Kathy's) responsibility to guide someone back to a closer relationship with the Lord. Tomorrow, because of stumbles in my own life, hopefully another Christian, with the Lord at her side, will reach out to help me bear my burden.

Yes, "Burden Bearers" are important in the lives of Christians.

CHAPTER TWENTY-TWO
He is There! He is Always There!

Twilight approaches. Streetlights flick on. Frosty raindrops click against the windshield. As you glance up, the sky is covered with billowing clouds. You drop your bag of kitty food, peanut butter, and fresh bread on the car seat, buckle up, and head for home. The temperature display on the dashboard of the car confirms your feelings — hurry before the streets become a skating rink. You notice your pulse beating more rapidly. You may even sigh silently, wishing spring would return.

What is happening? Uncertainty? Senior cautiousness? Concern for family safety? Memories stir not only of past winds, blizzards, or storms, but perhaps even of other moments of depression, uncertainty, worry, or fear. I enjoyed many trips around the sun, and there have been many weak days.

I remember a Christmas many years ago when my brother and family lived in Russell, Kansas. Each year I would journey to wherever he and his family were living to spend a few days of visiting, sharing gifts, and eating too much. That year was no exception. My Audi was loaded with gifts so I could leave directly after school was dismissed. Excitement was mixed with general classroom fatigue as I set the cruise control westward. Undoubtedly a book on CD entertained me as the miles slipped by.

The initial hundred miles were fine. And then...as I exited on the west side of St. Louis, the wind shield wipers started flipping unexpectedly. The engine sputtered and slowed. Strange smells emitted from the rear seat. (The battery for the Audi was located under the back seat in those days.)

My heart went into panic mode. A single young lady on the road at dusk, and the car was obviously experiencing problems. What should I do? I glanced up and there was an exit ramp inviting me to leave the highway. I turned off and, yes, rolled into a service station located immediately at the foot of the ramp.

The car was NOT working. It was evening rush hour and the number of cars on the road had increased greatly as everyone else was trying to get home also. I was in a strange place and still had several hundred miles to go. I must admit the short prayer I offered was tinged with a bit of fear.

The Lord was certainly with me at that moment. Although the service station did not repair cars, the owner knew exactly what to do and a plan was implemented immediately. He called the Audi dealer in St. Louis and made arrangements for his service truck to tow the car to the dealer. A quick phone call provided a room in a nearby motel, and a service attendant helped me load gifts and clothes into a rental car.

After spending the night in St. Louis, I made it to Russell, enjoyed the holiday, and on my return to St. Louis I located the repair shop, turned in the rental, and found my way home to Springfield in my own car. Hopefully I truly reached out to God.

God has made many promises. One writer counted more than 10,000 in the Bible. I have not personally confirmed that number but let's look at seven for a starter, each of which played some part in a safe and relaxing holiday that year.

I. I am your strength. I will dwell with you. "I can do all this through him who gives me strength" (Philippians 4:13).
II. I will never leave you. "Keep your lives free from the love of money and be content with what you have, because God has said, 'Never will I leave you; never will I forsake you.' So we say with confidence, 'The Lord is my helper; I will not be afraid. What can mere mortals do to me'" (Hebrews 13:5-6)?
III. I have plans for you to prosper. "'For I know the plans I have for you,' declares the Lord, 'plans to prosper you and not to harm you, plans to give you hope and a future'" (Jeremiah 29:11).
IV. I hear your prayers. "Then you will call on me and come and pray to me, and I will listen to you" (Jeremiah 29:12).
V. I will fight for you. "What, then, shall we say in response to these things? If God is for us, who can be against us" (Romans 8:31)? Load on your Christian armor (Ephesians 6:10-20) and more forward with faith.

VI. I give you peace. "A time is coming and in fact has come when you will be scattered, each to your own home. You will leave me all alone. Yet I am not alone, for my father is with me. I have told you these things, so that in me you may have peace. In this world you will have trouble. But take heart! I have overcome the world" (John 16:32-33).

VII. I will always care and love you. "Cast all your anxiety on him because he cares for you" (I Peter 5:7).

To this day I can still remember thinking, "What am I going to do? I am alone. My car does not work and darkness is advancing. Where in the world was my faith?" The Lord was there all the time. He did not prevent the car from having mechanical problems, but He certainly prepared a path to safety. He knew he gave me peace that evening both on the road and at the motel, alone, but not alone, for He will never leave me as long as I remain faithful. He heard my prayers and strengthened my faith. He was there.

Your Choice:
Snow covered, slick roads,
Potential accidents may
Produce
Fear
OR
Sun, shadows, sparkling
Streams,
Relaxation results in
His Peace
Where will you let your
Mind go in times of stress?

CHAPTER TWENTY-THREE
Abandoned? Missing in Action?

At the sight of twin toddler car seats sitting on the sidewalk, my curiosity button switched on. No children or adults are in sight. Where might the occupants of these safety seats be hiding? Did a pair of children escape, dashing off to grab a dish of pablum, followed by worried parents? Could they be invisible to human eyes? Should observers be worried and attempt a rescue mission? My imagination loves to wander around, inquiring.

Let's assume, for a moment, that twin kids escaped from the car seats and just wandered off. What would the parents do? Would they continue discussing prices of a new vehicle or split up and dash off in search of the missing two-year olds?

Jesus shared a parable of missing-in-action sheep. Checking his flock in at the end of the day, the shepherd reached number ninety-nine. He stopped. What had happened? Where was number 100? Leaving the multitude of sheep on the hills, our shepherd grabbed his staff and dashed in search of the missing wooly one. Was it hurt, mischievous, eaten by a wolf, or just still nibbling on a cactus? Regardless, he must find him and bring the wee ram home. Our Master continues his parable with, "In the same way your Father in heaven is not willing that any of these little ones should perish" (Matthew 18:14).

Probably that evening, sitting around the campfire, the shepherd celebrated the return of the one, but never even mentioned the sheep safe in the fold. So, Christ continues, "I tell you that in the same way there will be more rejoicing in heaven over one sinner who repents than over ninety-nine righteous persons who do not need to repent" (Luke 15:7).

Search and find is almost an automatic response for parents and others who love and/or are responsible for wandering young folk. These searchers leap over high walls, dash through corn fields, and run until weary, crying along the way. One goal motivates them. Find the lost. What happens then? Hugs, kisses, or maybe a special treat? But undoubtedly a short discussion on the behavior of the recently found, and how that behavior resulted in fright and worry by the adults. Why that discussion? People loved and cared for the lost.

Jesus continued his parables for the tax collectors and sinners listening that day. A woman has ten silver coins. One slips from her fingers and rolls away. Probably the floor of her home was dirt. She grabs a broom and searches for the one missing item. This coin, obviously, was extremely valuable, for she does a strange thing. She calls the neighbors over and says, "Rejoice with me; I have found my lost coin" (Luke 15:9). Then Jesus supplies the point of the story. "In the same way, I tell you, there is rejoicing in the presence of the angels of God over one sinner who repents" (Luke 15: 10).

Our trio of tales continues as the Master storyteller shares the experience we all remember, the tale of the Lost Son. The kid asks for his share of the family wealth, trots off to town, gets into trouble, runs out of funds, and then this Jewish lad ends up feeding the pigs. Hungry, and in total disgrace, he humbly returns to his Dad, seeking not to be restored as a son, but only taken on as a hired hand. Of course, Dad thinks differently. Spotting the grubby guy stumbling down the lane, he recognizes him, and filled with compassion, runs (not walks) to meet him. And then Dad did what many of us might have been reluctant to do, hugs his son, kisses him, and plans a party in his honor. The celebration begins.

We, of course, also remember the older, stay-at-home son, who pouts a bit and wishes that dad had made a fuss over him. Quietly his Father gives this heart-rending response. "My son, you are always with me, and everything I have is yours. But we had to celebrate and be glad, because this brother of yours was dead and is alive again; he was lost and is found" (Luke 15:31-32).

Why is Jesus sharing these everyday stories? His critics were questioning why he hung around with sinners. Why, they add, does he even eat with them? Our all-wise Father, instead of yelling at them for criticizing him, quietly shares three touching, but powerful, lessons about hunting for valuable lost items, and sharing that joy with others when recovery is accomplished. The priority was seeking the lost, not focusing on those already safely in the fold, or securely in the woman's hand, or reliably dwelling in the father's home.

Today I ponder. What is lost that needs to be found and restored to the Kingdom today in my life? Do I know a friend who has abandoned the church for many months? Have I closed my eyes for so long to those needing help that they have become invisible? Perhaps I have ninety-nine friends who are safely in the arms of Jesus, but what about the friend who is missing in action? Do I need to go searching?

Lost - Sought – Found

CHAPTER TWENTY-FOUR
V-Day -- A Time for Thanksgiving

**Roses are red
The sky is blue
God's great love
Reaches out to you**

Hopefully on Valentine Week, each of you remembered the Great Lover of all. The psalmist David said it so well. "Many are the woes of the wicked, but the Lord's unfailing love surrounds the one who trusts in him. Rejoice in the Lord and be glad, you righteous; sing, all you who are upright in heart!" (Psalm 32:10-11)

On the 14th, as I nibbled on a yummy dark chocolate from Pease's, my favorite candy store, I thanked my friend for her thoughtfulness. Wandering over to the kitchen window, my eyes blinked twice. Black and white feathers flashed by as a large eagle settled on the branch by the water's edge. God had just sent a reminder of his incredible creation. Once again, a quick little thank you.

Crunchy, icy sounds reached my ears as my feet carefully plodded out to retrieve the daily paper. With a near zero temperature outside, words of thanks to God froze in my throat. This lady prefers slightly warmer air. Once again, however, David had the word of the day. "When I said, 'My foot is slipping,' your unfailing love, Lord, supported me." And then another reminder followed. "When anxiety was great within me, your consolation brought me joy" (Psalm 94:18-19). Of course, David was not thinking of black ice on a driveway, but of his personal weaknesses. I am confident, however, that God was also watching over this clumsy lady as she treaded, ever so carefully, to the street.

My job on this earth for Him must still be unfinished, since I made it back to the warmth of the kitchen without smashing my nose and knees on the driveway. Guess I will have to keep pushing ahead. That is a thrilling idea for this time of thoughtfulness for our friends and for the Greatest Friend of all. "Hang tough" will be my motto until the next February 14.

Yes, thanks must fill my prayers, not just on V-Day, but daily. The greatest lover not only provides me with beautiful sights, delicious floral aromas, and protection from icy dangers, but even more importantly, joy and support during midnight hours of tossing and turning because of life's anxieties or uncertainties.

I am delighted that this special day causes me to pause and reflect for a few moments. Sitting at the computer, my mind wanders backwards in time. Suddenly I remember the red flowers sitting on my desk for a year. About a year ago I was resting on the sofa, recovering from knee replacement. The doorbell rang, and my friend and her daughter entered carrying a small vase with a trio of beautiful, artificial red roses. We sat and visited, shared medical stories and recoveries, and my heart was blessed. Today, while chatting with this same friend on the phone, I reminded her of her thoughtfulness and that the red blooms still greeted me each dawn as I wander by my desk.

Why, I ask myself, do I remember to say thanks and words of appreciation for kindnesses received from earthly friends, but so frequently fail to even murmur a mere word of thanks to the giver of all gifts? Am I too busy with daily tasks and responsibilities that I shut down my "thank you" button for God's gifts? Perhaps I just take God, and all He does for me, for granted. I just assume that blue herons, eagles, and red headed woodpeckers will continue to fill me with joy. They are present every day, as common as toasted flakes for breakfast. Nary a mumbled word to God in appreciation for common, everyday wonders in our world. Shame on me.

Time for a new resolution: "Lord, help me daily to praise you for your gifts."
May that be my Valentine Day resolution?

PS: No one will ever accuse me of being an incredible poet. Sorry for my revised version of the verse above based on the old favorite "Roses are Red".

CHAPTER TWENTY-FIVE
Meaningful Conversation with Teens

When was the last time you spoke with someone at least forty-five years older or younger than yourself, other than a relative? Oh! I know you can say hi to a teen or maybe even ask how they are, but I mean a real, meaningful conversation for four or five minutes?

Observation by this senior suggests that youth generally isolate into small groups and our over-sixty crowd moves to another corner of the auditorium or gathering area. Maybe we flash a smile if they are the offspring of one of our adult friends, but basically little to no intergenerational interaction takes place. Why might this be a topic worthy of an essay? What good or not-so-good could happen when "pimpled" teens and white-haired adults communicate with each other?

No, I'm not suggesting flirting, but lighthearted or serious sharing of ideas to help pass on traditions, knowledge, and open our eyes to the needs and challenges of people at each end of the age spectrum.

Our senior group at church recently visited with the student pastor and shared some thoughts with each other. It appeared that bits of shared wisdom and wit might help everyone. Hopefully some might be able to share life lessons learned from seventy years of hard knocks. Believe it or not, not all teens really want to receive those hints from their parents, but an outsider is another story.

And then, you say, why in the world would the arthritic generation want to know anything from a lively teen? Oh! Do you sometimes encounter technology challenges? Who is better than one who can solve computer or phone problems with his/her eyes closed? Agreed, they probably couldn't operate a four-line, hand cranked, phone on the wall, but unlocking your pocket communication instrument takes them a nanosecond.

We need each other. We learn from people who represent a variety of perspectives. Our history and culture must be shared, or our love of freedom may vanish. Who will be the leaders in fifteen—thirty years?

Not the silver heads, but the kids with the crazy jeans or frumpy hair. Our church nursery must be staffed with caring people, filled with God's love. Teachers of the new teens need to experience the wisdom of those ahead who traveled the road so rough.

A helping hand extends two ways. Youth need war stories and Christian wisdom, but wrinkled and bent humans need a strong hand helping them cross the foyer to the table spread with yummy casseroles and cookies. It's great to see a wide age range on the Lord's Day sharing the music leadership teams. Certainly, the adult guitar player begins to appreciate modern rhythms, and occasionally a hymn from the nineteen forties to eighties might begin to dance from the tongue of the teen making the drums rattle and roll. We need to bridge understanding and joy across generations.

Recently our youth prepared breakfast for our senior Bible class. Following the sharing of delicious eggs and biscuits, we gathered at small tables of three or four adults and two or three youths. All introduced themselves and shared a sentence or seven about their lives. The adults were then invited to each share with their table partners one bit of wisdom which they had learned from many years of living.

Switching gears, the youth were invited to ask any serious question about life or the Lord that had been bothering them, or of which they really wanted to have a deeper understanding. The adults then had the responsibility of sharing their wisdom. Probably no more than twenty minutes were involved, but the door of understanding between different age groups was nudged open. A second mixed age group session is planned in another month or two.

Could there possibly be another positive outcome resulting from increasing interaction between different generations of people? Both public reports, as well as observations in our own churches, suggest we have a problem. Especially among teens and those in the category of single adults; these groups seem to be vanishing rapidly from our youth groups and church pews. Their priorities no longer include following in the traditional foot-steps of their families. Acknowledging a love of God and meeting regularly to celebrate His love, is not for them. Life is too exciting or busy, or who knows what goes through the brain of a teen? Many do not even pretend to accept any connection with the church.

Maybe we need to initiate both spontaneous and planned situations for these humans of mixed ages to interact with followers of the Way. Back to our original premise — personal connections create friendships, bonding, and models for searching youth. Providing programs for same age groups is absolutely essential, but almost total isolation between different ages, is a tragedy.

The church is a community of believers. We are the family of God. Families care for one another through thick and thin. Communication helps, and that means a balance of two-way listening and speaking. Young people need to respect their elders, but elders need to model respect for teens. Ignoring the youth will result in a lost generation of Christ followers. Share from your heart/mind the love of God for each of His children. This love is more than a rote recitation of the Lord's Prayer, but deep understanding modifying our daily actions. Show you care, even as Christ cares for you.

Join me in a renewed effort to break the language barrier between all ages of our church family.

**Maybe find one youth for whom you will especially take the challenge of beginning meaningful dialogue.
Happy Chatting and Sharing**

CHAPTER TWENTY-SIX
Making a Joyful Noise

Power of a Song

What comes to mind when you hear the suggestion, "Make a Joyful Noise?" As I write these words on July fourth, the noise in the background is not really "joyful". Words like "burst," "distant and continuous pops and fizzles," or "little explosive noises" might be generated in my brain. The sound is not necessarily disturbing, unless one is trying to get a baby to sleep, but "pleasant sound" might not come to mind either. This evening, though, we will probably sit in the darkness with friends and enjoy the sparkling, sizzling, sometimes impressive displays in the sky. We will not be making melody, however, in our hearts, but perhaps remembering a bit of history such as Congress officially adopting the Declaration of Independence on July 4, 1776.

Psalm 100:1 suggests we need to "Shout for joy to the Lord, all the earth. Worship the Lord with gladness; come before him with joyful songs." Shouting may be a tad strong for me, as I prefer quiet, thoughtful worship music, but certainly I want to hear and share the joy of the Lord through words and sound.

While attending the funeral of a friend, a most unusual element of the service transpired. The audience was invited to join in the singing of a song. It was a hymn of love and thoughtful memories of Jesus walking in the garden with Mary Magdalene, shortly after the resurrection. A few voices began tentatively, but gradually, more courageous souls opened their mouths. The audience soon filled the room with joyful sound. Of course I appreciated the eulogies and loving comments shared by family and friends, but what lingers most are the memories of the melody "I Come to the Garden Alone" shared by the entire audience. In fact, a tear even slid down my cheek, for this song was a favorite of my own mother.

Why do you suppose the group singing touched my heart? For me, it is easy to tune out a single speaking or singing voice. When an entire audience - or at least most brave souls - join in, concentration and focus are increased. The individual is directly a part of the service. Each is personally engaged. Perhaps there is power in a song.

Shortly after that service, we had a time of singing hymns with a gathering of seniors at our church. To increase variety and personal involvement," the leader interspersed a few, brief comments and activities relating to the next hymn. Prior to "Praise Him, Praise Him," the microphone was passed around and audience members were invited to share a quick, personal praise.

Similarly, we were given a thought challenge prior to singing "When We All Get to Heaven." The leader asked us all to share who we are most anxious to meet when we leave this earthly environment. Of course, my response was my mother.

We had fun with "I Come to the Garden." A mini scavenger hunt took place. We were asked to find objects associated with a garden. One item on the search list was a seed, which was discovered in the form of a cookie with poppy seeds sprinkled on the top. Of course, we had to chuckle a bit.

The mood became more serious as we prepared to sing "Sweet Hour of Prayer." Each was encouraged to share a one or two sentence prayer of thanks with others at their small table.

Our time of joyful music concluded with the great favorite "Holy, Holy, Holy". A member had been invited to read aloud Revelation 4:8-11. What a great reminder as the four living creatures are described as never stopping their praise, saying, "Holy, holy, holy is the Lord God Almighty, who was, and is, and is to come." I'm confident each of us gets a little catch in our throat as we remember singing the old song, "Holy, Holy, Holy." God indeed is and will be merciful and mighty for all eternity.

Perhaps your friends might also like to echo our afternoon of memories, sharing, and singing. Surely you still have someone able to play the piano or guitar (softly) to help each voice stay on pitch. Remember to thank the leader for daring to be bold and venture into new worlds of sound.

The Lord will also rejoice as He hears His name being praised.

CHAPTER TWENTY-SEVEN
July - Delight of Many

Growing up, this phrase was heard frequently
in our part of the country
"I Scream,
You Scream,
We All Scream
for Ice Cream!"

Ice cream is a mouthwatering, creamy treat for nearly every child, adult, and even senior. What is your favorite flavor? Could it be Rocky Road, Peach, Pistachio, or Butter Pecan? The three most popular flavors are chocolate, strawberry, and then, of course the number one choice is vanilla. Any flavor containing nuts is tasty to my mouth. Just don't add a maraschino cherry on top. Sugar cones are preferred and I'll never turn-down a "drumstick".

President Ronald Reagan designated July as National Ice Cream Month in 1984. Apparently "The Ice Cream Capital of the World" is right in the back yard of Illinois. In 1994, LeMars, Iowa, home of Wells Enterprises Inc. and makers of Blue Bunny ice cream, was officially designated the world ice cream capital. I didn't even realize that bunnies liked ice cream, but maybe Iowa has a special species of blue rabbits.

As a youth growing up in Rolla, Missouri, I remember the little ringing bell, calling all children to the curb, clutching their money, while awaiting the Ice Cream man and his truck. The lure of Dairy Queen occasionally drew our car into their parking lot. Ice cream was truly a special treat for my brother and me.

July eighteenth is National Ice Cream Day. While thinking how to celebrate, a wonderful seed of an idea was planted in my brain. What if each of us decided to provide an ice cream treat for some staff member(s) at our church or synagogue? What surprise would warm the heart and cool the tongue of a stressed, hardworking employee? Could there be a group or an entire church team that needs recognition? Maybe some have spent days cleaning up following a bad storm or supervised a week at church camp with never-sleeping teens?

Several options popped into my head, which I will share. Perhaps these ideas will stimulate your brain to find cause for a special ice cream celebration for your circle of friends at church.

For example, pop into the office and invite one or more staff to join you for a milk shake or cone at the nearest ice cream treat store. Find a spot where you can sit around a table and visit a bit while licking the melting delight. Sharing stories and even expressing thanks for their faithfulness may be more long-lasting than just the calorie-filled cone.

I am close to a couple of youth from church who love ice cream. Occasionally we meet at a local dessert deli. They are given the chance to order whatever they want, and guess who pays the check? Although I know sipping malts is enjoyable, I do believe that a chat between teens and an older human also is a pleasurable experience for each. Missionary friends from Cambodia visit Illinois and send me an email of their pending arrival. I truly love crowding around a table, eyeball to eyeball, hearing about each family member's joys and the challenges of each of the family members as they spread the Word to people far away. Ice cream seems to be a perfect treat, as we talk and pray.

Thinking out of the box, try this idea. Go to your favorite ice cream spot. Buy an ice cream coupon to treat six or eight people. Think of a family with several children and pop the coupon into an envelope. Include a note encouraging them to have a family outing some evening, just for fun. Remember, some family budgets don't include $20-30 for a family trip to the local ice cream shop for the frozen, flavored cream delight. By the way, I just found the price of the most expensive sundae in the world—$1,000. I'm not suggesting you buy that, however.

Extra thought. Make up a fun six-to-ten item quiz relating to biblical references to food. Remember, Jesus fed the 5000, God provided the Children of Israel with manna and quail, and Elisha helped the widow pay off her debts and provide food for her sons. The sons gathered vessels from their neighbors. God filled the containers with oil, and the money from selling the oil saved the family. Perhaps the most meaningful food memory, though, is Jesus and the disciples experiencing the Last Supper. Tuck the quiz into an envelope with the coupons.

Do a little screaming.
Share a July treat.
Celebrate with the Lord and His workers.

CHAPTER TWENTY-EIGHT
Banana Peeling Pachyderm

Fussy Elephant

The long-lensed camera was carefully focused on Pang Pha, the famous 36-year-old elephant at the Berlin, Germany zoo. Rarely had eyes beheld the skill this huge, lumbering mammal might demonstrate that day. The photographer held her breath, hoping that her presence would not frighten our animal.

It was dinner time for our pachyderm. The zookeeper approached with a bag of food. She threw the beast a yellow-green banana, which Pang Pha caught and quickly ate. The second piece of fruit was mostly brownish. The fussy elephant tossed it aside. The third banana was yellowish-brown. The keeper and photographer held their breath. Would Pang Pha demonstrate her most unusual skill? Yes! Our animal friend scooped up this yellow-brown piece and swiftly moved it around and part of the skin was tossed to the floor. More waving of trunk and the pulp also fell to the ground. With a couple more shakes, the last of the pulp was released and the peel discarded.

Pang Pha stretched out her trunk, picked up the pulp with the tip of her tongue, and - about twenty seconds from toss to swallow - our friend peeled and consumed this rather ripe banana. For your information, elephants in captivity eat approximately sixty-six pounds of food a day. Three bananas equal about a pound. Thus, each would need to swallow around 198 yellow fruit each day. Maybe we should consider starting a banana farm in Germany and sell the produce to the zookeepers.

A bit of research revealed the fact that elephants like bananas, but rarely has one peeled them prior to popping it into her mouth. Pang Pha has not even taught her daughter how to eliminate the unwanted, ripe, brown and yellow spotted peel. Apparently, the body of an elephant is able to digest the peel.

What about people? Yes, we peel our bananas, but do we sometimes forget to shed actions and attitudes that make our personalities less attractive to the Lord? Paul tells us in Ephesians 4:22-24 to abandon our former way of life. Just for fun, think of peeling off "over-ripe" behaviors and thoughts. Paul said, "You were taught, with regard to your former way of life, to put off your old self, which is being corrupted by its deceitful desires; to be made new in the attitude of your minds; and to put on the new self, created to be like God in true righteousness and holiness." I just wish it were as easy to change my life and habits as it is to peel a damaged piece of fruit.

One might wonder how Pang Pha acquired the peeling technique. Zoo staff suggested that she watched them peeling bananas, and somehow decided to model their behavior. Thinking about the power of example, I was reminded how Christians are encouraged to be examples for new believers.

Paul used some strong words for the Philippians to consider, relating to the power of example. "Finally, brothers and sisters, whatever is true, whatever is noble, whatever is right, whatever is pure, whatever is lovely, whatever is admirable — if anything is excellent or praiseworthy — think about such things. Whatever you have learned or received or heard from me, (Paul), or seen in me — put it into practice. And the God of peace will be with you" (Philippians 4:8-9).

As the zookeepers watched their "wonder woman," they observed another interesting habit. Pang Pha would never peel a banana in a social setting with her daughter or another female Asian elephant named Drumbo. She would just pick up and swallow like the other "girls." Often, however, she would pick up the last banana and take it with her. If we had telescopic eyes, we might be able to catch her peeling and enjoying her after-dinner snack when she was alone.

Our fussy elephant, for some reason, sought privacy while performing this most unusual banana peeling practice. Maybe she was bashful or afraid that her elephant companions would make fun of her? Who knows why she didn't share this habit?

Could that also be true of Christians? Aren't we also sometimes bashful or timid when speaking about our faith with others or in public? We seem to want to be invisible followers of Christ. Yes, doing good deeds and helping others quietly is very correct. The scriptures, however, are also clear that we must let our light shine and be bold about our relationship with Him.

The Challenge Today
Go public with your faith.
Peel back your timidity.
Help others personally know about your friend Jesus.

(Note: Elephant picture is NOT Pang Pha. This shot was taken in Africa in 2015 by the author.)

CHAPTER TWENTY-NINE
Are You a Twin? Probably Yes!

Spring has arrived. The deer show up in our yard, nibbling away. Gone are our petunias, poking their heads out of the ground. Hosta disappears as fast as the green creeps out of the soil. No more fresh leaves on the redbud. Hello, dawn and dusk, and our lawn becomes the cafeteria for these lovely, four-footed creatures.

One morning, while exiting our lane, I spotted a mother deer standing in the roadway. Underneath her, several small legs could be seen. Slowing the car, I continued to watch. After a short while, there was movement, and mama sauntered toward the woods. Suddenly it dawned on me. A fawn was having her morning milk.

Then a second, startling observation—not one, but two babies were quenching their thirst from the mama milking machine. This was the first time I had ever observed a deer nursing, let alone twins. For a moment, a silent prayer of praise was lifted to the Creator of all. Although these four-legged creatures cause gardeners distress, they are beautiful animals, spots and all. Another miracle occurred this year among our deer on the lane. Apparently, triplets arrived to one mother, which I understand is a rather rare event. It probably means the death of even more hostas and newly planted trees and daisies.

Now, we get to the question, "Are you a twin?" Most of us will quickly respond in the negative, including yours truly, Kathryn. Continued reflection, however, causes me to change my mind. No, I don't have a biological twin, so why would I suggest I'm a twin? Paul, in Galatians 2:20, reminds us that, "I have been crucified with Christ and I no longer live, but Christ lives in me. The life I now live in the body, I live by faith in the Son of God, who loved me and gave himself for me." Christ and I are not two identical, physical bodies. However, when we believe and obey, the spirit of Christ comes to live within us. There is now a good me (Christ) and a sinful self (the physical me). One twin is my physical person (sin), while the other twin is the new "spiritual woman." We are to take on the mind of Christ. The first twin was buried in baptism when I proclaimed my belief and faith in God. How I wish that was totally true every moment, but the original twin controls my mind and actions too frequently.

So, what does that mean? It could be scary. If this "twin-ship" works, He, the Spirit of Christ, is inside my heart, mind, and soul. Paul again explains more about this Spirit that dwells within us. "You, however, are not in the realm of the flesh but are in the realm of the Spirit, if indeed the Spirit of God lives in you. And if anyone does not have the Spirit of Christ, they do not belong to Christ" (Romans 8:9). This is tough thinking. Apparently one cannot just be the "bad" twin or self, and at the same time continue to call herself a Christian. Paul reminds us in the next verse, that without the Spirit of Christ in us, our mortal body will die. With that Spirit who raised Christ from the dead living within us—bingo—we will receive new life (birth) for our mortal bodies, just as Christ was raised from the dead. Even Paul realized that was a very difficult balance.

Not only do twin fawns have spots, but so do human twins. Blemishes can spot our souls. Paul reminded the Roman Christians that if they lived according to the flesh, they would die. Those sin spots mean trouble. Action is needed. We must become God's children, seek forgiveness, and the blemishes (spots) will vanish, just like the spots of the fawns disappear as they grow.

In doing a study about deer, it appears that the survival rate of fawns is quite low. Perhaps God designed mama deer to have twins, thus increasing the chance of having at least one offspring survive. Unfortunately, that is also often true with young followers of the Lord. God survives forever, but many young "bucks" wander off from worship, fellowship, giving, and loving their live-in partner, the Spirit of God. Faithful followers must reach out to one another and feed each other from the bread of life, just as the spotted ones nibble on the grass and tree leaves or drink their mother's milk. Incidentally, one day, I spotted a couple of these wee ones attempting to eat snow covered leaves. I am certainly glad warm vegetable soup found its way to my table, and not snow-covered lettuce leaves.

Deer basically are quiet animals, but they can bellow and grunt. Hum! Sounds like some of us two-legged folk. Quiet can be good, but as the old expression goes, "Is silence golden, or is it just plain yellow?" I think how often this author bellows about some complaint, angry thought, discomfort, or delay in accomplishing my own wishes and goals. More of my life must be spent sharing the love of Christ to the world around me. Rather than bellowing, however, I need to let my good twin let her light shine brightly, maybe even in a very calm manner.

One day I walked into the office of one of our pastors, and there on the floor was a giant antler. I immediately inquired if he had eaten the deer, or just taken the antler for a souvenir. Having recently arrived from Montana, I thought he might be a hunter. His response, however, was, "Oh no! Bucks shed their antlers each year and grow a new set in spring." We too must shed the old "self of sin" and begin anew. For me, the need to request forgiveness and to shed my human weaknesses needs to happen more frequently than annually. Daily goofs, lack of faith, hints of a temper, unpleasant thoughts, or self-centeredness remind me of Paul's words in Romans 7:15-20. "I do not understand what I do. For what I want to do I do not do, but what I hate I do… As it is, it is no longer I myself who do it, but it is sin living in me."

Hopefully the Spirit-filled twin predominates in my life. Who dominates your life?

CHAPTER THIRTY
Job Opportunities...at 84?

Returning home following a two-week trip crossing the ocean on the Queen Mary, I had a surprise. My computer announced, "Employment Opportunities for You in 2019." Wow! I Could Go to Work! The job list included...

- Special Agent: Psychology/Counseling (Well, I do have a counseling degree from the U. of Illinois.)
- The Director of Research for the Illinois State Board of Education (I worked in education for over fifty years.)
- Dispensary Assistant Manager, Cannabis (I don't think so.)
- Customer Advocate (I love to stand up for the rights of people, but...)
- Administrative Support Associate for Lowe's (I have purchased bug spray at Lowe's. Would that qualify me?)

But the "top job" recommended, the one that really grabbed me, was Cardiology Physician. This one was reaction-worthy. In fact, I was laughing out loud. Taking care of someone's heart would be a joy, but ... This was advertised as a general, non-invasive cardiologist position. I reacted positively to the "non-invasive" aspect. Invite a person to my office and chat sweetly, or maybe just call the individual on the phone at a time convenient for them and visit as they munched their dinner muffins. No blood! No pain! Maybe no healing! Well, that caused a pause in my thinking. But, and that is a giant but, I had absolutely no medical qualifications. I have never even had a first aid course or a Girl Scout badge in quick splinter removal or stubbed toe repair. Why did this email think I was qualified?

For the moment, let's think a bit out of the box. Of course, 'non-invasive' must have a different meaning than my translation. Our Great Physician, Christ, also wants to take care of our hearts, but NOT in a non-invasive, casual, only-when-I-am-not-bothering-you manner. The Great Physician does want to interrupt our daily, humdrum behavior and cause drastic changes. Those changes involve our heart. Our actions must be revitalized as we clean up our attitudes toward others, and share God's love. Actually, He really wants us to have an "invasive" heart transplant.

I love the words of God spoken to the prophet Ezekiel in Ezekiel 36:26-27. God commanded him to share these words with Israel. "I will give you a new heart and put a new spirit in you; I will remove from you your heart of stone and give you a heart of flesh. And I will put my Spirit in you and move you to follow my decrees and be careful to keep my laws." That is invasive surgery. It was spoken over two-and-a-half thousand years ago by our chief spiritual surgeon, through his servant, Ezekiel—radical heart transplanting.

Maybe cardiology is not the right area of spiritual medicine for this lady. How do we really help others, as well as ourselves, to have a change of heart and mind? What really does a spiritual heart transplant involve? Apparently, God means for us to change our feelings, relationships, attitudes, and even our actions, which spring from our heart, including our mind. With no transplant, He says we will die. Hmm! That will bring unhappiness not only to the patient, but, as in real heart surgery, pain to our loved ones.

Paul says it so well. "Do not conform to the pattern of this world, but be transformed by the renewing of your mind. Then you will be able to test and approve what God's will is—his good, pleasing and perfect will" (Romans 12:2).

Should we be thinking about clogged arteries filled with impure thoughts? For example, our reaction to neighbors whose dog barks too loudly, world leaders who challenge our financial security, or a friend or casual contact who is especially handsome or attractive, could result in damaged hearts. Perhaps our spiritual veins need a transfusion of love for sinners, peace for our hearts, or transformed attitudes regarding our own self-seeking, self-serving attitudes.

As I continued to read the job description for a cardiology physician, I noticed no salary figures. Quickly conducting an online search, I found this headline: "Average Base Salary of $512,000 for Cardiologists." Whether this position in Springfield included such numbers, is unknown. But, if even close to that, I was ready to race out to our local medical university and enroll. Just thinking of how many lollipops and cuddly kitties I could buy made my heart sing. Then I stopped. Could financial gains clog up my system, preventing the wonderful challenge to share generously, to return to God what He really owns anyway, and provide for the needy among us? Was my focus on lollipops and personal wealth, rather than on serving the Kingdom? Oh, how often I need to be reminded that He owns my whole being, lock, stock, and tunic. A bit of heart cleaning is probably in order.

If we reread the background for Ezekiel's time in history, we realize that Israel had truly turned away from the Lord. Their lifestyle was an abomination to God. The people had disobeyed God's commands and He was furious with them, thus the order to Ezekiel to speak in a strong, focused manner. (I doubt that our prophet was excited about delivering that message.) I wonder if we today also need to rethink our behavior and attitude toward the Lord, and truly have a heart transplant.

As for Kathy, I believe the next job listed in that email is for me. I can't remember what I would be doing but I know the position is located in Phoenix. Golf, no furry coats or boots, and swimming every day sounds mighty exciting. I believe I will contact God directly, by social media, asking Him for a physical relocation. Then I will begin cleaning up the veins and arteries in my spiritual body, as I paddle around in my Arizona swimming pool.

The Bible reminds us that whatever we do for our career or vocation, we should do it all for the glory of the Lord.

CHAPTER THIRTY-ONE
Stillness - Solitude - Memories - Tears

What words flash across your mind when visiting the resting place of loved ones?

Recently, while returning home from Joplin, Missouri, I took a slight Interstate 44 detour. The green road sign announced Rolla, Missouri, my home for many years. Several months had passed since visiting the grave-site of my parents. Life was extremely busy: activities, volunteering, commitments, and friendships required a significant amount of time. The 600-mile round trip between my home and their final resting place also contributed to the sparseness of trips.

Although the sun was shining, the wind was blowing through the trees, causing me to grab a jacket. I opened the door, stepped out, and made the slow walk from the car to the stone bearing the name "Ransom," as I had done dozens of times before.

I stood silently, rereading two names etched below: Geneva H. (1909-1959) and John G. (1905-1990). My eyes reviewed the dates, noting that Mom died at the young age of fifty while Dad stayed around until eighty-five. I remembered how difficult it had been for me, as the time for celebrating my own fiftieth approached. My head just knew that cancer would invade my body and whisk me away, in like fashion as my mother.

Obviously, the Lord had other plans for this created one called Kathy. Perhaps my next birthday, eighty-nine, will also bring moments of concern as I reach, and pass, the age of my father. I truly pray not, however, as there are too many challenges and goals remaining on my bucket list.

No one was around that afternoon except a workman across the street, silently slapping paint to the graying walls of the store where my car rested in the parking lot. I was alone with my thoughts and memories. For a few minutes, happy times flicked by like a video as I visualized my gentle mother caring for people with love and kindness. Thoughts of a very hard-working Dad danced before me. Of course, I had to recall times with "Little" John, my only sibling, who has already joined my parents with God.

As I turned toward the West, I could almost see Ridgeview Christian Church up on the hill where John and I grew with grace and love for God as we worshiped. This was a church that put everyone to work swiftly. Even the youth were encouraged to participate and given leadership opportunities, causing many to graduate from high school and move on to full-time Christian service or become leaders in a local congregation. While in Joplin the preceding day, I had visited with another Rolla graduate, working in Christ's army for the Kingdom. The accompanying tears were a blending of sadness and joy. As I shivered a bit in the wind, a prayer formed in my heart and mind. It was a time of communion between God and this weary traveler. What a blessing to experience aloneness! Maybe I even wondered, what comes next in my life?

One of God's workers came to mind while composing this reflection. 1 Kings 18-19 relates Elijah's experience with God during a contest between the four hundred and fifty prophets of Baal and a prophet of God. Ahab, the king, was most angry that his prophets bombed out in the burning of the offering demonstration in which his guys failed to ignite the sacrificial fire. Elijah taunted Baal's prophets, and then quickly demonstrated the power of God, as he swiftly completed the sacrifice, despite jugs of water poured into the trench around the slaughtered bull. (Today, I would probably hack off the T-bone steaks for my dinner, prior to the sacrifice; a real No-No!) Stones, altar, water, wood, bull—all were consumed by the fire. Onlookers yelled, "The Lord—he is God!"

As a final act, Elijah commanded the people to seize the false prophets, and their lives were snatched away in death. Actually, the scriptures say, "They seized them, and Elijah had them brought down to the Kishon Valley and slaughtered there" (1 Kings 18:40).

What would you have done, if you had just ordered the death of these religious priests of Baal? "Elijah climbed to the top of Carmel, bent down to the ground and put his face between his knees" (1 Kings 18:42). King Ahab's wife, Jezebel, with anger and evil intent, warned Elijah that she would kill him.

Afraid for his life, the prophet ran. Leaving his servant behind, Elijah went a day's journey into the wilderness (solitude), sat under a broom tree, and prayed, "I have had enough Lord. Take my life," and then took a nap. Stillness may not always provide positive thinking. But God had other jobs for the sleeping prophet. He sent an angel to wake him, feed him a snack, and allowed him to snooze again. Following a second snack, Elijah was told to get up and he traveled forty days and nights, finally spending the night in a cave. Wow! Maybe I am glad the angel did not disturb my solitude in the Rolla cemetery. No forty-day hike for this wimp.

Bingo! Who appeared in the cave, but our talking angel? When asked, "What are you doing here?" Elijah's response was, "I am the only [follower of the Lord] left, and now they are trying to kill me too" (1 Kings 19:14b). Long story short, God finally spoke to Elijah in a gentle whisper, giving him his new assignment. Go! Do!

Elijah and I each experienced moments of stillness. His were far more dramatic than mine. Elijah heard God's voice in the soft whisper. Perhaps God whispered to me that day…

"Go Kathryn. Live faithfully for the Lord," as I pointed my car toward Illinois.

CHAPTER THIRTY-TWO
Garden Joys and Tragedies

Lunch was a joyful surprise. Not only was the food healthy, almost all the goodies were straight from the garden. My friend has a wee garden, about three by ten feet. Obviously, she does not raise corn and beans for a living from the produce generated on this tiny plot. Some surprising results, however, do arrive at our table during the spring and summer. Right now, zucchini is the KING of this tiny ranch.

Today fresh, curly lettuce, with bits of zucchini, red pepper, carrots, and chopped tomato bits, covered with a light dressing, tantalized my tongue. I was alerted, however, not to miss the surprise. I was to watch for four baby peas. Her pea crop had yielded one pod that morning, resulting in a quartet of tiny, green bites. My portion was just two, as we share at our home. The red and orange items were found in the local grocery, grown who knows where.

Mary Anne also made a wonderful sweet and sour zucchini relish. Thinly sliced zucchini sat for three days in a vinegar, sugar, and oil mixture. Tiny bits of onion, red pepper, and carrots joined the swimming zucchini. (The recipe suggested cucumbers could be substitutes for Mr. Z.) Recently we had so enjoyed sharing this with friends, that she repeated the process, recycling the dressing mix and popping in fresh vegetables.

Finally, my favorite item completed the trio of offerings. Each day the "chef" captured the squash blossoms. Therefore, a small plastic bag held several little blooms. Why would one possibly want to waste a squash blossom? She stuffed these fragile leaves with a mild sausage and baked them for a few minutes. Yum! Yum!

While enjoying this vitamin-rich, midday meal, a trio of biblical garden experiences came to mind. All will remember that first garden mentioned in Genesis 2, the Garden of Eden. The world had been created, but no shrubs or plants had sprung up. That was a giant problem. God had not sent any rain yet, and you know the other problem. There were no gardeners to care for the vegetation. God solved that situation. He created a guy named Adam and placed him in Eden, along with all types of vegetation. I don't know if there were any zucchini or cucumbers, but many plants were available for Adam when he became hungry.

Adam had the responsibility to care for this garden. Eventually, the challenges became greater than our lonely gardener could handle. God had a solution. He caused the man to take a serious nap, took one his ribs, and sewed him up. Oh-my! What a surprise for Adam when he woke up. God took that rib, made a woman, and brought her to Adam. Guess there wasn't any courtship fun, with trips to an ice cream parlor or jaunts through the park, prior to that union.

You can read Genesis 2 and 3 and discover the problems and challenges Adam and Eve faced. How sad. Those two listened to the crafty serpent and ultimately were thrown out of this incredible garden. Bottom line, these two followed bad advice, neglected their responsibilities, failed to remember God's command to not eat of a certain tree, and suffered for their unfaithfulness. Of course, there is a lesson for us also. God's Word overrides our own desires and wishes, regardless of how delightful they may sound. Satan can sneak up on any of us, if we are not alert.

We move around the world to Palestine for our second garden event. Jesus and the disciples had their last supper together. He shared many things with them, concluding with a lengthy time of prayer with his Father. The group then crossed over to the Kidron Valley, slightly northeast of the Old City of Jerusalem. Nearby was a garden, sometimes referred to as Gethsemane, or the "poison garden". Jesus frequently visited this area with his leadership team.

Two incredibly horrible actions took place here shortly before the crucifixion. While there, the soldiers came to arrest Jesus. How did they know where to find the King of Kings? One of his twelve betrayed him, Judas by name. For a few dollars, the traitor led the military detachment of soldiers to the very garden spot where his Master and the other eleven were resting.

This Judas, who made the decision to abandon Jesus, was the same Judas who communed with Jesus every day for three years. Sometimes friends do betray us, or maybe the reverse is true. Have you been guilty of betraying a friend? Or worse, have you been guilty of betraying Jesus?

A second sad event transpired in the same garden that day. Even though the omniscient Jesus knew his arrest was eminent, he had gone there, just as his Father knew he would. As the warriors prepared to take Jesus, the next discouraging event happened. Impetuous Peter drew his sword and struck the high priest's servant, chopping off his right ear.

Now, if someone had come to my defense in a similar type of experience, I would have shouted, "Yeah, Peter. Thanks for trying to help me." Our Savior, of course, did the exact opposite. He ordered Peter to put his sword away, and the officials arrested the faithful Son of God.

During that same evening, and even in the very same garden, Peter goofed again. The disciples followed the guards and Jesus and were waiting by a fire in the courtyard. While there, Peter three times denied that he was one of Jesus' followers. There was not much joy in the garden that day.

Perhaps followers even today become afraid, timid, or embarrassed, and they too, either publicly or silently, deny they are followers of the King. Silence often is not "golden," but just plain "yellow," a phrase heard often while I was a teen.

The third garden experience took place on the Mount of Olives, not far from Jerusalem and Gethsemane. This garden spot was the site of a newly dug tomb, not put into use, located not far from the place where Jesus had been crucified. Gloom and sadness covered the family, friends, and other followers of the Lord. About three days had passed since the burial of their friend in that tomb. Mary Magdalene went to visit, and found the stone rolled back.

As you know, we humans sometimes get very excited and distressed when the unexpected happens. Mary immediately thought the body of Christ had been stolen. While weeping and waiting, Jesus appeared, although Mary did not recognize him. He inquired why she was crying. Thinking he was the gardener, she asked where they had taken the body.

Then one wonderful word was spoken by Jesus: "Mary." As she heard her name, she immediately recognized him. Won't it be equally wonderful when we hear him speak our name someday? I don't know if he will say Kathryn, Kathy, Katie, KA, or Katrina, but I will be thrilled, regardless of which one.

Our tour of gardens found expulsion, a traitor, deception, and grief turned to joy. Maybe I need to take a quick visit to a garden and celebrate that wonderful resurrection day. For a quick review of the garden days in Jerusalem, turn to John, chapters twelve to twenty. Sometimes we each need to refresh our memories about happy events, as well as sorrowful situations.

Take the challenge today.
Read John's narration of those final events
in Christ's life on this earth.
Rejoice, HE IS RISEN

CHAPTER THIRTY-THREE
Burning Coals and a Burning Bush

Put on your thinking caps. If Moses lived in the twenty-first century, what form of communication would He have used to chat with the shepherds from Horeb? Undoubtedly USPS snail mail would have been too slow. Perhaps He might have selected a macOS Catalina 10.15.7 computer and sent emails back and forth from the pasture. Hopefully Moses would have had his battery fully charged.

What about cell phones? They come in all sizes, colors, and degrees of complexity. In fact, Moses might have appreciated one, as some phones are able to help you find a lost suitcase at the airport — why not a lost sheep on the hillside?

Think about today's fancy watches. God could have used one to communicate and catch our timid shepherd's attention. Even more importantly, the fellow in the pasture could keep track of the number of miles he walked daily. As a fringe benefit, Moses could monitor his blood pressure, especially when storms were rapidly approaching and he couldn't get the sheep to move swiftly enough for some shelter in the rocks. That would be enough to make anyone's pressure accelerate.

Well, Moses lived long before even the birth of Christ, so no modern communication tools were handy. God, however, still needed to get his attention. He wanted Moses to leave his sheep-herding job and go visit with the Pharaoh. The Children of Israel were slaves in Egypt and God was ready for them to leave and head for the Promised Land.

One interesting day, while on the far side of the mountain, an angel of the Lord appeared to Moses in flames of fire. The flames appeared to be within a bush, but the bush was not being consumed. Wondering what was happening, Moses went near this amazing sight. As he approached, God called out from within the bush, "Moses! Moses!"

That would certainly get your attention, especially when God's voice continued by saying, "Do not come any closer. Take off your sandals, for this is holy ground." Long story short, God and Moses had a conversation. God did most of the talking, and ultimately Moses obeyed. But then, wouldn't you, if someone spoke to you out of a burning bush that never was consumed? Our God is a forceful communicator. Check out Exodus 3 to read the rest of the story.

Many of us have heard the story of Moses and the burning bush since we were children. Recently I was reading an article in the *Restoration Herald* by Brian Shulz, minister at Kent Christian Church in Madison, IN. He shared an old story, by an unknown author, which made me immediately think of Moses.

A preacher decided to visit a man from his congregation who had not attended any church activities or services for many months. The preacher knocked on the man's door and was invited into the home. The stray parishioner gestured for the pastor to be seated near the brightly burning fireplace. As they were sitting down, neither man said a word.

After a few moments of silence, watching the fire blaze and crackle, the pastor moved a bit, grabbed the fire poker, and began to move a few coals around. Eventually he was able to remove one coal onto the hearth. The coal continued to glow a bright orange for a few moments, but then began to dim fainter and fainter. Eventually the coal was a dull gray, with no color at all.

The coal remained on the hearth as the two men remained in silence. After another few seconds, the pastor took the poker and poked the cold, grey, isolated coal back into the company of the other glowing embers. The secluded coal, now surrounded by the burning coals, quickly returned to a bright orange, providing heat and light for the two silent men.

The minister got up from his chair, put on his coat and hat, and prepared to exit the man's home. Just as the preacher reached for the doorknob, the wayward man spoke the first words of the evening's experience. "Nice sermon, preacher. I'll see you Sunday."

God used fire but spoke in an audible way to share his message with Moses. Our minister also used a blazing fire but did not speak a word, and his message was also clearly understood.

Hopefully the minister's message reminds us today that fellowship and worship in-person is necessary to keep the fire burning in our hearts. Christians simply need one another. We hold each other up, pray for friends, listen to their struggles, help clarify doubts and fears, or at times even suggest possible solutions for troubles facing a fellow worshiper. That is why I love the Lord's church and want to remain identified as a child of His family.

What's stopping you from joining the Lord's family?

CHAPTER THIRTY-FOUR
A Jar of Frozen Pears...

Have you ever been hungry? I mean *hungry*: hungry for lack of nourishment for maybe forty-eight hours or more. Your family is, "No-food-in-the-cupboards poor." Imagine yourself a small, growing child, and there is no food in the fridge. In addition, it is Christmas time, and the weather is wintry and frozen. Your home has limited heat. What are your options?

About a year ago I received an email from a friend. As I read his story, tears came to my eyes, followed by a bit of anger. These emotions, however, were shortly followed by an action plan. Let's share the story first.

Back in the day when I was somewhere between ten and twelve perhaps, it was going to be a bleak and empty Christmas. There was no money to buy food to have on Christmas Day. We couldn't even get a relief order.

Any money dad got, he bought whiskey. We didn't think or hope for a big Christmas dinner. If we, (I) got hungry, I would go down into the cellar and get a jar of pears or apples that mom had canned. They were frozen, of course, but I would take a jar, open them, and eat what I could.

One night before Christmas, I heard a car stop in front of the house and then take off again. I opened the door to see who it was. The car was gone. There was a box on the porch filled with groceries, everything that was needed for a good Christmas dinner.

We had no idea who left the box of groceries. We enjoyed mom's cooking that Christmas Day, thanks to our unknown friend. Dad, of course, was drunk.

It didn't take me long to figure out who left the box of groceries. It was one of my classmates, Mickey K. and his parents. I asked him about it when we went back to school, but he denied it. I didn't press the matter. Even after all of these years, I have never forgotten the kindness that was shown me that Christmas so many years ago.

A Friend

Today my friend has some serious medical problems. Unable to work for several years, his finances, once again, are in disaster, but things are, oh-so different! He has found the Lord and follows Him. He has a loving wife, children who care, and a church family who is supportive. That is a praise.

What about our Christian response to this wonderful story? Perhaps we could think of the Sermon on the Mount, when Christ reminds his audience, "So when you give to the needy, do not announce it with trumpets, as the hypocrites do in the synagogues and on the street, to be honored by others. Truly I tell you, they have received their reward in full" (Matthew 6:2-3). Share your wealth, but silence the guitars, and slip away like our youthful deliveryman.

But share we must. Perhaps only a few days remain until the special time arrives when we remember the birth of the Christ Child — God's gift to us. Who needs your kindness in this season of celebration? If Christmas is months away, surprise someone in need with a gift from an unknown friend.

Now, on His behalf, could we each take the challenge and partner with Christ to share with those needing a helping hand? For some it may be a gift of nickels, dimes, and/or hundred-dollar bills. For others, your cooking, sewing, painting, or childcare skills might find a worthy family worn out from struggles, but silently praying for some help. Gifts of time and friendship for the lonely, homebound, or strangers are just as important as silver dollars. Often thoughtful bits of kindness open the door to witnessing about God's grace and forgiveness for those who trust and follow his Word.

We are commanded in Proverbs 3:9-10 to honor the Lord and bring the firstfruits of our crops and labor to share with His Kingdom work. Guess I can't just bundle up the battered and blemished tomatoes, or wait until the final day of the month to decide what leftover coins remain in my wallet to make my donation for the needy. Perhaps "firstfruits" also suggest that waiting until I'm worn and weary to volunteer to help another is generally too late.

The Lord wants us to share our best. Hearing of a need for one of God's servants laboring in another country causes me to re-glance at my checkbook balance. Gifts of service and silver are each needed for the Kingdom.

Of course, emergencies arise and then His servants leap forward with the speed of jack-rabbits to give and do what ever is possible. Hearing of a family struggling to keep warm during the coldest winter for many moons challenges the Lord's team to quickly dig deeply in search of "Do Good Dollars," even if it means giving up an anticipated weekend trip to watch your favorite sport team trounce their opponents. Just think what that box of groceries meant to my friend that Christmas Day!

Paul reminds us in the fifteenth chapter of Acts of a wonderful example of giving. The Jewish elders in Jerusalem sent Judas and Silas to Antioch to encourage the Gentile believers. They demonstrated a double-barrel approach to giving: encouragement and support of believers of a different race. Each of us can encourage others, regardless of their ethnicity, financial status, age, or gender. Gift someone with love, hugs, or maybe a dozen frosted donuts.

Take the Gifting Challenge.
Be bold with sharing your talents and/or gifts with a child, family, homeless person, or lonely neighbor.
Create a long-time memory for one of God's Creation.
Remember, also, since God dwells in you as a Christian, the two of you are reaching out with love.

CHAPTER THIRTY-FIVE
A Trio of 'O' Words...

On a recent November morning, popping out to get the newspaper, I saw three robins. My first thoughts were, "What is wrong with me? I thought winter was advancing—not spring." Then a wee squirrel scurried across the lawn, and as I looked up, I saw a trio of deer watching me. Gracious, but it was like having a zoo in our yard!

Returning to the kitchen, I viewed through the window about 150 or so white pelicans waking up from their nap. As these beauties make their annual pilgrimage from the North to the South, I think Lake Springfield becomes a "recharging" station for them. For the last several years we have seen many of these gorgeous birds for a few weeks in the fall and then again in the spring. In addition, tucked into the water's edge, was a pair of blue herons and assorted mallards. Sorry, however, no Christmas partridge in a pear tree—just a sleeping turtle on a branch. As I said to a friend, "God is Great".

We tend to celebrate when amazing events happen. Joy abounds when a local sports team makes the state finals. A visiting choir thrills our hearts as performers proclaim God's Word through melody and inspiring words amongst a backstop of rock-style music from drums, strumming strings, and a huge guitar. Our hearts thrill with joy when visiting the newborn grandchild or a local botanical garden—evidence of God's creative genius. It is wonderful that we celebrate God. And yet ...

And yet, do we truly acknowledge His greatness? Have we been specific in our words of gratitude? Perhaps we are appreciative only when an event or happening touches us personally. When we view Niagara Falls with our own eyes, we murmur a word of thanks. A friend makes a remarkable recovery from an accident and hopefully we thank the Great Healer. A brilliant sunset, super brilliant grandchild, or healing of relationships among several family members stimulate words of heavenly gratitude. Each of these examples touch the individual in a personal way and certainly we must never forget to say, "God, thanks for your love and care of my family." But . . . have we unintentionally shrunk God to our own tiny world of needs? What about the "awesome" Creator?

For a moment, consider God's true greatness. Three giant "O" words pop into our thinking — Omnipotent, Omniscient, and Omnipresent. God is each of these unpronounceable words.

He is *Omnipotent* — all powerful. He created the world, the entire world, more than just our own personal backyard or the state in which we live. By His word, even more than our homeland, the good old USA, was created. Yes, He created the Mojave Desert, the Arctic Circle, Iran, and wee bed bugs. Such creativity! I can hardly create a pumpkin pie and He even created the pumpkins for me. Guess my prayers also need to thank him for the sand, ice, humanity, the entire world, and yes, even irritating bed bugs.

He is *Omniscient* — having complete, unlimited knowledge or understanding. God knows our problems, and we are glad He listens to our concerns, both those obvious to our friends, but also our hidden burdens. His knowledge exceeds what we individually are doing, thinking, or requesting. He knows our past, the present, and then the scary part - He knows our future, actually the future of the entire world and all small humans running around doing our own thing. We complain when our lives go wrong today, this week, or for a lifetime, but God holds the future in His hand. He prepares the way for us. No one gives him advice. He understands the universe and all within that space, including YOU. "As the heavens are higher than the earth, so are my ways higher than your ways and my thoughts than your thoughts" (Isaiah 55:9). Some trials today prepare us for the unknown future plans God has for us. He is an awesome caretaker.

Our Creator is also *Omnipresent* — present everywhere at the same time. Now think of that. No hiding from Him. Teachers are accused (teased) of having eyes in the back of their head as they catch a student misbehaving, even though there is no apparent eye contact. Imagine how great our God is when you think about how He sees everyone from Oslo to the Orient, while simultaneously watching the neighborhood sparrow fall from the sky (Matthew 10:29). It is impossible to play hide and seek with our Creator. No secret indiscretions, unkind thoughts, misplaced priorities, or just plain evil acts escape His all-seeing eye. Remember, however, that His arm is continually ready to reach out and support each of us in good times as well as tough situations. "My help comes from the Lord, the Maker of heaven and earth. He will not let your foot slip - he who watches over you will neither slumber nor sleep."…"The Lord will watch over your coming and going both now and forevermore' (Psalm 121:3-4, 8).

Enlarge your scope of thanksgiving. Think and pray "outside of the box" of your own self-interests and needs. Read Romans 11:33-36

CHAPTER THIRTY-SIX
Unwrapping the Gift

"Rip and Toss" or "Gently Unveil and Engage?"

December twenty-five approaches. Wee ones wait anxiously for the rising of the sun in anticipation of surprises. Seasoned adults approach the morning with mixed thoughts, knowing that human "alarm clocks" will sound off waaaaaaaay too early. As they observe the buzz of the family gathered before the real or artificial evergreen, hope springs eternal that shopping selections will be received with glee and appreciation. Soon the floor is littered with discarded ribbon, bows, gift wrap, and sometimes, even a broken or discarded gift. Do any of these words bring back childhood or parenthood memories?

Christmas celebration, as a child, was rather low key at the Ransom household. Youth at church annually presented their rendition of the birth of the King for beaming parents. Clad in bathrobes, hugging imitation sheep and staffs, while singing familiar carols, the parade would bow down before the crib holding a doll (occasionally a live baby). Youthful Mary and Joseph sat/stood guarding the Promised Messiah. Moments later, a trio of elaborately clad wisemen, clutching fancy wrapped gifts, would appear. Of course, we now know that the shepherds and the wisemen were not celebrating the birth simultaneously at the manger scene. Those wise fellows did not arrive until Jesus was a young child. It takes a while to travel by camel back from the East to Bethlehem, contrary to most public pictorial representation of the "Nativity Scene." All youthful participants, wishing each other a cheery Merry Christmas and clutching a bag of hard ribbon candy and a tangerine, would leave with rich memories of the Christ child planted in their hearts.

The celebration with family included just my parents and younger brother. All relatives lived too far west (Oregon and Washington) for us to share turkey, cranberry sauce, hugs, and memories. Gifts were simple, and certainly included needed socks or frocks along with a "wished for" dream or two. Parent presents were simple, as allowances were meager. But this I do remember. All members watched graciously as each gift was opened with a bit of tearing of paper, followed by wide eyes of joy, and words of thanks. Yes, I really think we expressed appreciation to our givers of gifts, either verbally or with actions suggesting thanksgiving.

One memory remains vivid. Each year, part of the celebration included the reading of Luke 2. Sometimes small figures of the birth scene were placed carefully on the footstool for us to move around as the story proceeded. As we grew older, brother John or I became the audio part of this celebration of the focus of the Christmas season. This practice followed my brother, as each year he and his family unwrapped Luke's recording of the promise of the most wonderful gift ever, the birth of the Savior.

After years of participating in early morning Christmas rituals, one observation becomes clear. There are two ways of discovering the hidden treasure beneath the coating of tissue paper: the "Rip and Toss" method or the "Gently Unveil and Engage" method. Group number one members grab a gift, yank off the string and paper, glance at the gift and toss it aside, while simultaneously grabbing gift number two. Little or no emotion, or expression, either orally or through glee in the eyes, is shared with the gift giver. By outward appearances, one wonders if this sharing of family expressions of kindness and love is just taken for granted by the receiver.

Then, a turn arrives for a member of group two to open a gift. Gently the fingers pry open the wrappings. The bow is untied, the paper is smoothed out as it falls off the gift. The receiver gently lifts out the item and begins to explore. Sometimes that means trying on the gift, or opening the pages of a favorite childhood tale, or beginning to assemble a new toy or tech tool. Other guests grow restless, awaiting their turn to proceed. But . . . one person observes, with joy, this total and complete attention to the new gift by the receiver. Yes, you know who, the gift giver.

And so, we come to the thought of the day. Each of us is the receiver of the greatest gift given—the gift of the Savior, who ultimately gave His very life as a sacrifice through death. What kind of receiver are we? Do we fall into the "Rip and Toss" category? We hear the Word, receive it briefly in our hearts, and even acknowledge Him as our Savior. But then what happens? We move forward with our lives and the daily humdrum of living, scarcely acknowledging His presence, let alone thanking the Giver of the gift. Perhaps we attend a weekly community time of worship, but have we really engaged with the giver of the "Gift of Eternal Life?"

Then, think about category two, "Gently Unveil and Engage." This person thoughtfully listens to the "opening" of the Word, as the story of Christ is shared. She explores the gift through study of the Bible, witnessing, and watching the lives of mature Christians. While the world waits, she begins the assembly stage of this life as she attempts to create a person of love, joy, peace, long-suffering — images of the original Giver of life. What joy that slow development of a follower must bring to the Giver of all good and perfect gifts!

Which type of Receiver do you wish to be?
A "Rip and Toss" receiver?
Hopefully, instead, you become a
"Gently Unveil and Engage"
receiver of God's gift to each of us.

CHAPTER THIRTY-SEVEN
Curmudgeon - Long in the Tooth

Everything is just hunky-dory for our meeting. I'll put on my best bib and tucker. Heavens to Betsy, you'll see the whites of my eyes, arriving in my jalopy, before you can shake a stick. There will be a carbon copy of the contract, prepared on my Olympia Typewriter. Although the guest speaker is only knee-high-to-a-grasshopper, thou will be able to follow along on the mimeographed copy provided.

By now you are wondering, "What in the world happened to Kathryn? Has senility overtaken her thought processes? Sounds like the author regressed to early or mid-nineteen hundreds." Maybe she has, but take a moment and identify as many archaic or obsolete words in the first paragraph.

Apparently, words are easily discarded, as time slips by. Who in the world uses a mimeograph today when the handy Xerox zips out copies in seconds? Translators of the King James Version of the Bible used the words thou, thee, and thy. I doubt any modern mama would put on her best bib and tucker or refer to her young child as knee-high-to-a-grasshopper. Words do vanish or acquire different meanings.

Society, also, has invented several words which imply disrespect for those of us with white or gray hair. Perhaps you've heard an older person referred to as an old fogey, coot, geezer or even worse, a curmudgeon. The latter implies a bad-tempered person who is generally old. The phrase "long in the tooth" was a seventeenth century phrase referring to aging horses. The older the horse, the longer the teeth became. This is not necessarily a positive reference as people describe an older person as "long in the tooth."

Rotten garbage, storm damaged tree limbs, or worn-out jammies may be discarded, but not people. Certainly no one must be discarded or ignored, but today our focus is on the over-sixty crowd. Despite an abundance of wrinkles, or using a walker, or the fact that one's driver's license is history, there are still ways to keep us engaged. We are each valuable in the sight of God. We find in Job 12:12 this thought-provoking question. "Is not wisdom found among the aged? Does not long life bring understanding?" Take time to share knowledge with the younger crowd.

Paul's comment in 2 Corinthians 4:16 is so encouraging. "Therefore we do not lose heart. Though outwardly we are wasting away, yet inwardly we are being renewed day by day." Paul had experienced umpteen challenges in his life, most of which none of us could have handled, yet he tells the Corinthians not to lose heart.

Sometimes society appears to want to relegate "over-sixties" to the dugout or an isolated cabin in the back woods of northern Wisconsin. Take a quick survey and remember some of our leaders who were well past mid-life. Astronaut John Glenn returned to space at the age of 77. Julia Child wrote a cookbook at the age of 87. Our Illinoisan architect, Frank Lloyd Wright, was still designing homes at age 91. Even Kathryn Ransom, at age 88, anticipates her second book will be published by 2024.

What makes the difference between these "alive" leaders and a lonely lady, lounging on the lawn all day? Why do some bent, bearded, and wrinkled men move boldly forward with life, while others stay on the couch all day, driving their spouses or adult children to distraction? Up, up, and away. Get moving and serving.

The July 2023 Mayo Clinic Health Letter suggests that people who live long, healthy, happy, and productive lives are just ordinary people who refuse to equate age with illness and inactivity. Staying active seems to keep the muscles working. Interacting with people helps retain conversation skills and stimulates the brain. Assisting others by writing letters to the lonely, making mud pies with children in the nursery, mowing the church or neighbor's lawn, or even helping plan a popcorn party for teens, presents challenges and reasons for leaping out of bed at eight a.m. Well, for some it might be ten or eleven before you need to arise and leave to help serve the funeral dinner at the church.

Seniors can provide valuable models for younger adults as they work side by side on various community and family activities. Create mixed aged committees and boards, thus helping leadership blend wisdom and talents of the past and the present. As we age, we have experience in reaching out to help and recognizing signs of those needing help. Who better to encourage an overworked, struggling pastor, than a Christian with forty to fifty years of being a part of the family of God? Know some first-time mothers in overload? Start a New Mothers Support Group, exchanging ideas for soothing a weeping baby or a distraught father. Don't forget to add a cup of tea.

> **David, in Psalm 71:9, 18, expresses a final prayer for you, Dear 'Long in the Tooth'. "Do not cast me away when I am old; do not forsake me when my strength is gone…**
> **Even when I am old and gray, do not forsake me, my God, till I declare your power to the next generation, your mighty acts to all who are to come."**

Keep On Keeping On

CHAPTER THIRTY-EIGHT
Soda Jerk

Retirement day arrived late 1993. Happy, relaxing days were anticipated, as my mind hopped around golf courses, visited lands of sand, snapped photos of leopards sunning in trees, or just imagined the soft rocking of a river boat. The absence of an alarm, driving home in evening traffic, and making work deadlines created rainbows in my head. Of course, thoughts of helping within the community also brought joy to my being. Life would be glorious. I anticipated surprises, maybe even limpy legs as my bones grew older. Of course, the rest of my body would stay young, vigorous, and vibrant? Ho! Ho!

Shortly after turning in my office keys, I had an invitation impossible to dismiss lightly. Our neighbor, John, owner of an old-fashioned drug store with a soda counter, remembered a dream of mine—to be a "jerk," a soda jerk. Would I like to work behind the counter for a week and try my skills of mixing, blending, smiling, and yes, even inventing new soda creations? Well, that was like dangling a giant worm before a starving fish. Of course, I would love to be part of the staff for the week.

Prior to launch day, a brief lesson was shared by this gracious giver of joyful anticipation. We spent some moments operating the milk shake shaker, identifying pieces of equipment, investigating secrets of the finances and cash register, and locating various supplies. Other loyal, long-time employees were introduced, and I'm confident they wondered what in the world would happen to their calm, daily stream of guests when this wild woman would begin upsetting the daily routine.

The day arrived for the new 'soda jerk' to start. Wonder of wonders, friends began to arrive. With clumsy hands and smiling face, I began fulfilling the various soda requests. In anticipation of their needs, I had also acquired a few new supplies for the counter — some flavored sherbets and containers of fruit juice. Yes, I was going to create a Ransom Special. A simple poster announced . . .

New — Kathy's Fruit Floats
100% Pure Fruit Juice
Diet Lemon-Lime Soda
Fresh Fruit Sherbet or Shaved Ice
Flavors: Tropical Fruit or Raspberry
Special Price - $1.75

For fun, I brought a book to the store entitled, *Soda Jerk*, poems by Cynthia Rylant. It remained on the counter during my fun week and people autographed and often wrote a few words. As I reviewed their comments, I discovered that my chocolate sodas and banana splits were outstanding. A favorite comment concluded with, "What a fun way to begin your retirement. We enjoyed your treats. You seemed to enjoy them," Judy and Laura. One day a great friend, Elizabeth, provided a harp concert. I thought maybe I had died and made it through the pearly gates. It was so beautiful.

The comment, however, which continues to speak to me and is frequently reflected in my writings was, "Good for you, Kathy! You just proved it's never too late to realize your dreams," Donna. The Lord absolutely expects us to 'keep on keeping on' until life is over. I often think of eighty-year-old Moses starting out across the desert area leading the Children of Israel on a forty-year hike prior to their entering the Promise Land.

Now, twenty-six years later, at eighty-four, another dream was realized, becoming a published author rather than soda jerk. The apostle Paul also made a radical career change. From persecutor of Christians to persecuted for his Christian beliefs, he suffered in prison, preached, encouraged the discouraged, and yes, he too became an author. As the Holy Spirit directed his thinking, he penned the majority of the New Testament letters to the early church. He challenged, anguished, encouraged, instructed, and prayed for these struggling new Christians. No, I will never make a career writing nor begin to have Paul's impact on followers of the Lord, but each of us, in our own small way, must use every gift God has given us to proclaim His word. As I pen these words, my unspoken prayer is, "Lord, may these words draw someone closer to you, encourage another, or renew the spirit of engagement in a reader."

One last surprise awaited me following six days of scooping ice cream, making shakes, and creating fruit floats. John, the owner of the drug store, handed me a framed picture — my pay for the week. The two-dollar bill pictured has been with me since that day. I certainly appreciated both the opportunity to serve, but also the token for my memory bank. This, however, is minor, as I anticipate the heavenly Father knocking on my door and saying, "Well done, my faithful servant."

Remember, "Each of you should use whatever gift you have received to serve others, as faithful stewards of God's grace in its various forms" (I Peter 4:10).

CHAPTER THIRTY-NINE
The Value of One

In February 2019, we traveled to Jerusalem and Egypt, including a cruise on the Nile. One of the more engaging activities included a walk through the livestock market in Daraw. As the group neared the site, the excitement and noise mounted. Crowds of people, pickup trucks, and live animals created a cacophony of sounds.

The weekly market was bustling with cows, goats, camels, and sheep, yes, hundreds of sheep. People jostled each other, bargaining for the price of livestock. Money exchanged hands. People were serious shoppers.

In the first century, this would have been the "agora," a place where goods exchanged owners, or merchandise was sold. The root meaning was "to collect," or a "town meeting place," or "resort of the people." Hundreds of people were gathering, meeting, and exchanging items that morning.

In addition to animals for sale, occasionally we saw huge tarps on the ground, covered with various types of farm supplies for sale. Another tent sold a variety of liquid refreshments and provided chairs for resting while smoking water pipes.

Jesus and the disciples frequently visited the marketplaces, wandering, I imagine, much like we did that chilly day in Daraw. There was, however, a gigantic difference in the disciples' marketplace travels. We wandered everywhere, with cameras clicking, staring at the robe-clad folk and pickups loaded with noisy beasts. In Mark 6:53-56 we find Jesus near Gennesaret (Sea of Galilee area), almost overwhelmed with people. The crowds were not merchants selling goods, but mobs carrying sick on mats, requesting "physician" Jesus to touch their loved ones, restoring them to health.

We, too, saw people with a crutch or limp who, I am certain, would have welcomed the heaven-sent healer. Everyone was important to the Master when He visited marketplaces during His travels. Thinking back to our visit, everyone still is important to Jesus today, even each wiggling lamb that was being cared for that day.

Marketplaces in ancient times, as referenced in Matthew 11:16, were open recreations areas for children, where the young would sing, dance, and play. In addition, unemployed would come, seeking employers needing temporary day workers (Matthew 20:1-6). There was no evidence of "Worker Needed" signs or gatherings of people soliciting day jobs during our visit, but perhaps we just did not look in the correct corner of the mob scene.

Believe it or not, preliminary hearings in trials were also located in the early marketplace. Paul and Silas were seized and dragged into the public area to face the authorities. Paul had called on a spirit to exit a female slave whose owners made much money from her fortune-telling skills. These guys were mad as hornets that their source of revenue disappeared (Acts 16:16-21). They decided to arrest, accuse, and try the duo. I'm glad trials are a bit more private and organized today.

Jesus even chats about a special group of "Publicity Seekers," sometimes referred to as hypocrites. These Pharisees, in their long robes and fancy tassels, wanted to tell the crowds what to do, but failed to follow suit. They liked to be seen, praised, and acknowledged as special banquet guests. So where did they go? Into the marketplace to be seen by many. We find in Matthew 23:3-12 that Jesus suggests we consider ourselves servants, avoid pretense, and remain modest, remembering that the Messiah is the greatest among us.

Today, instead of a special marketplace, our country relocates these various activities. But they still happen. The unemployed can go online, or watch for "Help Wanted" signs. Children gather in grassy fields, playgrounds, or YMCAs to share moments of joy and/or competition with friends. Merchants seek prime locations in which to sell and barter their baskets, bread sticks, and buggies. County and state fairgrounds provide temporary housing for animals needing new homes. Courthouses replace a public square for trials.

But one thing remains a bit similar. The proud and the popularity seekers still parade around, perhaps on the street, at the fair, or via the Big Three — television, telephone, or news print. Is it possible today to find those folk implying, "Do as I say, not as I do?" Surely none of us knows anyone in that category wandering our sidewalks and homes!

As the smells, noise, dust, crowds became almost overwhelming, I was suddenly reminded, not of multitudes of men, boys, and multicolored sheep, but of a parable of Jesus recorded in Matthew 18 and Luke 15. The Master tells about the shepherd who leaves ninety-nine sheep in the fold to go in search of the one who wandered away. Today we were overcome with hundreds of animals. I wondered if one of the shepherds that day had left behind a single sheep. Perhaps it had a sore toe or was feeling ill. Maybe it was too skinny to sell. Regardless, the sheep was missing.

Believe it or not, the Lord used the sheep to represent people. Ninety-nine men and women may be worshiping and serving, and that is praiseworthy — but are we as concerned about the lonely boy, the absent widow, the angry denier of God, or the weary follower who are not celebrating and hearing the Word of God preached? Where is that one-hundredth individual? Our responsibility is to go in search and bring him home. I wonder how effective I am in searching for the ONE that is lost. Each individual sheep/person is valuable in the eyes of the Lord.

Despite the negative aspects of the marketplace, one is reminded that Jesus spent much time there. Why might that be? Yes, that was where the everyday people - the lost "human sheep" - were, so that was where Jesus did His teaching, healing, and modeling for the twelve. Witnessing and preaching must not be hidden behind walls, inside our homes, or only with other believers. Paul and Silas, despite the beatings they received, witnessed while in the inner cell of the prison, fastened with chains. They were bold, and God was with them. Surely, I can do no less.

I ask myself, "Am I witnessing boldly?"
Each Soul has value in God's eyes.

CHAPTER FORTY
He Hears

Life is good. I relaxed while gulping down twin tacos and a creamy cherry dessert. The cafeteria of Ozark Christian College, located in Joplin, Missouri, was filled with smiling teens with holes in their jeans, nibbling, visiting, and texting. One student actually appeared to be preparing a lesson. Rather soft music, with a beat, blended with the chatter and laughter. Other adults joined us, competing for chairs in this pleasant room filled with delicious smells. A common purpose drew us to Joplin that day. We were attending the 2020 Preaching-Teaching Convention sponsored by the college.

As I sat alone, in the midst of a crowd, my mind drifted backward sixty-seven years to this same city. The year was 1953. A new phase of my life was beginning — college life. The campus had moved from a single building on a hill to this sprawling array of attractive, but functional, buildings seated on the rolling hillside. What a difference!

Memories, both of good times and rough, filled my gray head. Friendships remain after almost seven decades. Images of Moses, Joseph and David flashed by, as I remembered how my professor of Old Testament history brought to life these ancient leaders of the Children of Israel. Regret crept in, remembering the study of Greek, which to this day is still "Greek" to this modest student. Looking around, I spotted pictures of professors and staff from those early years of the college, and a smile spread across my face.

Suddenly my knee appeared to be twitching, as if memories were causing this movement, and why not? It spoke to me in sympathetic vibes, as together we remembered my first ride on a man's bike with hand brakes. The fall evening was warm, as a friend and I climbed on borrowed bikes for a short ride. A sudden stop on a gravel area found me catapulting over the handlebars, resulting in an overnight stay in the local hospital. The next thing I remembered that evening was the wife of the college president calling my mother, suggesting she drive the two hundred miles from Rolla, Missouri and consult with the attending physicians regarding my treatment. The x-ray reported the news that my dorm, with no elevator, had suddenly increased in navigational difficulty. Climbing three flights of stairs on crutches was certainly a challenge.

What a difference sixty-seven years had made! Three nights I fell asleep in the home of my first roommate of so many years ago. She graciously opened their home to this conference pilgrim. As I climbed to the second floor to rest my head, celebration crossed my lips that no crutches were required.

For three days my hungry mind feasted on the lectures and sermons of prayer, hope, promises, and challenges for Kingdom engagement found in the book of Acts. My emotional battery arrived dead, desperately needing recharging in God's power strip. Slowly the power indicator went from zero to eighty-five percent charged. Fifteen percent undercharged. Hmm!

And then it happened. My chirping cricket phone buzzed as I munched on my taco. Grabbing the phone, I dashed to a quiet stairwell to communicate with a friend. Her opening words caused me to pause, breathe deeply, and then mumble, "Please repeat what you just said".

"This is Kerma" (director of our church camp back in the Springfield, IL area). "We have just received super news. A member of an area church left a gift for camp in his trust/will. We will be receiving a very nice sum for the camp."

The camp had purchased a piece of land (Cypress Point) adjacent to the current camp grounds. The trustees had arranged for a loan, a loan that was coming due in just about a month. Would this gift help us reach our needs? Approximately $20,000 remained to complete the purchase. Many folks had been praying fervently that God would help us find friends of the Lord and the camp who could help us reach that goal. We had about forty-one days left to find those funds. Although my faith is strong, and although I continued to tell "self" that God walks with us in this financial journey, I must admit that moments of depression would creep into my midnight thoughts. I waited quietly for her follow-up sentences. Was this gift a much-needed new van to transport campers, a collection of fishing gear no longer needed by this donor, but which could be used during camp with young, novice fisher-people, or . . . ?

She continued, "The trust leaves us approximately $80,000." I gulped, paused, gave a frantic word of thanks to the Giver of all perfect gifts, and then cheered in Kerma's ear. What an answer to prayer! I pondered, "Why am I so weak in faith at times?" Many had been praying. We said we believed. Why did I have moments of doubt? I don't know that answer, but it thrilled me when Kerma assured me that undoubtedly the camp trustees would allocate a portion of that gift to be used to complete the loan.

We concluded our conversation and I returned to my solitary thoughts and uneaten taco. Then Paul's words to the Ephesians flashed before me. Please read Ephesians 3:16-21, making special note of verses twenty and twenty one: "Now to him who is able to do immeasurably more than all we ask or imagine, according to his power that is at work within us, to him be glory in the church and in Christ Jesus throughout all generations, for ever and ever! Amen!" He heard our prayers and responded.

What a conclusion to a glorious week! My emotional battery was recharged. Look out world! I'm on fire.

Thanks God — Yes, You Do Listen

CHAPTER FORTY-ONE
Disaster to Delicious...

Once again, this non-chef found herself in great distress. Guests were to arrive in a few hours, and completing food preparation was on the fast track. Pork was thawing. Potatoes were scrubbed, ready for baking. Spinach was washed, trimmed, and waiting to be mixed with cranberries, onions, caramelized pecans, and a yogurt dressing. And then it happened — disaster.

My mind pictured the bite sized sausage-cheese appetizers described in full color on my computer screen. I envisioned my guests complimenting the chef on her clever creation as they munched away. I carefully mixed the ingredients, baked them according to directions, and extracted them from the oven. Troubled thoughts crossed my brain waves. Why don't these golf ball-sized items look tasty? The cheese should have melted and mixed with oil from the sausage. Staring at me were wads of dry, flour-covered, crumbly bits. Gathering courage, I reluctantly popped one into my mouth. Yuck!!!! No way would this item make it to my appetizer plate that evening. Tragedy!

Revising my menu a bit, other delicious tidbits were arranged and presented as the troops arrived through blowing weather and cold, but one question remained. What would I do with the meatballs? They were not only golf ball-sized, but almost sufficiently hard enough for actual use on the fairways of the local golf course. Ditching a pound of sausage and a similar amount of extra sharp, cheddar cheese made my conservative heart send out "no-no" signals. That evening, tucked under the covers, memories of a pleasant evening danced in my head, but a little, dark cloud hung in the background. I'm wasting good food. And then ... an idea for recycling appeared.

The next day the skillet appeared, and a new recipe was created. Crumbling the "golf balls" into the pan, with a bit of oil, a modest splash of milk, and some additional seasoning, (whatever I found in the cupboard), I created a cheese-sausage gravy. A pair of baked potatoes provided a mattress for my gravy creation, and along with broccoli left-overs, a delightful meal was gobbled down. Now I must add that probably a blue ribbon at the state fair would not follow, but no food was wasted.

Life often follows this same path. As newborns, we are sweet, with incredible potential predicted. Years pass, and that beautiful creation becomes stained with unlovely thoughts and actions. The Lord peeks down through the clouds, and just shakes His head. That evening He probably mumbles, "What a waste of a life! Shall I throw her out?" And then, as we listen carefully, perhaps by reading and hearing His Word, we realize that a "new recipe" has been provided. Because of the sacrifice of His Son, we can have a new beginning.

The apostle Paul is among the super examples of a life of disaster changed to an incredible Christ-focused journey. Saul, as a young man, stood by, lending his approval of the stoning of Stephen (Acts 8). This "tough golf ball" guy went from house to house, dragging off believers to prison, both men and women. The early church members experienced fear. Undoubtedly the church leadership discussed ways of wasting this focused fellow of destruction.

But God had another recipe for Saul's life. The new plan took two directions. Initially, as Saul focused on destroying the church, God watched the early Christians quickly desert Jerusalem. As they emigrated everywhere, they preached the word. The new recipe for enhancing the Kingdom was built from bad decisions by Saul and revised by the early disciples. God was the chief chef as the plan developed.

It appears that sometimes fear can bring out the best in people. In this case, the fearful developed courage to speak up and tell others about Christ. For some of the believers, I am certain, this was a real challenge. Our question today should be, "Am I sharing the gospel wherever I travel, whether down Main Street of my hometown or to the outermost points of Illinois, the United States, Europe, or the entire world?"

Part number two of God's plan unfolded around Saul. As this man of destruction breathed out murderous threats against the Lord's disciples, (Acts 9:1) God created a different strategy. Saul, on his way to Damascus, is interrupted by a voice calling out, "Saul, Saul, why do you persecute me?" (Acts 9:4)

Struck blind by God, he meets up with Ananias. This disciple got a special call from God, ordering him to dash off to Damascus, to the house of Judas on Straight Street and have a chat with this persecutor of Christians. That courageous fellow listened to the Lord and followed instructions. (Acts 9) A new life was born. Saul changed his name to Paul, and the Lord used him in a marvelous way.

What about folk of the twenty-first century? Can God change hard golf ball beings into "appetizing," new creations? Of course. Peter suggests a pattern. "Therefore, with minds that are alert and fully sober, set your hope on the grace to be brought to you when Jesus Christ is revealed at his coming. As obedient children, do not conform to the evil desires you had when you lived in ignorance. But just as he who called you is holy, so be holy in all you do; for it is written: 'Be holy, because I am holy'" (I Peter 1:13-16).

God can make something beautiful of our lives.
He can take a life of disaster and
make it a 'delicious' recipe for others to follow,
if and when we turn our wills over to him.
I'm still open to his tweaking of my soul and actions.

CHAPTER FORTY-TWO
Paul's Final Travelogue

Recently information surfaced, reminding me of my college days. A friend in Lumby, BC, Canada sent me an email. As I read Caralyn's note, I smiled and enjoyed happy thoughts of my college experience, but even more importantly, about Caralyn and her husband, Don.

While Caralyn was sorting boxes, she discovered a wonderful reference book, *The Works*, Vol. 1, No. 3, December 16, 1953. *The Works* was a publication that shared news related to Ozark Bible College students. Embedded in the text was this tiny mention of a freshman student familiar to me. "The name chosen for the 'Mission Group' at Ozark Bible College is World Watchmen." The next sentence made me smile. "After the song service, led by Don Renken, and assisted by Kathryn Ransom at the piano, Jack Albee took over the business part of the meeting."

My first reaction to the comment was, "I have absolutely zero memory of 'The Works', or the Mission Group, and certainly not of the particular session." Yes, I did play the piano a bit, but I'm confident that was the one and only time my name has ever been recognized in print discussing my keyboard skills. I played the notes on the page with few, if any, additional flurries.

The next sentence is the one, however, that made me laugh. Since this was a campus-focused publication, students must have been questioned about how they planned to spend their Christmas holiday. Here it is, friends. Apparently, I made this comment to the interviewer: Kathryn R: "Go home to Rolla, MO, sleep for two weeks, and refuse to do dishes."

One of the ways I helped support myself was to work in the college kitchen, including doing dishes. In those days there were no automatic dishwashers. The job helped pay the bills, but it was a rather repetitive occupation. I suppose my mother encouraged me to change my mind and grab a dishtowel when I arrived home, but I did chuckle as I read my quote from years ago. Incidentally, today one of my favorite household chores is doing dishes. I just love the feel of the hot water on my hands, and the quick clean-up of the after-meal mess.

Caralyn's e-mail reminded me of Paul's trip to Rome, as recorded in Acts 27-28. I flipped to the chapters and started refreshing my mind of his adventurous trip. Fortunately, he recorded great details of these final days of a life dedicated to witnessing and spreading the Word.

For fun, we will pretend his notes were in travelogue format. Perhaps this abbreviated record of the challenges of his trip, under guard, from Jerusalem to Rome, may help you appreciate what commitment Paul possessed. This writer would have jumped overboard long before the trip ended. And so our review begins: (Exact number of days is not clear, so we will use the word 'Entry' in place of a specific day or date.)

Entry...
1. I, Paul, along with other prisoners, board a freighter bound for Italy. (Remember, Paul reminded the courts in Jerusalem that he was a Roman citizen, and therefore should be tried by the Romans.)
2. We landed in Sidon. The prison staff allowed me to go to friends so they might provide for my needs. (I guess eating is allowed as a prisoner, but you must hunt up your own Italian sausage or pizza.)
3. We sailed near Cyprus, but strong winds, on the open seas, made sailing difficult. We went ashore at Myra.
4. Same as above
5. The centurion guard found a ship sailing for Italy and put us aboard. We made slow headway for many days, as weather did not allow us to stay on course. We were forced off course and landed at Crete.
6. Moved down the coast today, but strong winds made sailing tough. We have lost a lot of time. I warned the captain that a great disaster was a possibility, bringing potential loss to ship and cargo, and to our own lives. Unfortunately, our centurion guard ignored my suggestions and listened to the pilot and owner of the ship, and moved on. The pilot did not want to spend the winter in Fair Havens, but rather in Phoenix, a harbor in Crete.

7. Today the weather was terrible. The wind was so strong that the crew was forced to hoist the lifeboat on board. We understood they feared running aground on the sandbars of Syrtis. In fact, they even passed ropes under the ship, just to keep it from falling apart.
8. It is now the third day of the fierce winds. No sleep last night. The storm is raging. The crew began throwing the cargo overboard, and rumor has it that they will begin by hand, to throw the ship's tackle overboard.
9. Several days since I have written in my log. We have all given up hope of being saved.
10. No one has eaten for many days. All aboard are starving and showing great signs of stress. Yesterday I stood up before the crew and reminded them of my advice not to sail from Crete. I added that if they had listened, we would not be in this pickle right now, including the loss of their cargo. Tomorrow I may make another suggestion, if there is no immediate improvement in our condition.
11. Well, today I changed my tone. I urged all aboard to keep up their courage. I then made a wild statement. I told them that not one of them would be lost; just the ship would be destroyed. You can imagine what their reaction was to that statement. Who in the world is this "crazy" guy who can't see with his own two eyes that we are doomed? My next sentence shocked them. I shared that the previous night an angel of the God to whom I belong and whom I serve, stood beside me and said, "Do not be afraid, Paul. You must stand trial before Caesar; and God has graciously given you the lives of all who sail with you." What an unexpected visit, but I trusted the angel's words, and attempted to demonstrate my faith to the sailors. Nevertheless, I added that they must run aground on some island. Guess I will just have to trust my God, take one day at a time. Probably many of the individuals were extremely frightened.
12. Fourteen nights in the storm on the Adriatic Sea and all are getting weary. It is midnight, and the sailors seem to sense, even in the dark, that land is approaching. Some of the crew were taking soundings and found the water was only a

hundred and twenty feet deep. At the next reading, the water depth had lowered another thirty feet. You could see the fear increase as the men anticipated crashing into the rocks. Before I knew it, they had dropped four anchors, hoping to avoid a total crash. I was surprised to see them praying. Then I observed a strange event. The sailors were preparing to lower the lifeboat. I quickly found the centurion guard, and said, "Unless these men stay with the ship, they cannot be saved." Thank goodness they listened and cut the ropes and our lifeboat drifted into the darkness. We all waited anxiously. I'm certain no one took a nap.

13. Dawn arrived. I urged all to eat, since they had not eaten for fourteen days. We must survive. I assured them that not one would lose a single hair from his head. Actually, I took some bread and gave thanks to God right in front of the entire crew. Don't know what they thought, but I felt the need to say, 'Thank you God'. As you can imagine, all two-hundred seventy-six people aboard eagerly consumed food. In fact, I think they each ate as much as they wanted. The crew then began throwing the grain into the sea to lighten the load.

14. It is daylight. No-one recognized where we were, but we could see the bay and a sandy beach. The captain decided to run the ship aground, if possible. They cut loose the anchors, untied the ropes that held the rudders, hoisted the sail and headed for the beach. Well, the weather did not co-operate. We struck a sandbar, and the bow stuck fast. We couldn't move at all, and the ship started to fall apart. I must say, that about then, my heart started to beat very fast. The crew decided to kill all the prisoners, rather than having us escape. Then a wonderful thing happened. The centurion really wanted to spare my life and persuaded the crew to change plans. Swimmers were ordered to leap into the sea, and a make-shift gang plank was designed for non-swimmers, thus enabling everyone to reach shore. Once on shore, someone must have studied their geography and recognized that we were standing on the shores of Malta. I was amazed at the kindness shown to each of us by the local people. They built us a fire, even though it was cold and rainy. Their hospitality was so

appreciated. We had other adventures, but I will write more when we finally reach Rome. The crew and prisoners were each grateful for a safe landing. God certainly pitched in and saved us all.

Reviewing a bit of history, whether your own or that of Paul, God's great warrior, brings moments of wonder and amazement. Paul did make it to Rome for a trial. During that time, he made one final speech. What courage this man of God demonstrated.

May each of us have courage to be bold, even in times of great stress and challenge.

PS: Paul had a serious experience but was provided with an opportunity to demonstrate to the local people that God was with him. Turn to Acts 28:1-6 for a quick review of the miracle that day on the beach.

CHAPTER FORTY-THREE
A Life Experiencing Transformation

Lessons from a Caterpillar

During some private time of reflection, I was reading Romans 12:1-2. One phrase caught my attention. I swiftly re-read. "Therefore, I urge you, brothers and sisters, in view of God's mercy, to offer your bodies as a living sacrifice, holy and pleasing to God — this is your true and proper worship. Do not conform to the pattern of this world, but BE TRANSFORMED by the renewing of your mind. Then you will be able to test and approve what God's will is — his good, pleasing and perfect will."

I was intrigued with the concept of "transformed." Apparently, Paul challenged the Christians who wanted to be pleasing in God's sight, to change. He cautioned them to offer their bodies as a sacrifice, but first they needed to be transformed. Paul did not expect them to suddenly change their hair style or begin wearing cowboy boots, in order to be transformed. What was he encouraging them to do?

What does Paul's challenge have to do about creeping caterpillars? Their story might be an analogy helping in the understanding of the conversion or "interior transformation" of our bodies and minds. These fuzzy bugs undergo four entirely different stages over their lifecycle. The word "metamorphosis" is used, and literally means to change form. The new creature, the colorful, winged flying insect, catches our eye, and makes us smile. Its entire being, from inside-out, became new. Growth and time transpired. There was an egg. The "larva" or caterpillar emerges. Stage three is referred to as the chrysalis, and finally the beautiful butterfly we each love flits around our garden.

Our author said transformation happens "by the renewing of your mind." Transformation relates to brain or attitude change. These Christians were told to "not to conform to the pattern of the world." Obviously, Paul expected a major overhaul of the lives, the thoughts, and actions of these early followers.

I remember, some time ago, a friend sharing a life-changing experience her daughter witnessed in her job working with homeless people in a shelter. The person involved, whom we'll call Jim, seemed to be angry continually. He acted as if everything wrong was everyone's fault but his own. He would sometimes be having a good day, but as soon as my friend's daughter (we'll call her Jennifer) would say anything within his earshot, he would go into a terrible tirade.

Another person at the shelter remembered sharing a jail cell with Jim and decided to talk to him. Jim commented that he was in deep, deep pain because he had been banned from seeing his two-year-old granddaughter. Apparently, Jim had been her primary caretaker since she was born. He missed her dearly.

During her next visit, Jennifer again met with him. She asked if he would want her to get a card from the card cabinet and send it to his daughter's house, but addressed to the granddaughter. She added that the worst thing that could happen is that someone would throw the card away without sharing it with the little one.

Jim immediately told her that he couldn't read or write very well, so our wonderful support staff wrote the message that he dictated. Rules of the center required that to use one of the cards, you must work fifteen minutes for a card, envelope, and a stamp. Jennifer got him a stamp and asked him to mail the card.

The next week when Jim returned, he was a totally new man. He had been able to see his granddaughter the past Saturday and Sunday for a few hours each day. And I quote, "It's like it transformed him."

The child called Jim, "Pop-Pop." He doesn't have service on his phone, but he takes pictures now and always shows them to Jennifer when he sees her.

Jim hadn't worked in twelve years, because of his felonies. He thought it was hopeless to find a job. Nevertheless, he allowed Jennifer to create an account at a local personnel agency. She also shared some companies who hire felons. Yes, this story has a double happy outcome. He had an interview the next week and was immediately hired.

The heart of Jim was beginning to be truly transformed. One day he shared that he wanted to get something "girly" for his granddaughter. Jennifer went the second mile. She found some bows and a bow holder that she was no longer using and gave it to Jim to take as a gift.

Appreciate the final quote from our everyday angel. "This story isn't about me being nice to someone. It's just an example of how someone can be transformed when another intervenes and advocates for him." It helps when you understand that his rudeness was coming from despair and deep pain, not from just wanting to be a "jerk"

Is this not the concept Paul was encouraging the followers to embrace? Get inside the head of another and try to understand what causes each to exhibit anger, selfishness, or to get off track and lose focus on their need for life-changing actions along our journey as a Christ follower? We each need to help another refocus and grow.

Of course, since each of us also wanders away, or ceases to mature, we too will need a hand-holder as we attempt to be transformed by the renewing of our minds and actions.

The Great Hand-holder, God, will be ready to also help us in our transformation, if we reach out for assistance.

CHAPTER FORTY-FOUR
How Big is Big?

When is your zucchini ready to eat? Do you pick them at two inches, or must they resemble the size of a banana, or do you prefer them large enough to work as a club - handy to bop the head of an invading Martian entering your kitchen? Is a child described as "big" when she is able to crawl, or when she leaves home with a packed suitcase and college catalog in her hand? For me, Labrador Retrievers or Alaskan Malamutes are large, and a new-born kitten is tiny.

Big is an interesting word. We think of New York City as the Big Apple. Big bands often make a big noise, and Big Brothers help others in a big way. You may have observed the Big Dipper in the night sky. Daniel spent time in a cage with a lion, sometimes referred to as big game. Hopefully many of us are big-hearted but not big-mouthed, spreading unnecessary information about others.

The April 2023 issue of National Geographic caught my attention with an announcement relating to size. Apparently, our world population has now reached the wild number of 8,000,000,000. Spelled out, that is eight billion. I must admit I have not conducted a personal head count, but my dinner table will be unable to seat all 8 billion for a potluck supper some winter evening.

As enormous as the population of the world, or as gigantic as an elephant is in relation to a mouse, that is absolutely nothing compared to some sizes of our universe. When we don our sunglasses and glance at the sun, it looks rather small. Then we read the sun is ninety-three million miles away, with a diameter of 864,938 miles. Can you imagine the little guy that had to dig a tunnel through the center of the sun, and then run back through with a tape measure, in order to discover that number to report to his boss? Would you believe that you would have to drive 2,715,396 miles to make it all the way around the perimeter of the sun? Of course, however, your car would melt before you even had the engine started for the trip. Those science guys must have a better way of measuring.

Now, hold your breath. That brilliant ball of sun is large enough to fit about one million Earths inside of it.

I'm not talking about the dimensions of Illinois, or the United States, but of the entire body we call Earth. And we have the audacity to think the US is a large, important country? Our country is rather like a pink gumdrop as the solo item rattling around in a giant, totally stripped down, empty ocean liner.

Big gets bigger. Hang on! Perhaps you have heard of Betelgeuse, a red giant, classified as a "semi-regular, variable star." You can guess by now, that it may be a tad larger than our sun. If you said that, you win my imaginary prize for the day. Checking out various online sources, Betelgeuse is seven hundred times larger than our sun and 14,000 times brighter. Imagine the Lord creating these two stars, our sun and Betelgeuse, along with multiple other stars on the fourth day of creation. He was a very busy God. No wonder on the seventh day He was ready for a rest. (Genesis 2:1-2)

As I sit in awe, reading these facts about God's creation, I think how very small I am. Yet, we know He cares for each of us. His Son took five little loaves of bread and a pair of fish and fed five thousand men along with women and children. (John 6:1-14) It is almost beyond my comprehension that God's eye notices even when a little brown sparrow falls to the ground, and at the same time knows how many hairs we have on our head. (Matthew 10:29-30) Incidentally, I keep him busy, as my hair seems to fall out rather rapidly these days.

An even tougher job is mentioned in Matthew 18:20: "For where two or three gather in my name, there am I with them." Now just close your eyes and imagine. Think how many followers of God meet, especially on the first day of the week. God is in their presence, whether meeting on land, in the air, or in a flowing stream. We cannot think small when we contemplate our Father in heaven. He is everywhere.

Perhaps Paul's comments to the Christians in Corinth are an appropriate finale for these thoughts. "Therefore we do not lose heart. Though outwardly we are wasting away, yet inwardly we are being renewed day by day. For our light and momentary troubles are achieving for us an eternal glory that far outweighs them all. So we fix our eyes not on what is seen, but on what is unseen, since what is seen is temporary, but what is unseen is eternal" (2 Corinthians 4:16-18).

Maybe some of you will remember the old hymn, "When We All Get to Heaven!" The author reminds each Follower that the gathering in heaven will truly be a day of rejoicing and shouting words of praise and victory. Let's grab our hymnals and begin practicing right now. We will need to be ready to praise God with our voices when the BIG day comes.

That will be the BIGGEST day in my life.
I'm ready to celebrate in a big way.

CHAPTER FORTY-FIVE
Green Apple Experiment

One late summer afternoon my friend needed some exercise. She wandered into the park adjacent to our home. She enjoyed the breezes and the voices of youth hitting the little white ball into left field or popping out. Eventually our walker passed an area with a few apple trees. Noticing that several small, imperfect lumps of green decorated the ground, she gathered a few and brought them home.

Eight or ten immature apples sat on a plate on our counter for a few days. Then the "chef," who prefers creating her own concoctions, decided to attempt a batch of applesauce. Now for real cooks, this is no challenge. I could have searched online for a recipe, but what did one really need to know to make one of the simplest desserts in the world?

As a pan of unmeasured water began to boil, I diced the green fruit into small hunks. I cut away the seeds, stems and rotten parts, but left on the skin. I was certain the skin contained all the healthy vitamins. Just to confirm my intuition, I checked online. What do you know? A raw apple with skin contains up to 332% more vitamin K, 142% more vitamin A, and 115% more vitamin C than a peeled apple. Guessed right on that decision.

I tossed the small pieces into the boiling water and zipped into the computer to check my email. Scurrying back to the stove, I realized more water would prevent a burned taste to my sauce. In addition, sugar seemed like an essential addition to the pot. A small number of calories found its way into the now-bubbling fruit. I popped the lid on the pan and checked on my wash in the other room. I also scanned a page from a book explaining the intricacies of Ecclesiastes; I was reading the book for a class I was teaching at church.

As I folded the dried clothes, I suddenly remembered that applesauce usually has some extra seasoning. Could it be cinnamon, or is it nutmeg? Cinnamon won out, and sprinkles landed in the pot. Watching the bubbling bits, I grabbed a little fork and started smashing. This maneuver minimized the appearance of the skins and made the mix less like lumpy oatmeal. Whoopee! Maybe this was going to work, but a bit of sticking to the pan suggested I throw in more water and stir more rigorously. I thought the flavor would be better if the pan were covered and the apples were steamed. The problem, however, was this: if I left the lid on, I couldn't continue to smash the less hard lumps of apple. Smashing won out.

A quick taste. More water, sugar, and cinnamon were added to enhance the flavor. Smashing with the fork made little progress, so a new tool was found with a larger, forked surface. More water was added. The moisture seemed to evaporate very swiftly. Lumps were disappearing. Hope began to enter my thoughts. Maybe, yes, maybe we will have dessert for dinner.

Sampled a bite. Smiled. Turned the stove off, and grabbing a spoon, located the chief chef of the household. This would be the ultimate test. She tasted it. She did not grumble, nor, however, did she suggest we increase our production line, bottle up jars of applesauce, and sell to the other residents at our senior living center.

Reflecting on the day's experiment, I thought about people in relation to the applesauce story. We start life much like the green apples. As "greenhorns," we hang onto, not a tree, but our parents' hands. Gradually, as we celebrate several birthdays, we leave the shelter of the family tree, and venture out of the shade, and into the bubbling "hot water" of life.

Beware however, because our personalities can quickly change. Sometimes the changes cause scars, as we experiment with various lifestyles, actions, and the making of new friends. Perhaps youth who had been faithful worshipers and workers at their church, find little or no time for celebrating the Lord. The bruises of life might be called "sin spots" on the soul of God's creation. Help is needed to remove those spiritual sin spots, just like we cut away the bruises and bug spots on the apples.

Applesauce, for most people, improves with the addition of water, sweetener, and spices. In John 7:37-38, Jesus had something to say about water. "On the last and greatest day of the festival, Jesus stood and said in a loud voice, 'Let anyone who is thirsty come to me and drink. Whoever believes in me, as Scripture has said, rivers of living water will flow from within them.'" Jesus is our source of living water and life.

Let's consider another analogy. As we love others, demonstrate evidence of the fruit of the spirit being part of our daily behavior, (e.g., long-suffering, joy, kindness, peace) and put Him first in our lives, we will show evidence of seasoning. This will be pleasing to God.

Sometimes, however, the lumps of sin in our being need smashing out. Cutting out sinful habits and thoughts is tough. One apple was so full of rot, it went directly into the garbage disposal. When we ask for forgiveness and attempt to refrain from repeating the same errors, others around us will smile, and desire to "taste" our friendship. God will be glorified, and we will avoid God's garbage disposal plan.

Become part of God's
'Green Apple' Sauce Plan for Your Life
Signed — Chef K. Ransom

CHAPTER FORTY-SIX
Parasites Plagued Royal Thrones

Royalty and palaces seem to go together. Frequently during our international travels, we've had the privilege to wander through ancient homes of kings and queens. Usually as we approached the entrance, our feet walked by carefully groomed lawns. Our eyes admired magnificent beds of flowers, sometimes shaded by huge, ancient trees. Undoubtedly the royal leader rarely, if ever, found the need to trim the trees, or water the grass. Servants, during Biblical days, would have provided the energy to care for the exterior of these magnificent, royal homes.

Entering these huge mansions or palaces, my heart would skip a beat. Immediately my knees ached, thinking of crawling on the floor to polish the marble. Undoubtedly company would never have entered through the heavy doors. The residents would be so busy dusting the self-portraits displayed, that there would have no time to rustle up plum pudding or a zucchini quiche.

Truly, however, visitors are often a bit overwhelmed as they wander through these structures which are not so very old. My overall impression often included a feeling of coldness and isolation.

Ballrooms were huge, while bedrooms could have just enough room for a bed, chair, and maybe a dresser. Of course, there would be the lower, lower level where the servants would spend their leisure time.

One room, however, was missing in the very old mansions and castles — the bathrooms or latrines, sometimes referred to as the "Royal Thrones". Beside the bed there might be a china container, for use during the sleeping hours.

Historians have continued to dig and search for ruins even older than the castles into which my feet have wandered. Recently, in the Old City of Jerusalem, an incredible find was unearthed dating back to biblical times, over 2,700 years ago. A pair of biblical-era, stone toilets was found, probably created around the end of the Judean Kingdom. These toilets were not flushable but did include cesspits. They were very rare, owned only by the elite.

Perhaps you are thinking, surely not. Toilets 2,700-3,000 years ago? Take a quick glance at 2 Kings 10:27. King Jehu was the ruler. You can read the entire chapter and review his relationships with Baal, and the events surrounding this verse. Today we are only looking at the unexpected word that pops up in verse 27. "They demolished the sacred stone on Baal and tore down the temple of Baal, and people have used it for a LATRINE to this day." The design is not like our modern, porcelain, flush unit, but this is more effective, from my perspective, than the Greek hole in the floor. Been there — tried that. Yuck!

What made this find even more thrilling for archaeologists was what was found under these stone objects — dysentery parasites. These two hunks of rock, pictured above, showed evidence of diarrhea. First found in 2019, their microscopic examination revealed the eggs of a host of parasites including whipworm, roundworm, tapeworm, and pinworm. The samples were found in the sediment beneath the pair of stones. (Sounds like a lot of worms to me — Guess one could have gone fishing with a can of those creepy crawlers.) Sanitation standards have certainly been upgraded in our twenty-first century.

Their findings seem to represent the earliest known evidence of Giardia duodenal, home of the parasites accounting for dysentery. Dysentery is spread by feces contaminating drinking water or food. The absence of any sewer system designed to protect the water families drank, made it inevitable that pure water was seldom available. The heat and flies of these warm countries just enhanced the contamination. Drinking beer and eating bread also contributed to increased diarrhea. (Undoubtedly this is information you were so eager to know.)

No wonder the Old Testament includes ample information of the sanitation laws. Standards of sanitation were primitive, but did include rules for careful cleansing, including frequent washing of hands with running water, especially if exhibiting signs of a health condition or coming into contact with something considered unclean.

Read Leviticus 15:4-27. You may find the guidelines for sanitation and cleanliness in this passage interesting. Isolation was another expectation for those with signs of illness. Perhaps that sounds familiar as we attempt to forget Covid-19 requirements of separation.

The Great Physician and His Father certainly attempted to keep their family healthy, even with no modern conveniences. He still cares about us. We just need to listen to his guidance and obey.

I truly appreciate His love for each of us.
I am also grateful for modern "Royal Thrones"
and sanitation conditions.
What about you?

CHAPTER FORTY-SEVEN
Pineapple Party

Pineapples were once so valuable, people rented them for parties. Renting extra tables or chairs, maybe a tent or a tux, is not uncommon, but pineapples? In the 1700's, party hosts who wanted to make a splash called up an entirely different business. They needed pineapples.

What message were they attempting to quietly convey to their guests? The message was: "We are extravagantly wealthy." Today we dash to almost any major grocery store and grab one or multiple rough-looking pineapples, and scurry home. There we struggle to extract the delicious, juicy, yellow fruit from the tough outer skin on our tasty tropical fruit.

Pineapples were mostly imported, and terribly expensive. In the eighteenth century, a single pineapple bought in Britain could cost as much as $8,000 in today's money. They were dubbed the "king of fruits."

In fact, Queen Elizabeth II is remembered for a pineapple party. She received pineapples as a wedding gift in 1947. The governor of Queensland, Australia, sent five hundred cases of canned pineapple. This would have been quite a party, especially since two years after the end of WWII, Britain was still experiencing rationing. What a treat for the guests! Incidentally, the foliage atop a pineapple is called the "crown," a rather fitting gift for a Queen.

Jesus also attended a wedding party where there was a shortage of an important item. On the third day of the wedding, the wine ran out. The host must have been embarrassed. Jesus' mom encouraged her son to provide a gift for the host. Six stone water jars were filled with water. Problem solved. A miracle transpired. Following a tasting of the new wine, the master of the banquet was amazed at the quality of Jesus' gift (See John 2). I'm certain the wine lovers of the party were also pleased that an even better quality of wine was produced nearing the end of the wedding celebration.

Isaiah records a description of an even more spectacular feast prepared by the Lord. "On this mountain the Lord Almighty will prepare a feast of rich food for all peoples, a banquet of meats and the finest of wines" (Isaiah 25:6). The Lord's party will include all people, not just the Queen of England's royal friends.

A few interesting facts popped up while preparing this piece. You can eat pineapple skin as it turns orange, when ripe. Actually, it should be a part of a healthy diet. Pineapple peels are neither poisonous nor toxic. If, however, the fruit isn't ripe, there may be some burning sensation on the tongue and throat. Even eating a bit of the harder core of this healthy food has nutritious value and helps keep your digestive system healthy.

I found some intriguing facts about this delicacy. A pineapple takes up to three years to grow and mature into a plant. Only a single pineapple on a plant. A pineapple is not an apple or pine. Actually, it is a berry, or truly a mass of individual berries fused to a central stalk. A record-breaking pineapple weighed in at eighteen and a quarter pounds, enough for several parties.

New Christians also need time to mature and grow in their faith. In fact, each of them must continue to study and dig more deeply into His Word. This white-haired writer finds she must continually study, just to keep her computer knowledge up to speed. I consult youth, friends, and professionals to help me accomplish a product up to the standards of today. So, too, must I keep digging deeper into the Bible.

Recently I began teaching a series on the book of Ecclesiastes. Although my heart yearned to share the thoughts of the author, my brain yelled, "I don't have sufficient information to teach this." With the opening verse, "'Meaningless! Meaningless!' says the Teacher. 'Utterly meaningless! Everything is meaningless,'" I felt challenged. I've studied the Bible for far more than the three years it takes for a pineapple to mature, and I still need to dig deeply. New and deeper depths of learning help keep us fresh and ready to share God's Word with others. Who knows, I might need to share at God's final gathering.

I'm Ready for a Party with the Lord.
Come Join Me.

CHAPTER FORTY-EIGHT
Sterilized Tomb

Seven days and counting. The walls began to close in on the human. Impatience, boredom, and fear. Yes, FEAR, filled her every thought. Would escape ever be possible? Her mind pictured her home. She visualized the tree shaded surroundings located on the shore of a peaceful lake. Maybe even a goose family was plodding down the lane near her driveway. A friend patiently waited to provide transportation to freedom.

Prayers for release and healing had been sent skyward multiple times during the preceding week. Where was God? Was He on vacation or just too busy helping another petitioner? Maybe He had given up on this restless, bed-bound female, thinking she had lost faith or had not prayed diligently enough. How she wished the medical staff would utter the magic words, releasing her from this sterilized tomb called a hospital.

As sadness crept into her thoughts, the passage in Isaiah 40:31 seemed to come in focus. "But those who hope in the Lord will renew their strength. They will soar on wings like eagles; they will run and not grow weary, they will walk and not be faint." Good gracious, how long must one wait and hope? Was God so busy watching hummingbirds flitting around on earth seeking nectar, that he had forgotten her? Weariness seemed to attack both body and soul. As the hours slowly ticked by, her body and soul were exhausted and emotionally drained.

Picking up her phone lying on the sheets, she searched online for Isaiah 40 and read the chapter. God's children were in distress, as the Assyrians held them captive. God's voice instructed Isaiah, in 40:1, to "Comfort, comfort my people, says your God." As she read further, once again, the greatness and caring capacities of God became so very clear. She had almost forgotten what the Sovereign Lord could do, how He cared for all, and how magnificent and gigantic his deeds were as He tenderly held his children in his hands.

Reaching verses twenty-eight and twenty-nine, a few tears came into her eyes. "Do you not know? Have you not heard? The Lord is the everlasting God, the Creator of the ends of the earth. He will not grow tired or weary, and his understanding no one can fathom. He gives strength to the weary and increases the power of the weak."

What a blessed thought! Certainly, many friends must also grow impatient and weary with life, even though they are not in a hospital. Probably parents feel imprisoned at home, as they care for children or an elderly parent or spouse. How could she encourage associates feeling imprisoned in a job or life situation that mentally or physically seemed to strangle them, creating an attitude that death might be more rewarding than the pressures of daily living?

Her mind flashed to the lonely people confined to their home or care center, with little or no ability to go or meet friends and visit. She tried to think if she had the courage to share the promises of God, found in Psalm 46:1-3 with others. "God is our refuge and strength, an ever present help in trouble. Therefore we will not fear, though the earth give way and the mountains fall into the heart of the sea, though its waters roar and foam and the mountains quake with their surging."

Putting the phone down, she closed her eyes and said a small prayer. She prayed for guidance and courage, not only for herself, but for boldness, enabling her to reach out to another human.

Finally, with patience and glorious care by the medical staff, an escape did happen. Walking into her home that afternoon was such a joyful, thankful experience. The word "heaven" even slipped into her thoughts.

Even Jesus may have experienced joy as He shook off the funeral garments in which he had been bound. He stretched and then walked out the open door of the borrowed, unused tomb where he had resided for about three days. His Father looked out for His Son. He will also look out and care for His children.

Tattoo that promise on your heart and trust.
You can escape your fears and loneliness.
Then eagerly await your trip to your new heavenly home.

CHAPTER FORTY-NINE
Alone and/or Lonely? What About You?

Five o'clock rush hour. A mother slowly makes her way through the traffic, her mind reviewing the executive decisions of the day at her insurance agency. Quick supper plans are needed, as she debates picking up a sausage pizza for the second night or warming four cans of soup with extra vegetables and hamburger thrown in. She remembers that Hank's team plays for the finals at 7:20 and Tim is out of acne meds. Her mother-in-law called, wanting to discuss birthday plans. Oh! Yes, the cat needs to go to the vet before dinner. Her eyelids blink with tiredness as she dodges the kid on the bike in the crosswalk.

Anticipate what her prayer might be that evening as she tumbles into bed, hearing the clock strike midnight. "Please God, provide me with a few moments of 'alone' time to relax and chill out. Let my internal battery recharge. God, help me take these moments and reflect on YOU and your love, so I can remain patient with my family. I so need time to just be free from challenges, responsibilities, and pressures. My appreciation for my family, job, and you is gigantic, but, some days God, I just want to 'pull out of life', sit on a tiny island, and watch the surf splash onto the shore. Give me time alone."

Two blocks down the street, Hannah sits staring at the TV, watching *Gone with the Wind* for at least the seventeenth time. The rocker squeaks, disturbing the wee mouse hidden under her unused, dusty chaise lounge. As she nibbles on a dry, cheese sandwich, the crumbs scatter on the floor, mixing in with dust balls, and a few orange peels from breakfast. Her eye watches the clock slowly tick, tick, tock in a monotonous distraction. The mail comes with seven catalogs for auto parts, grape jelly samples, and trips to Mars, along with five requests for money from groups unknown to her. As she searches the letters there is not a single personal note from family nor friends, even though today she celebrates her 60th year on earth. Three bills tumble to the floor, waiting for her to write checks.

Time drags on as another day of inactivity becomes history. If only…and her mind wanders backwards to the days when the house was filled with noise, hustle, baking smells, and homework scattered on the kitchen table. She remembers those aching legs, and frantic shoving of the wash into the machine, while answering the phone. So many joys then, but she was too busy to appreciate them. Now the void filling her life is almost unbearable.

Perhaps her prayer might include some of the following thoughts. "Oh God, how I need a friend! My life is like an empty tin can, filled with rotting smells and emptiness. No engagement, no joys, no friends, no one needs me. Woe is my life. I know you love me but Where are You? God, I go to church, but no one speaks to me. My arthritic hands are unable to toil in the garden or knit sweaters for freezing children. The phone remains silent 24-7. Days drag into night and back into dawn. Please, Lord, oh, please Lord, send me a friend. Help me find usefulness in my life. Goodnight, God."

Two wonderful people but, Oh! How different are their lives. One prays for aloneness. The other craves some noise, activity, and purpose. I must confess there are times in my life when each of these scenarios has provided a personal challenge. Age has little to account for this dichotomy in my life. I must, however, admit that person #1 matches my thoughts more frequently. The bustle of daily responsibilities, matched with personal desires and pleasures, so jam my daily twenty-four hours, that when I crawl under the covers, I just pray for silence, peace, and the ability to learn to say, "No".

Then the dilemma. With my eyes wide open, and a heart that cries easily, I see hurting people, tasks that crave workers, friends that need handholding, or a pleasure invitation that makes my heart sing with joy and desire to attend. With a battery that recharges swiftly, I dash along. Then the world crashes. My patience grows thin. The horn on my car honks more quickly. Thoughtless words pop out of the mouth, resulting in an injured spirit of a friend. Time to chill and take a week off to a deserted island, or a cruise on the Nile.

Life is not fair, it seems. Some folks have too many tasks while others rock quietly in the dark of their room, waiting for action. What can we do to balance out these needs? Matthew 28:20 concludes with the promise of God, "And surely I am with you always, to the very end of the age." That even includes today, in the midst of your own battle with "alone" vs. "Loneliness." Chat with Him. He is right there beside you at night as you cry out. "Cast all your anxiety on him because he cares for you" (I Peter 5:7).

God, through the voice of Moses, tells us, "Be strong and courageous. Do not be afraid or terrified because of them," (the enemies the Children of Israel would be facing as they entered the Promised Land) "for the Lord, your God goes with you; he will never leave you nor forsake you" (Deuteronomy 31:6). Yes, whatever our situation, God will be sitting right there "with" you, even in the darkness of your loneliness.

But my challenge to each of you today, is to bring balance to your own life. If you are overloaded, find a lonely Christian to at least pray with you. Call him or her when your heart is breaking with tension and fatigue. Share some of your burden with them as they plead silently to be needed. If, however, you occupy the rocker of loneliness, open your eyes. Step out of your emptiness and find a frantic mother who needs a listening ear, or an extra-large bowl of soup for the family's evening meal.

Let's help each other — the too-busy and the too-lonely. Don't, however, forget the Lord in that new partnership.

CHAPTER FIFTY
Invisible...Maybe a 'Hammock' Moment

Sad, lonely, without friends, a feeling of desertedness? Cartoonist Stephan Pastis, in the March 8, 2020, edition of "Pearl Before Swine," has Pig ponder the topic of loneliness. One frame truly caught my attention. Our author reminded us sometimes when we feel we are "unwanted" we also may feel invisible. Words of wisdom from the lonely pink porker.

Previously I discussed the concept of "Alone" and "Loneliness." We spent many words describing the needs of the busy mother, pressured CEO, and teens with classes, sports, and social life, as each attempted to find a balance between engagement and personal time. Their lives were crammed with interaction, responsibilities, and relationships so heavily weighing on them, that a half-hour retreating to the backyard hammock was a perfect reward. "Alone" is a word they envy. A moment in God's prayer closet, speaking quietly to their best friend, is a rare, but cherished event.

The discussion also introduced the opposite situation. Isolation in a nursing home, absence of friends and social connections, immobility, or lack of feeling needed, produce gigantic mountains of pain and sadness. Days drag into weeks, into months and moments of depression. God created us to relish relationships and purpose in our lives. These folk yearn for a piece of action. This writer suggested the need to somehow make connections between folk in Group A and Group B. Hand-holding and helping hands blending together might reduce the stress for all parties. (Perhaps elbow or toe bumping is appropriate in today's post-pandemic world.)

Today, let's take a second look at this balancing act--the blending of a purpose-filled life combined with need for reflection, quiet, and peace. Pig, the comic strip porker, introduced the idea of "invisibility" and the concept of the absence of feeling needed or the lack of purpose in life. He needed friends and a sense of being wanted. Again, the word "invisibility" has double meaning. The over-engaged person craves moments of invisibility from the world — thus the hammock for shut-eye or "closet" for prayer moments. But just the opposite is true for the "invisible" person, lost from her community, lacking purpose, or perhaps sinking into depression. No isolated swinging bed under the trees is needed for her. Moments of meaningful connections, relationship-building opportunities, and a feeling of purpose in life require an entirely different intervention. (Maybe some even need to find a hammock opportunity where friends gather to relax, read, and share tales from their lives across age differences.)

A friend shared a story about a five-year-old riding home from school, and absolutely driving her mother bananas. The mother is frustrated and annoyed at her daughter's "mood". Annoyance filled the mom's thoughts. Finally, after several hours, the little girl looked up at her mother, with tears in her eyes, and said, "I'm just tired, Mommy." This mother recognized that children, as well as adults, can be stressed and need attention. Mama immediately drew a lavender bubble bath, gave her daughter a face mask, lit some candles, and allowed her to sip apple juice and read her books. A new kid appeared, the happy, energized, youngster who needed alone time for renewal.

Stress from the day's interactions needs moments for "social distancing" and reflection. Hop in that hammock and begin a lively discussion with God. Actually talk out loud to Him, as you share your woes, griefs, pains, desires, and challenges. Wait and listen for His voice of peace to respond. Keep your eyes open for life changes designed to reduce your pressures.

Walking into a large auditorium or meeting, crammed with totally unknown folk, the concept of invisibility enters my mind. Suddenly I wish I could just disappear. Where will I sit? Is there anyone with whom to converse? Why did I come? Or, even more appalling, am I wanted among this group of folk, perhaps of a different race, financial situation, talent pool, or age group? Let me just vanish. How crazy our world is! We need people, but we need peace and quiet. We crave purpose and companionship, but too much of a good thing causes tears to spill from our eyes.

I started this piece prior to our changing world and new guidelines designed to provide increased Covid-19 safety measures for each of us. What a coincidence! As the stories flooded in, I recognized folk in both situations. Isolated in their homes, except for rare trips for pizza or filling a prescription. People were calling, texting, or seeking out a visit with the neighbor while getting their mail. Some lonely ones were volunteering to bring food/medicine to others who were afraid of venturing out. Then we had the huge group on the front line, helping with health and safety needs. Their hours were long, and the danger was ever present. The prayer on their hearts might be, "God, just get me home safely for a shower, ten hours of sleep, and quiet moments of solitude."

The wonderful promise through all these times is this: God is with us, He cares for us, and He offers His arms out to us for rest. Paul reminds us, "Don't fret or worry. Let petitions and praises shape your worries into prayers, letting God know your concerns" (Philippians 4:6-7, The Message).

You are never alone once you accept Jesus as your Lord and Savior. He has promised to never leave or forsake us.

CHAPTER FIFTY-ONE
Hurting - Healing Heart

During the recent pandemic experience we were daily encouraged to stay apart from each other. Many newscasters, as well as some medical professionals, strongly suggested that standing six feet apart in the grocery store, restaurants, schoolrooms, and even churches would hopefully reduce the spread of this horrible virus. Regardless of how one feels about that strong suggestion, the result created another problem. We were often isolated.

I believe however, we do need each other, especially in times like these. We are told to draw close to Christ who will hold our hand, walk with us, and dry our every tear. Prayers from friends and believers prop up our weary spirits. Yes, physically, during Covid-19, we were reminded to practice safe distancing but, and that was a large "but", that did not mean we could not remain close to family and friends in other ways.

As I approached time for major open-heart surgery, friends and family were important. Prayers, cards, calls, and visits helped me over hurdles of depression and loneliness. Yes, I prayed, and had conversations with God—often even in the middle of the night. Because of recent conversations with other Christ-followers about the concept of "with God" versus "following God," I would actually visualize Him sitting in the chair by my bed and having a conversation with Him.

In an effort to build relationships and connections with my surgeon and her team, I had as a goal to share a comment with her just prior to surgery. As we exited the elevator on the way to the operating room, there was a moment's pause. I asked them to wait just a second. I then shared, with the doctor and part of her team, that hundreds of people around the world from Hong Kong to Austria to Chatham, IL were praying, not only for my well-being and quick healing, but also praying for her and her team, as they attempted to restore my hurting heart. I have no idea what she thought. I wanted, however, to both witness, as well as build a bond or relationship, in addition to just receiving her medical expertise. I do know that I could not have had a more caring, kind friend throughout the ten days I was in the hospital.

That relationship/friendship continued later, as I met with her and two of her closest staff, at my one-month checkup. Her kindness, and the love that radiated from our visit that morning in her office, will remain with me for a long time.

Is that not also the kind of relationship the Great Physician wants with each of us? Have you really had that conversation with the God doctor, requesting healing of either your physical or spiritual breakdown? Have you invited friends to pray that your closeness with the Master will be enhanced? My doctor became more than just an expert in her field of surgery. That day she became a friend, who later demonstrated she cared about me as a person.

How do we build that relationship, whether with a doctor, family member, friend, or with God himself? Psalm 27:8 suggests that first we must seek Him out. "My heart says of you, 'Seek his face!' Your face, Lord, I will seek." I sought out a moment to seek the face of my surgeon in the elevator. I initiated the action to bring us closer together through bonds of friendship. In the same way, seek out God!

Deep friendships evolve as we spend quality time together. We shared my fears and dreams that evening when the doctor sat quietly by my bedside, after her long day in surgery. I listened quietly to her words of explanation, confidence in my healing, and acknowledging that depression often follows heart surgery. She knew. She shared in a quiet manner, and drew my heart, because of her thoughtfulness. She was honest, but I knew she cared.

Have I had that type of conversation with the Great Physician? Have I laid bare my heart's concerns and then really listened to God's reply? I was totally quiet during my post-surgery conversation. I was focused on every word the doc said. Do I follow those same procedures and quietly listen to God as I read His word? Do my eyes simply glance at the words of scripture, while my mind is focused on daily activities or challenges I am about to face? What kind of a focused listener am I? If I want that true relationship with God, the One who is going to heal my heart, I must turn off my own channel of words, thoughts, or focus, and tune in totally to what He is saying to me. He will begin to be a true friend that is like a brother.

Going alone is lonely. I watched a tiny turtle one day, slowly, oh-so slowing plodding down from a rock. I took a quick photo, and thought, "What a lonely life, as he is about to step off into that pool of water." Even during COVID 19, with forced separation, we had to find ways to make connections with others. But we have this promise: "And, I will be a Father to you, and you will be my sons and daughters, says the Lord Almighty" (2 Corinthians 6:18). Yes, just as the great song promises, *"He Holds My Hand."* As I wrote this sentence I was listening to that song, with a lump in my throat. I know he loves me. He is my keeper from day to day. He holds my hand in moments of gloom. I'm clutching it tightly because I need that friend, as he safely leads the way. Together we will work to heal my hurting heart.

Let Him hold your hand.
"For I am the Lord your God
who takes hold of your right hand
and says to you,
Do not fear: I will help you"
(Isaiah 41:13).

CHAPTER FIFTY-TWO
He-She: Talking to God

Silently the gray haired "she" lay in bed. Thinking, yes thinking! Alone! A bit of fear and depression filled her mind as "she" reflected on her recent triple bypass and aortic valve replacement surgery. Nine days, alone in the white room, hooked up to cords, wires, and machines. Poked, stuck, and weighed throughout the dreary hours of darkness. Weary eyelids attempted to sleep, but the peace of dreams and rest eluded her.

"She" needed a friend, a companion, a listening ear. Her heart cried out for relief and patience from this new self to which she was attempting to adjust. Questions filled her mind. Will the incision hold? What limitations will my body require, as "she" begins to enter the real world in a few days? Will a cane and rocking chair be her constant companions in her future days? A "little old lady," this "she" does not want to be. Perhaps being unable to drive, golf, write, or travel became moments of worry, sometimes eliciting a tear or two.

What could "she" do to escape this room of misery, discouragement, and sadness? Then, after one of her brief moments of shut eye, "she" awoke with a start. Of course, what was wrong with her? How could "she" forget, just when "He" was most needed?

Let "she" introduce you to him. We will call him "He." "He" cannot be seen, literally touched, nor audibly heard. "He" however, is not a figment of "she's" imagination. This fellow has been her personal friend for over seventy-eight years. As a six-year-old, "He" was more a friend of her mother, but as the years flipped by on the calendar, "she", too, began to know him more intimately. Although invisible to her human eye, "she" began to understand a great deal about "He."

Since the beginning of time, this fellow had lived everywhere, all the time, available for anyone to call a friend. In fact, "He" actually spent some visible time on our planet. For nearly thirty-three years "He" became like "she", a person of flesh and blood, not just a spirit. "He" had friends and enemies.

"He" was a teacher, much like this author, but oh, so much brighter. In fact, "He" was omniscient (all knowing and understanding). "He" had a cluster of a dozen young men who followed "Him" for about three years, learning about this friend, and later becoming teachers themselves. They also, thank goodness, recorded many of "His" teachings and actions for people like "she" to study.

"He" brought an entirely new perspective about life; a life "she" needed to grab hold of during these fearful hours in the white bed. "She" began that night to remember some of the lessons "He" had shared with his early followers. Love! Love your enemy, as well as those who love you. Forgive, walk with him through troubled waters, seek peace, and so many other teachings.

Trust Him to care for you through raging storms as well as in a peaceful canoe floating down the river of life. "He" promised in his teaching to be with his followers. Could that really be true, that dark, tearful night as "she" struggled to remain positive? Well, what about when Solomon in Proverbs 3:5 said, "Trust Him with all your heart; do not depend on your own understanding?" Would "He" really watch over "she," care for "she," and maybe even figuratively tuck "she" under the sheets without bothering the tubes, patches, and scars?

Then vaguely, some long lost words crawled into "she's" memory. "The Lord is good, a refuge in times of trouble. He cares for those who trust in him" (Nahum 1:7). "She" immediately dug into her thoughts. What was wrong with her? Had "she," in her private self-pity, forgotten "He" would be her island of safety that evening?

On a roll, "she" remembered what Paul had written. "Now may the Lord of peace himself give you peace at all times and in every way. The Lord be with all of you" (II Thessalonians 3:16). How could "she" have forgotten? "He" promised to bring peace to the restless, the lonely, and the scared ones. "She" let her mind wrestle with that concept and then "she" gave herself a talking to. "Get with it," "she" said. You are not alone. "He" is right here in this room with you. Didn't the passage say, "The Lord be with all of you," even a frightened, old lady "She?"

Well, that was a game-changing thought. "She" decided to try that idea. In fact, "she" spoke out loud in that quiet room. "She" imagined "He" was sitting in the chair by her bed. Thoughts began to form in "she's" mind. Words tumbled out her mouth. "Please, 'He,' hold my hand." I am so delighted you are with me tonight. As you know, "she" has been through a tough few days, but just having you sitting with me brings relief to my weeping heart. We can hum a tune together, discuss ways for "she" to experience peace, and most of all, reassure "she" that we can always be partners, walking hand in hand, through life together."

As light began to creep through the windows that dawn, "she" relaxed for a brief nap. Waking with a smile on her face, and her hand still reaching out to "He" who calmed her soul during the wee hours of the night, "she" felt peace. Yes, "He" was with "she" then as well as today.

What a joy to introduce my friend to each of you readers, as we each continue to walk with Jesus.

CHAPTER FIFTY-THREE
Birthday Wish

Once again, the calendar reminds me another twelve months have vanished into history. Eighty-eight years ago, John and Geneva Ransom were the proud parents of a wee little Ransom by the name of Kathryn Ann. Born in Portland, Oregon, and on the go ever since, I'm delighted to celebrate.

A friend sent a sweet card expressing the idea that birthdays are really the beginning of a new year, and a new tomorrow, thus providing an opportunity for new challenges filled with hopes and dreams.

Hopefully, a riverboat cruise on the Danube will find me blowing out candles and celebrating another 365 days of joyful life. More importantly, however, are the challenges of the greeting — it is the first day of anticipating a year of opportunities to live life to the fullest, to smile and encourage others, and above all, to celebrate the joys of being a Christian.

Even as a gray-haired, plus-eighty lady, I see the world as open to possibilities, thus avoiding boredom and uselessness. My eyes just need to snap open and my antenna to charge to capture those opportunities for being creative, helping others, worshiping the Lord in spirit and truth, and remaining active.

For some seniors that may be hopping in a car or on a bike and visiting others, golfing, and remaining strong, or working at your computer, sharing words of wisdom or kindness with others. At this moment in life, I am so grateful that my physical body and brain are sufficiently nimble to allow me to keep active.

Other seniors may be confined to a single room, in a chair, with kind attendants helping with daily needs. The challenge changes a bit, but a year of possibilities remains. Perhaps it is an extra smile or happy birthday hello to those assisting you or passing your room. Others may have a cell phone with which to chat with someone needing a moment of conversation to share a joy or concern. Maybe it is blowing imaginary kisses to friends and family miles away.

Incidentally, your cell phone is a perfect camera for capturing pictures through your window of God's sun, rain, clouds, or a goose waddling on your yard. Take a snapshot of the hummingbird on your feeder and forward a copy to a niece or ornithologist. Who knows, but you might have captured the "picture of the year" or started a twelve-year-old on a new adventure of identifying birds. Turn on your imagination switch and let the Lord direct you in new adventures.

Personally, I'm eager for this new year of living on God's earth. One goal included getting a second book on the market. Today, as I wrote this piece, I settled on the name for book two — *More Ransom Notes: Walk with Joy*. I'm convinced that each of us will stay younger and more alert if we keep active and thinking and doing.

Won't you join me in celebrating "Tomorrow's Opportunities?"

CHAPTER FIFTY-FOUR
One Bean at a Time...

My niece and family from Oklahoma paid a visit to Springfield. Actually, I expect, they wanted to check and see how the "old lady" was doing after her heart surgery.

A great time was had, but with a young child, there always seems to be a story. Dinner time arrived, and we roasted hot dogs over the fire pit. The menu also included baked beans. Suddenly I noticed that our two-year-old, while sitting on her father's lap, was carefully poking her fork into one bean, and then into her mouth it went. This was repeated over and over, one bean, eat, one bean, eat, while the family patiently waited for her to eat her fill.

That was slow, but the next morning we reached a lower water mark. Hash browns were on the plate of one diner. Then, you know what happened. The wee one entered the scene. Her little fingers reached out and plucked up one tiny piece of hash brown, popped it into ketchup, and ate it. Over and over, a single piece of fried potato went into her mouth.

Later that evening, memories drifted through my brain. I reviewed the patience of that two-year-old. What about self? Does the one-at-a-time philosophy find a place in my life? Yes, I thought. The first day after arriving home from ten days on floor six (cardiology area) of our hospital, I was eager to once again explore the world--well, at least part of it.

Taking a friend with me, we ventured out the front door for a walk. I had been assured that exercise was essential to recovery from open heart surgery. We tentatively stepped off the stoop and started down the drive. By the time we reached our mailbox, I was exhausted, and we returned to the safety of a living room chair.

Day two dawned and a repeat performance was attempted. As we began, I said aloud, "Let's try to get to the first mailbox down the road." Success, and then the return to safety. Day three we made it to the second mailbox, day four to the third, until about day nine we were down the road by box eight. Each day one more box was set as a goal, until finally the body and the mind cooperated and we were able to walk half a mile, and finally a mile. Victory!

How did that happen? Goal setting, patience, struggle, and never giving up. One day at a time of setting a new goal, and then patiently working to accomplish that goal. Matthew shares words of Jesus in 6:25-34, reminding us, "Therefore do not worry about tomorrow for tomorrow will worry about itself. Each day has enough trouble of its own." My family was eagerly hoping that our 'one bean at a time' person would hurry. This author continued to be discouraged as her walk took her only two houses, then three, and on and on and oh, so slowly. She wanted to be back to normal and conquering the world. Worry that life would never again be full of activity flooded her mind. My, but little faith filled her head. What did Jesus say in Matthew? "Do not worry about tomorrow."

There are 86,400 seconds in every day. Our focus should be on creating quality time for that day. Actually, the author of Hebrews suggests, "But encourage one another daily, as long as it is called 'Today,' so that none of you may be hardened by sin's deceitfulness" (Hebrews 3:13).

Encourage each other. That is an interesting challenge for Christians. Even a recovering heart patient could reach out and encourage others with a phone call, note, or email. Maybe instead of wishing to be back to "normal," my mind and actions needed to focus on others. James in 3:13 reminds us that understanding folk will demonstrate their good life, including deeds done in the humility that comes from wisdom.

The Christian is challenged each day, one day at a time, to help others, thus witnessing for Christ. Our family waited patiently for the "one by one bean eater" to complete her meal. Am I that patient in my Christian life as I focus on helping others, OR do I want a month of Sundays to be accomplished in twenty-four hours? We are not to worry about tomorrow but to focus on today.

That, however, probably does not say we should never have a huge goal for certain days in our lives. Our bean eater was finally ready for dessert. Campfires suggested the tasty treat created from graham crackers: melted chocolate "smores." When the little one was offered one, she carefully rejected the graham cracker and hot marshmallow, and grasped only the melting chocolate slice. Instantly, her eating habits changed from single bean to, you guessed it, attempting to cram the entire chocolate slice into her mouth. My phone camera recorded a charming photo of the end results: a mouth full of goodies, and a face and two hands covered with melted chocolate.

Perhaps that is the final reminder for eager beavers for the Lord. Stay focused on one "bean" at a time. Reduce worry about the future; instead, keep your eye on the cross. Witness to others by helping, caring, praying, inviting, sharing, and in general, reaching out to family, friends, and strangers, just for today. Some days, however, may be graham cracker "smores" days, filled to overflowing with love that bursts forth on our faces with smiles, cheer, encouragement, and concern for others.

Just don't worry about tomorrow.

CHAPTER FIFTY-FIVE
He is Risen...

It was a cool, fall day as I returned from a trip to Joplin, Missouri. The week was wonderful. I reunited with lifelong friends during a visit to share information about my current challenge — telling folk about *Ransom Notes*, my first shot at authorship. Renewing tales and adventures from 1953 with my college roommate was exciting.

A highlight, however, was a surprise. Following a presentation to a group at Spring River Christian Village in Joplin, I was invited to one of the guest rooms to see a resident. What a surprise! There was Mrs. Gayle Boatman, wife of Don Earl Boatman, president of Ozark Christian College during my twin years of enrollment. She was quick to share that my eighty-four years of life was a mere drop of time in comparison to her 105 years and seven months of serving the Lord. Legally blind, her excitement for life and living produced a target for my remaining years. The Lord is good.

Returning home, I exited Interstate 44 and drove into Rolla, Missouri. More memories sizzled through my brain and brought a few tears to my eyes. Rolla was my hometown for several years, and two very precious folks had found a resting place there on a green, tree-covered hillside: my parents. Reading the dates on the tombstone, I was reminded that my mother scurried off to a far better home at the age of fifty. Yes, even though God is good, there are still times my heart longs for a motherly hug.

A different trip - to Jerusalem in 2019 - likewise resulted in moments of celebration, tears, and hope. During our walks around the city, we passed a quiet area with hardly a tourist, but our guide paused. Yes, we were standing at the possible location of one of the most glorious memories for Christians. Many think it may be the tomb where Christ paused for about three days. There was no tombstone marking the spot. Nobody remained hidden from us. The space was empty. Thieves did not cart his body away. He has risen. Our Savior is good because he is gone.

I've shared three memories for our review. A trio of related events, but you say, "How can they be related?" Memories! Memories! Memories! Stage One involves recognition and acknowledgment of Christ as your Savior. We are His servants, committed to living a life according to His direction. We must let our light shine and encourage others to join us in that new birth and dedication to a life of service. What a great goal for each of us!

Gayle Boatman was a perfect example of that commitment — a commitment lasting over 100 years. Even though legally blind, each day she is busy typing away on her old-fashioned typewriter, with a couple of stuck keys. When a key is not working, she must feel around, and "unstick" the key. The problem is that with almost zero sight, she could not read where the message stopped. She must guess and then continue typing tales of her family, designed for initiating future memories by grieving loved ones. Yet, with eagerness and pride, she handed me a copy of her day's labor.

I almost cried as I stumbled through her beautiful thoughts. I wished, however, that she had had a composing instrument which allowed verbal input. Yes, she is living the committed, Christian life until the end.

Stage Two initiates a period of memories, a mixture of joy, sadness, regret, and renewal. As I stood that fall afternoon looking at a stone monument, quick scenes of history flashed before my eyes. Words of thanksgiving passed my lips as I remembered the marvelous example my Mother modeled for her daughter, a life of sharing, caring, and sacrifice. Although she lived only half of a lifetime compared to Mrs. Boatman, my mother reflected a Christ-like spirit until her final breath, that afternoon so long ago, as I held her hand.

I wondered what memories others might review, when someday my ashes are found to the right of the family marker. Paul reinforces this thought as he writes to the Christians in Ephesus. "For this reason, ever since I heard about your faith in the Lord Jesus and your love for all God's people, I have not stopped giving thanks for you, remembering you in my prayers" (Ephesians 1:15-16). In both life and death, memories are precious. Give thanks.

Stage Three highlights the memory of every follower of Christ — the empty tomb. Death is not the finale of our lives. Jesus paid that ultimate sacrifice, was crucified, but - oh me! - He rose and returned to our promised, future home. Remember again the words of Paul in 2 Corinthians 4:13-14: "I believed; therefore I have spoken. Since we have that same spirit of faith, we also believe and therefore speak, because we know that the one who raised the Lord Jesus from the dead will also raise us with Jesus and present us with you to himself."

Memories of Life, Death, and Reunion

CHAPTER FIFTY-SIX
Celebrate New Life

A friend sent me a photo of her azaleas. I hope each of you can bring into focus some beautiful evidence of God's creativity, as we remember the celebration of Christ's resurrection. Pretend you have returned to that first century. It is a glorious day in Jerusalem on the hillside where you left your friend three days ago. Imagine you are one of the women who discovered the empty tomb. The cemetery is empty. No crowds. Just sleeping soldiers, weeping women, and one of God's angels. People who loved the Lord gathered to care for Him. They came in fear, anticipating a closed grave and wondering who would be able to roll back the stone.

What a wonderful surprise! The entrance to the grave was wide open — open for all to see, walk in, and observe the absence of the Lord. No one was barred. Even though, in the beginning, the women feared the body had been stolen, they continued to seek help finding Christ. As they approached, the angel acknowledged their presence, and spoke to them. "Do not be afraid, for I know that you are looking for Jesus, who was crucified. He is not here; he has risen, just as he said. Come and see the place where he lay. Then go quickly and tell his disciples: 'He has risen from the dead and is going ahead of you into Galilee. There you will see him.' Now I have told you" (Matthew 28:5-7).

The tears were turned to cheers, smiles, and maybe even a restrained hug. (I don't know what method of greeting was common between women and men in the first century.) I know I would have given a hug, if it had happened in this century. The risen Lord was found — or better yet, He found the women.

Just pause a moment and imagine the celebration. Their beloved, who had been killed, was alive again. I wonder sometimes if followers of the Lord today have become blasé about the resurrection. We have heard the story so many times. We know it happened. We believe with all our hearts that it is a promise for our own future resurrection from death to life with God. But, and that is a sad "but," we fail to exhibit either silently in our hearts or overtly with our neighbors, the same joyful exaltations these Jewish ladies showed that first morning. I don't believe cartwheels or trumpets appeared, but smiles, a quickness in their step, and eyes that danced with joy surely happened. Perhaps it's time for us to re-evaluate our own outward signs of joy and appreciation for the gift of eternal life.

When I think of an azalea bush (and really most shrubs), I think of the dead-like branches from November — March. Then, wow! What happens? A tiny green tint, gradual greening of the limbs, a bit of a bud, and bingo — the gorgeous blooms. The bush appears to be resurrected for our appreciation.

But then, my mental image changes. I envision what happens when azalea bushes are trimmed. They are pruned, chopped off, and reduced in size. It took "major bush surgery" to produce such a beautiful new life. But is that not also true of followers of the Word? We, too, especially during times when we remember the resurrection, must apply major surgery to our lives.

Paul reminds us this is necessary if we are to produce fruit. The fruit of an azalea is its beautiful blooms. Our fruit must be love, joy, peace, forbearance, kindness, goodness, faithfulness, gentleness and self-control (Galatians 5:22-23). These "flowers" are identified by their resulting actions. As the Holy Spirit transforms us into kind people, for example, we demonstrate kindness toward others. My flowers of peace may result in trouble-free nighttime snoozing or perhaps a lack of fear about tomorrow.

Perhaps the pruner of our souls needs to help each of us clip off some unworthy actions because we are often unable to do this ourselves. Actually, John shares a comment by Christ. "I am the true vine, and My Father is the gardener. He cuts off every branch in me that bears no fruit, while every branch that does bear fruit he prunes so that it will be even more fruitful" (John 15:1-2).

Maybe, if we stretch this analogy just a bit, we can translate it apply to the person who acknowledges his or her unworthiness, sin, and sorrow. Self-pruning of hateful thoughts, anger, or selfishness must take place. This individual is then revitalized, and bingo. Once again, there are new blooms celebrating and shining forth as witnesses to Christ's resurrection of our soul.

Today, may we bloom and shine for those confined at home, but also to those with whom we connect electronically. Share the great news, wherever your steps take you, on this glorious day the Lord has given us. His plan is so incredible that it makes my heart ache when so many people know so little about Him.

CHRIST IS RISEN
Christ Lives
Christ Lives in Us
Share the Word with Others
Go Forth Rejoicing

CHAPTER FIFTY-SEVEN
Dragon Musings...

Date: April 11, 2013.
Location: Perfume River in Hue, Vietnam.
Participants: Fifteen travelers
Action: Exploration of Vietnam and Cambodia
Highlight: Meeting the Dragons

Fifteen tourists spent April 10, 2013, at Halong Bay, "the bay of the descending dragon," before flying from Hanoi into Hue. As the bus headed for our hotel, it stopped at the river's edge, allowing us to view the ten-day old dragon bridge at the edge of town. The giant golden head, followed by a pair of humps, was thrilling to view. From our spot on the riverbank we were able to really appreciate the sparkling newness of this monster.

The next day, we boarded watercraft to visit the Thien Mu Pagoda. Although I thoroughly enjoyed the pagoda, my eyes focused on several small boats, each with the head of a wild-looking dragon on the bow. I was impressed by how clever they were, especially since this writer is fascinated with this weird beast.

Peter Paul & Mary's "Puff the Magic Dragon Who Lived by the Sea," was a favorite song. Fairy tales of fiery beasts caused my imagination to wander afar. But a favorite dragon memory involves a group of fourth graders taught by yours truly. Our fourth-grade reader had a story about a dragon, and this silly woman decided that her class of inner-city kiddos would create a little drama for the kindergarten children at the school. Of course, the center of the production must be a giant, movable, dragon, capable of breathing smoke (really fire, but not a good idea in a school gym filled with five-year-olds). The classroom desks were moved around in order to create a large working space for this papier-mâché monster. A carpenter friend created a wooden frame, probably fifteen to twenty feet long. For several days, students took shifts covering the area with double sheets of newsprint dipped in the floury paste. Green paint was applied. Students worked on the script and others, four at a time, practiced slipping under the frame to become the legs for moving the beast. The date for the production was almost upon us, when a student reminded us that this dragon must breathe smoke. What can we do?

I don't know if some parent was creative, but the following day, one of the boys brought in a short piece of hose which we inserted up the neck of the dragon and onto the edge of the mouth. The student, then walking under the head, would blow flour out the hose at the right moment in the play. What genius! Who said kids can't be creative? The five-year-olds created much applause and our fourth graders beamed from ear to ear. Of course, the teacher was rather pleased herself and even remembers, to this day, the challenge of getting the monster out of our classroom door on its way to the gym. Yes, we had to break the tail a bit to get around the corner and down the hall.

To complicate the construction, yours truly had just broken her left arm while trying to learn how to roller skate. Thankfully the students, even though only nine and ten, were very resourceful and a super time was had by all. For those teachers reading this, half the class would be working on studies while the other half participated in the construction. After a period of time, the teams would shift roles. It is amazing how speedily and focused young kids can be when challenged with something they truly enjoy doing.

A few days ago, I read a bit of information that stimulated my thinking about dragons. Liquid nitrogen was poured on cheese puffs and allowed to set for a few moments. The cheese puff would become very cold. Pop the puff into your mouth, and you can breathe smoke out through your nostrils. That process would have solved our smoking dragon problem. CAUTION. Use a plastic, not glass, container in which to place the cheese puffs. Search online for more details and safety precautions.

Now, let's transfer my love of dragon lore to the scriptures. Isaiah 30:6 (KJV) refers to a "fiery flying serpent." Later translations use 'darting snakes.' Fiery flying serpents might even be a forerunner of my imaginary dragons. Job describes Leviathan, probably a sea creature. "Flames stream from its mouth; sparks of fire shoot out. Smoke pours from its nostrils as from a boiling pot over burning reeds" (Job 41:19-20). Smoke-breathing Leviathan makes me think of dragons. Scholars debate the issue. Some chemists confirm that certain animals today are capable of "breathing fire," suggesting, for example, the bombardier beetles, who genetically can produce an internal explosion in their abdomen and then expel a jet of boiling, irritating liquid toward their attackers.

We find another marvel in Revelation 12:3 — an enormous fiery-red dragon with seven heads and ten horns and seven crowns on its heads. Verse nine defined this beast. "The great dragon was hurled down — that ancient serpent called the devil, or Satan, who leads the whole world astray. He was hurled to the earth, and his angels with him." This red fellow, Lucifer, is not one we want as a companion nor do we want to follow, as his motives are not for our safety nor good. Thank goodness chapter twenty of Revelation reminds us that someday God intends to take care of this deceiving, evil fellow.

This is a quick review of the good, bad, ugly, and even funny side of a creature sometimes referred to as a dragon. The only one of which I am really frightened is the "red" fellow, Lucifer. Give thanks for God's promise to utterly destroy Lucifer.

God and the Lamb Will Reign Forever
We Win
Revelation 22:1-5

CHAPTER FIFTY-EIGHT
Tired of Waiting?

Say "Yes" to "Rest"

Do you ever just want to yell? Are you sometimes exhausted and emotionally drained? Perhaps you even feel alone, wondering, "Does Jesus even remember who I am?" Have you ever momentarily felt God has forgotten you? Perhaps subconsciously you wondered if He might be just sitting on his throne, having a snack, and watching hummingbirds flitting around hunting nectar. Why would He help me in this moment of frustration?

Well, maybe your outlet for frustration is crying, or jumping off tall buildings into a rose bush or a swimming pool below. There are moments in my life when patience eludes me. *Waiting* is a key trigger for harsh, thoughtless words springing from my mouth. Waiting seems like a waste of time. Ugh!

The other day, my car stopped at the drive-up window for a pharmacy. I handed the information to the person at the window, and indicated I would like to have a refill. After assuring her that I really was Kathryn Ransom, born on a particular date, many years ago, and providing her with my current address, we got to the subject of the visit. She continued looking at her computer, left for a moment, and returned with a white bag in her hand.

I blinked twice and asked her what she had. She replied it was my medicine I had just ordered. I replied, "I just handed you the prescription. How could it be ready?" And then I heard the strangest answer.

"Oh! You are listed as 'Automatic Refill.' Our office in Carol Springs fills your prescription whenever they think it is time, ship it down to Springfield, and we have it ready for you."

I quickly assured her that I did not have automatic refill. "Would you please remove that note from my record. I will call when I need my next refill." I paid the bill and returned home.

While putting the medicine into the refrigerator, I noticed the words "Use by 9-4-2023" printed on the label. Since there was a three-month supply, and only about thirty-eight days until the medicine should be consumed, there was a problem. By now, my frustration was building. Picking up the phone, I called, or rather tried to call, asking to speak to the pharmacist.

Nine minutes and ten-seconds later, I finally reached a very kind and helpful pharmacist. The label error was acknowledged. She explained the meds would be valid for the entire three months. The problem was, I wasted one-sixth of an hour on the phone. I was frustrated, silently screamed inside of my head, and pounded the keys on the keyboard with a bit more vigor, as I continued working on my jobs for the day.

Why was I impatient and upset with a few minutes of wasted time? Everyone makes mistakes. I'm certain I'm not the only person who loses patience, however. Why? Apparently when a human is especially tired, pressed for time, or in general not relaxed, negative consequences can result. Had I forgotten momentarily to ask God for patience? Fits me to a tee. It makes me envious of people that seem to be able to remain calm through frustrating moments.

The apostle Paul, in Philippians 4:4-7, admonished his brothers and sisters in Philippi, whom he loved dearly, to "Rejoice in the Lord always. I will say it again: Rejoice! Let your gentleness be evident to all. The Lord is near." Then he adds this statement that is so hard for me at times. "DO NOT BE ANXIOUS about anything, but in every situation, by prayer and petition, with thanksgiving, present your requests to God. And the PEACE of GOD, which transcends all understanding, will guard your hearts and your minds in Christ Jesus" (capitalized by the author for emphasis). Perhaps I need to learn to hum a tune or sing a hymn, thus keeping my frustrations inbound while I trust in the Lord.

Being gentle and understanding is a worthy goal for each of us. The challenge is, how does one remain gentle and understanding in the heat of a frustrating incident in your daily life? Patience disappears. Weariness creeps through your heart and bones. Funny thoughts pelt through your brain. "Surely this is not happening again. I don't want to grumble and complain, but how could this or that irritation be repeated so frequently?"

God was concerned about His children and their frustrations and behavior. He directed Isaiah to speak to Jerusalem. The first words from God in Isaiah 40:1 are so tender. "Comfort ye, comfort ye my people." (Incidentally, George Frideric Handel's *Messiah* has a beautiful piece reflecting this thought.) Isaiah reviews all God has done for them, and then God has Isaiah ask the question, "Why do you complain, Israel?" (Isaiah 40:27) God will not grow tired or weary of helping us. Even though we grow tired and weary, and we stumble and fall, He will be there and hold our hand.

The thirty-first verse then tells me exactly what we need to do when we are frustrated and weary. "But those who HOPE in the Lord will renew their strength. They will soar on wings like eagles; they will run and not grow weary, and they will walk and not be faint" (Isaiah 40:31). God is our refuge and strength and will be there to help.

The problem is, I forget to Stop, Pray, and Calm Down. I forget that the Lord will not grow tired or weary as a helper for me. I don't know how God does it, but that was the promise Isaiah shared with the group. He will give me strength, but I must listen, by reading His Word, and then respond to Him through prayer.

I believe, however, there is another element essential for the reduction of life's daily frustrations. It is called REST. Perhaps you have also experienced nights of restlessness and lack of sleep. One night is not a problem, but if we fail many nights to have sweet dreams, we grow weary. As we experience lack of shut-eye, frustration expands.

Take a moment and inventory your list of challenges, chores, and potential crises facing you. Turn the problem(s) over to the Lord. Pray as you tumble into bed, "Lord, help me tonight. Relax my mind, and allow me to seek your wisdom, in order to accomplish the potential mountains of life facing me tomorrow. Provide me with patience." Then one last phrase, as you pull up the covers,

"Yes, God, help me sleep."

Believe it or not, as I pray this prayer many nights, sleep arrives quickly. Mornings become a new day of joy, filled with anticipation of great opportunities to witness for the Lord, minus huge moments of destructive frustration.

Pray:
"Lord! I need your help with rest tonight.
I want to be a good witness for you,
a witness that is patient, helpful,
and thoughtful all day long.
I can't do it alone. My hope is in you.
Please, I do want to soar on wings like eagles,
and not grow weary; to be able to walk all day,
holding your hand.
Goodnight, Lord"

CHAPTER FIFTY-NINE
Making Melody in Your Heart

A friend residing in an assisted living area had trouble walking and standing up. She mentioned one time that whenever she needed to get on her feet she would begin to sing, "Stand Up, Stand Up for Jesus," and it worked. What a great idea. Paul reminded the Christians in Ephesus to be careful how they lived. They were told to "be filled with the Spirit, speaking to one another with psalms, hymns, and songs from the Spirit" (Ephesians 5:18b-19a).

My friend, as she sang her "stand-up" song, was really indirectly witnessing daily. When my spirits are down, or I'm feeling especially tired, I find myself whistling a happy tune. It is not always a religious melody, and in fact, many times no melody is being followed. I just whistle random phrases, but as I whistle, my thoughts seem to move from focus on myself and the current challenges, to a more joyful, positive attitude. Crazy, I know, but amazingly enough, my attitude does move upward on the happiness scale.

Paul implies that as we speak and sing, we are to do it with/for one another. Our singing helps encourage and strengthen others, even if some of us are a bit off tune or screaming loudly. Of course, we can sing while isolated on a desert island or in our garage, changing the oil in our jeep, but community singing is encouraged by the author of Ephesians.

Hopefully each of us, as we gather together for worship, joins in the main part of the service where everyone can be an overt, active participant, not just a listener. The challenge for some worshipers relates to the songs selected. They are often new tunes, with unfamiliar text, and perhaps played at a volume sometime unpleasant to our ears. The yearning for the familiar causes my spiritual heart to shed a few invisible tears.

Ephesians 5:19 continues, "Sing and make music from your heart to the Lord, always giving thanks to God the Father for everything in the name of our Lord Jesus Christ." There is a third entity involved. We are to speak to one another BUT sing to the Lord. Even though the community of believers is singing and listening to their neighbors, our focus, both in the message and with our thoughts, must be a gift sent to the Lord.

The real challenge of this scripture revolves around our heart. Now that is interesting. How does our heart make music? I thought my vocal cords and lungs produced the joyful and/or off-key sounds. What does my heart contribute? Does this mean that music played by piano, guitar, cymbals, CDs, or cow bells is not worthy? Of course that is not what it means.

Certainly, instruments may be part of worship music, but somehow our heart must be involved. Physicians hear my heart frequently, but standing in a worship service, I must admit, I have never heard a heart singing on or off key. Singing is making melody with our mouth but also with our heart.

Reviewing the definition of heart, as used in the scripture, we find an enhanced meaning. The heart includes our mind, soul, spirit, or really one's entire emotional nature and understanding. It is not limited to the pumping machine in our chest. We use the expression "have a heart" but we aren't suggesting the individual divvy up sections of her eight-ounce pumping machine and give it away. The phrase encourages someone to be merciful, show pity, or be reasonable.

We use phrases such as "he has heart" or "let's have a heart-to-heart" conversation and assume the person will think about what they say, to use the mind, and share or show feelings. If we are "singing and making music in our heart to the Lord," we are sharing our feelings of love.

Lyrics for "Holy, Holy, Holy"
express praise and adoration for the Lord.

Lyrics for "Take My Life and Let It Be"
petitions for help developing a consecrated life,
using our hands in service, and requesting
our voices sing in ceaseless praise.

Notice that the emphasis is not about the quality of our singing. Instead, we are to consciously focus our minds on the message, as we mouth the words of praise to the Almighty.

Sing, we must. Sing, making melody with our mouth. Singing as a community is encouraged. Singing to the Lord is Paul's charge to us. Singing is part of worship, not the city's choral society. The challenge is, how do we blend the music preferences of the vast age span in our congregations? Thoughtful and scripturally accurate lyrics are an absolute requirement. Melodies that encourage harmony of voices, with limited redundancy of phrases, are appreciated, but bottom line, all must be designed to praise our Savior.

Go Forth Together, Singing a Happy Tune to The Lord

CHAPTER SIXTY
Cruise Liner or Battleship

Come See — Be Served
Part 1

Preparations are moving ahead for fun, relaxation, and celebration of the author's eighty-eighth birthday. Even seniors tend to be weary and long for more than just a nap or walk in the park. The Lord makes a suggestion, encouraging us to action. "Come to me, all you who are weary and burdened, and I will give you rest" (Matthew 11:28). Apparently, He understands the concept of fatigue and burn-out.

Tickets are in hand for a flight to Budapest, with reservations for a European river cruise on the Danube River, aboard the *M/S River Adagio*. My brain is anticipating being a guest and being cared for by a dedicated staff. History with Grand Circle Cruise Line causes my mouth to water, as I dream of tasty cuisine. Trips ashore in Bulgaria, Czech Republic, Hungry, Serbia, and Romania will be led by talented and knowledgeable guides. I will appreciate several days as a pampered guest.

What more could one want? Cruise ships are designed for customers to be served, coddled, entertained, and kept happy. The experience is rather passive. The staff will serve, while the paying customers recharge, as they participate in joyful activities. Gripping their luggage, several days later, the guests walk down the gang plank, hopefully rested and ready for daily routines. Vacations and rest can restore a weary heart.

Could this also be true of Christians? Worshipers arrive each week, plunk themselves down on the pew, and wait for the service to begin? Like passengers on a cruise, each anticipates music of their preference, preaching by an entertaining pastor, and the opportunity to partake of the Lord's Supper. Some will sing, but many just listen, maybe daydream, and yes, anticipate plans for lunch with family, after service.

Sixty minutes later, people exit the church building, after shaking hands and greeting friends, and return to their daily routine. Hopefully each experienced spiritual restoration and recharging of their souls.

David acknowledged that, "The Lord is my shepherd, I lack nothing. He makes me lie down in green pastures, he leads me beside quiet waters, he refreshes my soul" (Psalm 23:1-2). Hebrews 4:9-11a tells us, "There remains, then a Sabbath-rest for the people of God; for anyone who enters God's rest also rests from their works, just as God did from his. Let us, therefore, make every effort to enter that rest..." We need a time of reflection, worship, and praise.

There are additional boats that also bring time for relaxing and renewal. Some require a bit more engagement and focus from the boater, but generally provide rest, with less stress. We think immediately of paddling our own canoe, or sailing along, letting the wind provide the power, as we pray the boat stays upright. After a day of stress, Peter and the boys were out in their boat, with the Lord napping, when the wind grabbed the sail and almost turned a time of rest into a wreck (Matthew 8:23-26). Thank goodness the Master woke up and took control.

Maybe sometimes we need to cry out to the Lord, like the disciples that afternoon, acknowledging our need for his support. I remember the days when we first began taking our small sailboat out on the main body of Lake Springfield. The wind blowing through our hair and the sun shining was relaxing, but I was scared to death. I just knew the wind would gust and these inexperienced sailors would lose control, forcing us to appreciate our life jackets, and wonder how we would ever return to the boat or the shore. Too many rely on an old saying of my brother when young, "Own self do it," and then wonder why we continue to be in trouble, discouraged, weary, or worn out in our relationship with the Lord.

Worship is essential, but other moments of relaxation may also be medicine for both our physical and spiritual health. The ancient saying, "All work and no play makes Jack and Harriet dull persons" will always be true. We need time to pray, have devotions, and contemplate God's love for us.

Cruise ships and recreational boats are not the only answer, however, for our lives. Being served is delightful, whether on a cruise ship or in a worship service. Others provide the service.

But, and this is a gigantic BUT, Christ needed rest AFTER He had served others through his preaching to the crowds and training of his leadership team. Part two will provide some thoughts on the service half of the team, so don't get too comfortable after reading these comments. Anticipate some challenges in Part 2. Right now, however…

Find a Cruise Ship or Recreational Craft
Come Aboard — Be Served and Renewed

CHAPTER SIXTY-ONE
Cruise Liner or Aircraft Carrier

Serve — Go Tell
Part 2

Rest is crucial to survival and peace in your life. Vacations often provide battery recharging time. Cruise liners contribute to restoration. Alternative recreational craft, e.g., paddle boats or pontoons, also provide relief for many individuals facing stress and fatigue in their lives. The basic principle of cruise liners involves the individual coming to see, enjoy, and above all, to be served. The client chooses when to isolate or when to enjoy the daily offerings provided. Fun, relaxation, and restoration of peace often are an end product.

Worshipers participate in weekly services, not as a vacation, but seeking an opportunity to focus on God, his love and grace, and to celebrate and say, "Thank you God for all you do." As we stretch our analogy, the element of come-see-and-be-served relates to a worship service. Pastors, priests, and support staff basically are responsible for the service. The worshiper then selects where to connect and become engaged. Some elect to sing, most participate in the Lord's Supper, and who knows which person tunes in the "sermon channel" or instead daydreams or plans the activities for the rest of the day. Hopefully most have renewed energy and focus. A charged battery is mandatory for keeping our light shining brightly for the Lord.

Now, the challenge. Today we want to switch roles. "Go" is a key element for a Christ follower. Go into all the world, go into the highways and byways, go into battle wearing the armor of God - these are charges for each soldier of the Cross (Ephesians 6:10-17). Thus, we must think about changing from a cruise liner to an aircraft carrier, from the concept of "come, see, and be served" to "Go, tell, and serve."

Battleships, submarines, and/or cargo ships come to mind. We want to focus for a moment on aircraft carriers. Humans found on these vessels are not there on vacation, not to be entertained, or to be served. These people have been called to serve, to go to war, to defend our country, to even go into fierce battle at times. They are prepared to attack and defend, to stand and deliver.

Although it has similar goals, each type of military vessel has unique tasks to perform. Let's take a quick review of the special skills and functions of aircraft carriers. They are similar in size to many cruise ships, housing close to eight thousand people. That is about the size of my hometown back in the 1940's. I cannot imagine the entire population of Rolla, Missouri aboard one vessel. A super aircraft carrier may be twenty stories above the water and about as long as the seventy-seven story Chrysler Building is tall.

Its unique purpose is to launch fighter planes. An efficient crew can launch a plane every twenty-five seconds from an incredibly short launching strip. Every crew member has a specific role, from the captain to the person stocking the ship's vending machines. They are to equip, prepare, launch, and receive returning aircraft, back from the crucial assignments away from the mother ship. The battle, however, is not at the home base. The planes are designed to go forth and fight and serve.

Churches should model this role. Yes, action happens aboard the mother ship, but the real goal is to go, find, protect, and fight. Is that not what Christians should see as their function? Certainly, we need to rest and recharge through worship, but to go, serve, and fight Satan and his arrows is our true mission. Just as the planes are launched rapidly, so we must each leave the "mother ship" to go and serve.

There are multiple roles for workers both at the home base and for the fighter planes. Not everyone can be the captain. In fact, we have only one captain, the Lord. Some will repair engines, while others will clean, feed the troops, maintain the food supply, or manage the communication system. The mechanic is as important as a fighter pilot, for without a fully functioning, healthy plane, the pilot is unable to attack the enemy. I cannot even imagine the multiple roles assigned to the eight thousand or so people, old and young, skilled and novice, aboard the ship. Each must perfectly perform. Likewise, with our churches, we need the home team to serve at the launching site. But then, everyone else must assume other tasks that help win the war against Satan.

Think what must happen to a military recruit who decides to just sit in the lunchroom or exercise area, and ignores completing his day-to-day tasks. Not a pleasant thought, I'm certain.

It might be interesting to take a survey of the worshippers in our local church. We could see how many reach out during the week in some type of support for the Kingdom battle or how many leave the church building and basically make no other connections to serve or help with the cares, problems, or tasks of the family of God.

**Come, See and Listen is our time of rest
and recharging or internal focusing.
Remember, also, the planes leave the "mother ship"
and go in search of external problems or needs.**

**"Therefore go and make disciples of all nations,
baptizing them in the name of the Father and of the Son
and of the Holy Spirit, and teaching them
to obey everything I have commanded you.
And surely I am with you always, to the very end of the age"
(Matthew 28:19-20).**

GO FORTH, TELL and SERVE

CHAPTER SIXTY-TWO
Power of the Song

Strains of the Lord's Prayer filled my office, as the Mormon Tabernacle Choir shared their talent on You Tube. Their clear voices assisted in switching on my brain, as my fingers began to record my thoughts. God's model for our prayers, recorded in Matthew 6:9-13, caused me to pause for a brief morning chat with my Master. Songs can be powerful, as we take our daily walk through life.

Never underestimate the value of making hymns a part of your life. Paul reminded the Colossians that God's word may be shared through singing. "Let the message of Christ dwell among you richly as you teach and admonish one another with all wisdom through psalms, hymns, and songs from the Spirit, singing to God with gratitude in your hearts" (Colossians 3:16).

Paul also told the Ephesians to sing and make music from their heart to the Lord, always giving thanks to God for all things. As we sing our favorite hymns repeatedly, the message becomes embedded in our hearts and mind. Perhaps songwriters should quote scripture for their lyrics, thus helping more of us learn God's Word.

The messages of some songs help us express our gratitude to God. "For the Beauty of the Earth" reminds us to raise our voices in praise to the Lord, our God. Even the well-known "Hallelujah Chorus," from the Handel's *Messiah*, is filled with moments of thankfulness and praise. My first real connection with Handel's glorious music occurred while in high school. Our choir was invited to join the Missouri School of Mines men's college choir in Rolla, Missouri. What a thrill for a teenager to join more mature voices for a concert. My heart grows sad when I realize how few youth and adults today have the opportunity to join multiple voices in harmony, singing God's praises.

Singing builds community. During much of a worship service the audience plays a quiet, listening role. The song service provides an opportunity for the listener to become an active participant. The joy of hearing voices quietly singing next to you unites worshipers and promotes social bonding and feelings of togetherness. Worshipers are a part of the family of God, coming together for fellowship. Visitors and the lonely potentially have an opportunity to figuratively join hands with other believers, building a sense of belonging and even joy.

Upon hearing "When Peace Like a River," sound forth from any source, I immediately want to sing or whistle along with the professional musicians. The words bring peace into my heart for at least a few minutes. The emotional me weeps quietly as I attempt to sing about this peace that flows around me and I acknowledge that it is well with my soul.

Three great messages emerge from the lyrics — sadness, grace, and heaven. What more powerful sermon than the reality that sorrow and grief are a part of our lives? Stanza two acknowledges we all sin, but the grace of God, through the death of His Son on the cross, is worthy of praise. Then our musical sermon concludes with the final trumpet call, announcing life eternal with God. Yes, "It is Well with My Soul."

Spiritual songs have the power to shove us into action. Even the simple "Take Time to Be Holy," influences our agenda planning for the day. Is prayer and a short devotional time scheduled into the busy calendar of citizens of the twenty-first century? Frances Havergal took Mozart's melody and added a powerful petition to the Lord, as he wrote "Take My Life, and Let It Be." The lyricist asks God to take our life, hands, voice, finances, and even our will and love, and use them for Him. Singing those words truly causes me moments of pause and internal review of my life and actions. It is impossible to avoid a quick time of self-reflection when singing the final line as the words admonish us to give it all to the Lord.

The real challenge today, as we think of worship and music, is blending the interests and preferences of different generations. Inclusion of organ, piano, choirs, drums and/or guitars, as well as volume control, present huge differences in audience preferences. Even the decision to stand or remain seated, while singing, varies with individuals. The bottom line, however, is that we need to blend all our voices in praise to the Lord.

I close with David's challenge for each of us in Psalm 96:1-2, "Sing to the Lord a new song; sing to the Lord, all the earth. Sing to the Lord, praise his name; proclaim his salvation day after day."

Even the Children of Israel were challenged to action, following their exit from Egypt. "Give praise to the Lord, proclaim his name; make known among the nations what he has done. Sing to him, sing praise to him; tell of all his wonderful acts" (Psalm 105:1-2).

Join me in Praising the Lord Through Song

(Note: Listen to the Mormon Tabernacle choir online and start your day with a prayer.)

CHAPTER SIXTY-THREE
Cluck Cluck and T-Rex

Could Chicken Little be a descendant of Barney, the children's purple cartoon dinosaur?

What a shock, as I read the headlines on my computer of today's apparent source of "all wisdom." Hold your breath. Could it be true: Chickens really are descendants of dinosaurs, walking the Earth as one of the closest living relatives to the Tyrannosaurus Rex? A site popped up on my email called "Interesting Facts."

Now, I admit, I am drawn to strange and interesting thoughts and facts, as they often become the skeleton of an idea for a Ransom Note. This possible fact, however, made my eyeballs blink three extra times. Further online searching continued, most saying that scientists really consider all birds a type of dinosaur. I will not go into much other basis for this alleged, dramatic fact, except to say, in 2008, scientists performed a molecular analysis of a shred of 68-million-year-old Tyrannosaurus Rex protein. They found it linked to a variety of proteins in many different animals, including our little fluffy, humble chick. (By the way, how much is a "shred" of protein?)

The scientific knowledge is far above my education level. This senior sees little, if any, overt similarities between a rugged, mean looking, thirty-forty feet long, seven-to-nine-ton, ugly, huge-boned creature, and the wee, yellow, fluffy, future source of my breakfast scrambled eggs. There was a small note that perhaps baby T's were possibly covered in feathers, so maybe that would help make a chicken connection. But then, what do I know about chromosomes and genetic lineage?

I'm glad they did not find dinosaur protein in my blood samples when preparing for heart surgery. Our family has not even done extensive genealogy studies to trace our ancestors. There is, though, a heritage connection which I am thrilled to acknowledge. Paul, in Romans 8:14-17 helps us trace that lineage:

"For those who are led by the Spirit of God are the children of God. The Spirit you received does not make you slaves, so that you live in fear again; rather, the Spirit you received <u>brought about your adoption to sonship.</u> And by him we cry, '*Abba*, Father.' The Spirit himself testifies with our spirit that we are God's children. Now if we are children, then we are heirs — heirs of God and co-heirs with Christ, if indeed we share in his sufferings in order that we may also share in his glory."

We are adopted children of God, which makes us part of His family, with the family name "Christian." Adopted children and biological children are legal equals. Granted, a molecular analysis of protein of these siblings will not match, but each has equal ability to inherit.

We each belong to the human race, and as Christians we also belong to God's family. The Ephesians learned that whether Jew or Gentile, they were "no longer foreigners and strangers, but they were fellow citizens with God's people and also members of his household, built on the foundation of the apostles and prophets, with Christ Jesus himself as the chief cornerstone" (Ephesians 2:19).

Scientists undoubtedly spent many moons of study to make a possible chicken and T-rex Connection. Determining genealogy connections in any family can be difficult. My relatives are constantly trying to uncover our own family genealogy, including using technology from DNA testing services. Who knows what future advances will occur as people seek to understand their heritage.

My question today is, how much difficulty would others experience if they searched to discover your adopted heritage with God? Do you know a silent follower who either intentionally, or simply by neglect, fails to make public his family of God connections? Would an adopted member of Christ's family skip opportunities to share publicly his Christian identity by missing worship, failing to witness in daily conversations, or rarely becoming part of the labor team any family/church requires to function smoothly?

Our researchers studied, I'm confident, for weeks. I must also add, however, that in Genesis 1:24, God said, "Let the land produce living creatures according to their kinds: the livestock, the creatures that move along the ground, and the wild animals, each according to its kind. And it was so." Birds and lizards are of a different kind, so you don't need to worry about your pet chicken suddenly becoming T-Rex.

God, however, is all knowing. He can recognize His children. Individuals may hide from friends, but their heavenly Father knows His children. God does not have to find a family "protein connection." Therefore, let each of us be proud of our heritage, sharing with others the invitation to become members of God's family.

Be a Living Descendant of His Family and Invite Others to Join Your Adopted Family

Postscript: Just for fun, a search I conducted found only two references to chickens in the New Testament and none in the Old Testament. Matthew 23:37 and Luke 13:34 basically express the Lord's sadness as he looked over the city of Jerusalem and said, "Jerusalem, Jerusalem, you who kill the prophets and stone those sent to you, how often I have longed to gather your children together, as a hen gathers her chicks under her wings, and you were not willing" (Luke 13:34). The thought that Jesus cared so much for others and made this mother hen analogy, makes my heart weep. Mama hens try to protect their families.

Then I tried to visualize a dinosaur reaching down from his huge body, but with arms only three feet in length, cuddling his baby offspring. The image is not soft and tender. Apparently, T-Rex three-foot arms would be similar to a six-foot human with five-inch arms. This would be a tough job for a human or a dinosaur to protect their young.

I'm glad God is caring for each of us and holding us in His arms.

CHAPTER SIXTY-FOUR
Kings T and J

School bells rang for the final time in late May 1962. My heart raced with anticipation. Summer plans were incredible. A group from Lincoln Christian College planned a seventy-six-day Holy Land adventure, beginning with an Atlantic Ocean crossing on the Cunard *Carinthia*.

Seven days on the sea, beginning on June 8, with a scheduled arrival home on August 22, would be bookends for a bus/train trip through sixteen countries from Scotland to Egypt. During that trip we would visit the burial sites of two famous individuals, King T and King J.

The contrast between the two is stunning. King Tutankhamun spent his life in the lap of luxury. He became king at the age of nine in 1334 B.C. With the help of several advisers, this fourth-grade-aged pharaoh reversed many of his father's decisions. The "boy king" ruled for less than a decade and died at age nineteen. In 2010, scientists did find traces of malaria parasites in King T's remains, which may have been the cause of his death.

In mid-July, our tour group arrived in Egypt by train. After time in Cairo, we moved toward Luxor and the gigantic pyramids. The Valley of the Kings is the site where many pyramids are located, but also includes crypts buried deep in the rocky hillsides, designed to be safer from looters than the pyramids.

In 1922 British archaeologist, Howard Carter, and his team, discovered a stairway, leading to the tomb of King Tut. Three years later, they found a sarcophagus carved from a block of quartzite. It contained three nested coffins, one inside the other. The innermost coffin was made of about 243 pounds of solid gold. The king's mummy still lay inside.

The four rooms of the burial chamber were packed with some 5,400 objects, including disassembled chariots, bows, arrows, shields, as well as over 200 pieces of gold jewelry. Incidentally the archaeologists not only found three golden beds, but also another six, more practical beds, for the comfort of the young king's eternal rest. For the Egyptian, the rooms were packed with everything Tut would need to live like a king for all eternity.

By contrast, King Jesus' body was placed in a borrowed tomb. It is estimated that preparing King T for burial took about seventy days. Joseph of Arimathea requested the body of Christ. Given permission, "Then he took... [the body] down [from the cross], wrapped it in linen cloth and placed it in a [new] tomb cut in the rock, one in which no one had yet been laid" (Luke 23:53). A friend, Nicodemus, brought a mixture of about seventy-five pounds of myrrh and aloes. This took just a few hours, and the stone was then rolled to cover the entrance.

The women who had followed Joseph went home and prepared spices and perfumes, but as it was the Sabbath, they waited until the first day of the week to place them with the body. It was a simple burial in a small opening in the rocky ground. There was no gold nor other items to help King J live for all eternity in the closed area. Nothing was offered from faithful followers but tears.

And then, came the rest of the story, which you know. Returning early in the morning, Mary Magdalene and the other women discovered the empty tomb. Nothing. There was nothing but strips of linen lying in the tomb and the cloth that had been wrapped around Jesus' head. No gold, chariots, or even a pair of sandals. EMPTY.

Life-sized, lifeless statues of soldiers guarded the Pharaoh's burial chamber. He did not escape. Live guards watched the tomb of Jesus but were unable to stop King J from exiting the single-room, stone chamber.

Today He reigns in heaven, seated at the right hand of His Father. King Tut's innermost coffin and remains can be found in the Grand Egyptian Museum in Cairo, Egypt.

King T was buried with his treasures. Christ was buried alone. We are His treasures, celebrating the empty tomb every day.

As I peeked into that empty tomb in 1962, I said a prayer of thanksgiving. Our God is great. He promises His followers will also leave behind empty graves.

Now that is something to rejoice about.
I Thessalonians 4:13-18

CHAPTER SIXTY-FIVE
Sauerkraut Apple Gravy

Kathy's Cooking Academy

Great chefs create culinary delights. A recent "treat" listed online made me catch my breath: Octopus Sucker Sashimi. Regardless of the price, I believe I would rather order a peanut butter and black raspberry jam sandwich. One listing of gourmet food included a spinach, corn, and cheese grilled sandwich. I probably could enjoy that combination. My one opportunity to taste raw octopus occurred in Italy and was not the highlight of my eating career. We each have food favorites.

Frequent readers of this epistle know that I stumble into cooking opportunities occasionally and wonders never cease with the end results. My experience with Cream of Green String Bean STEM Soup was, well, one for the record books. Read about this culinary marvel by turning to page thirty-seven in my book, *Ransom Notes: Moments of Reflection, Courage, Engagement, Worship, and Humor.*

Today, however, we will share another experiment. Sunday dinner was history. I was in charge of clean-up since my friend had cooked a tasty pork roast with a sauerkraut/apple combination plus other support items. As I reached to wash the Dutch Oven, I spotted some leftover juice from the roast, as well as bits of sauerkraut and apples. It smelled delicious. Should I trash this leftover or . . . and then my head said, "Make something delicious! Don't waste food."

Did I dare create a gravy that could be used with leftover pork and potatoes? Why not? Quickly removing some of the extra sauerkraut/apple mixture, I placed the liquid on the stove, grabbed a bunch of flour and mixed it with a gob of water. In nothing flat the liquid thickened. Sneaking a taste, I smiled. Yum! Yum! A bit tart, but what a rich, brown calorie-laden goo.

I popped it into the fridge and waited until evening. I volunteered to make us a hot roast pork sandwich with no bread and use up the leftover mashed potato, covered with the gravy. My concoction was carefully taken to the table, and I held my breath as Mary Anne took her first bite. She was kind, cleaned her plate, but probably will not repeat my creation. I, on the other hand, loved the strange blend of juice from the pork, tart apples, and a few strands of sauerkraut. Leftovers can be yummy in your tummy.

Maybe, you my readers, know someone experiencing a "leftover life." What do I mean? For years some of your friends and partners with whom you worked and worshiped, were on the front line helping. Greeting, cooking, visiting, listening to hurting people, or even rocking crying babies in the nursery kept them busy. Camp deans needed workers, and off your friend dashed to help. The missionary trip is scheduled. Five adults are needed to accompany the youth on their journey to learn about spreading the Word to others. Guess who volunteered to use their own vacation time to accompany those over-active, dedicated youth on a life changing journey? Yep! Your friends or spouse who are now isolated in their small apartments, mentally replaying glorious days of helping others. Could they feel like life's "leftovers?" Maybe even some reading this today have had moments of feeling like unwanted, throw away servants for God.

Perhaps silent tears or boring hours of being confined to a wee room crowded with pictures of sacred memories are your current reality. Maybe the fear of reaching out to help another interjects itself into your existence today. Your energy level is zero. Pain creeps throughout your body. Sleepless nights are filled with regrets, boredom, or even discouragement. In general, you feel like "leftover sauerkraut and apple juice." *No one needs me. No one visits, nor even calls or emails me.* "Poor Me Syndrome" creeps in and you or your friend withdraw even more. Pain, fear, and loneliness increase, much as a tiny snowball rolling down a long hill accumulates the icy white stuff, until the lump of snow/pain is the size of the bottom of a large snow person. It's a crazy analogy, but I guarantee each of you know at least one person fitting this description.

So, what do we need to do? Hmm! Be creative. Remember, God created you. (Psalm 139:13-14) He KNOWS YOU and your needs before you even ask. (Matthew 6:8) He made you and cares for you like a loving parent. But He needs you to stay connected. Teens graduate from school, begin working and raising a family and then they seem, too often, to forget parent connections. The parent yearns for a call, card, or even a drop in for a quick cup of soup with their son or daughter. Just because we are unable to perform certain tasks, it does not mean we are useless in God the Father's sight. He needs our wisdom, experience, focus, dedication, example, kindness, and thoughtfulness to support new believers on His service team. Maybe you can even crochet or stitch up garments for Inner City Mission residents needing help. One blind lady I know, receives forty handmade diapers daily that need turning inside out. She then sends them to the seamstress who sews them into the finished product, diapers for children in the local hospital. For the first time in days, my friend feels useful and needed.

Thank God for his support of you for so many years, but rededicate your life. Pray. Pray as you search for people who need a call of encouragement. Send emails of kindness to church leadership. Pray out loud in your chair for the mission team or camp program that is working on staying afloat. Take a youth or young parent out to the ice cream store and just chat a bit.

Offer words of encouragement. YOU are not useless. You must become useful. God does not allow us to quit, just because we are 87, move like a snail, or no longer can play soccer. Don't wait for someone to knock on your door for help. Reach out for options. Surprise the Lord, as you re-enter the Lord's volunteer work force.

Find rusty, creaking, lonely, but caring people and help them find new recipes for restoring sparks to their lives.

I am not a culinary expert. I will never become famous for my gravy creation. But I was able to create a tasty meal. So, you too, can help create action plans for others or yourself to re-join the ACTIVE army of workers for the Lord.

Recycle - Renew - Retread - Relearn
Restart - Reaffirm - Revive - Repent

CHAPTER SIXTY-SIX
The Empty Grocery Cart...

The wind was blowing that late, fall afternoon as I drove into the grocery parking lot. My mind dashed through several tasks still uncompleted on my "to do list." Parking the car, I noticed out of the corner of my eye a strange sight. Dressed in a hat and shabby, oversized coat, an elderly, fragile-looking woman was attempting to pick up about six or eight large plastic bags, her purse, and containers. She would get several in her hands but then had to lower one or two in order to reach for another. The juggling act continued as I scurried into the store. My mind switched from the woman with bags to the best buy on avocados and raspberries.

Checking out, I dashed to the car while mentally reviewing the remaining items on my to-do list. Reaching the perimeter of the parking lot I looked twice. There was the elderly lady, pushing a grocery cart toward a pile of plastic bags and containers. What was she doing? Could it be that she intended to load everything into this wheeled container? Where was she going? I expect I mumbled to myself, "What a sad situation!"

Then, just before pulling onto the main street, strange thoughts grabbed my heart, mind, and conscience. This lady needed help. Who was around to help? You! You, Kathy, must stop, turn around, and determine what help she requires. As my car paused near the grocery cart, I opened my window and inquired where she needed to go and if I could give her a lift. Bag in mid-air, she paused, looked at me, and nodded yes.

Clearing off the car seat, I suggested she place the bags and bundles in the back seat and tell me where to take her. We pulled out, heading north without any clear idea where we were going. She mumbled continually and I finally determined that she had bags containing unknown items that needed to go to a homeless shelter. Following her guidance, we approached the first possible location, a church which was now closed for the day. Without a pause, she swiftly changed directions and off we drove, as she chattered away about helping people, and some men needing the blanket she had in the bag. Truly, truly, I had no idea what we were really doing.

Arriving at location number two, I stopped, while she retrieved one or two of the bags and entered the shelter area. Shortly she returned, replaced a bag in back and I inquired, "Where to next?" Lunch time was nearing, and I finally determined that she needed to get to St. John's Bread Line. She apparently was telling me it was early, but she could wait outside. She appeared thrilled, as she would be at the front of the line for food when the doors opened.

She gave very clear directions. I zipped through back streets, into an alley, past commercial trash containers, and then into the parking lot where lunch waited. As she prepared to depart with her bags, I reached across the seat, suggesting we hold hands and pray. I have no idea what requests I sent heavenward, but I know God heard us that morning. Good-byes and thank-yous were exchanged as she lifted the parcels out onto the pavement. As I drove away, she was tugging her treasures across the parking lot to a wall where she planned to rest until the doors opened. My heart cried, imagining her burden, day after repeated day, lugging her belongings around, finding food and occasionally money to pay for cheap shelter. That day, in my car, her special wish was for warm housing.

Will I ever see her again? Probably not unless, perhaps, I volunteer at the bread line. Is she the only person burdened down? Absolutely not! Perhaps you, too, are carrying a load of loneliness, poverty, family discontent, shaky marriage, or personal guilt. David, the psalmist, sent a petition to God. "My guilt has overwhelmed me like a burden too heavy to bear… I groan in anguish of heart… My heart pounds, my strength fails me; even the light has gone from my eyes" (Psalm 38:4–10). Take a moment and read the entire thirty–eighth Psalm. Obviously, David was experiencing remorse and sorrow for sin in his life.

So, what did he do? He petitioned God to not forsake him. And then, just as I would, David prayed, "…Do not be far from me, my God. Come quickly to help me, my Lord and my Savior" (Psalm 38:21–22).

We are such impatient creatures at times. David wrote about his burden. Where have you hidden yours? Perhaps deep within your mind you hide that giant millstone of worry. Others may find a buddy with whom they can confide. Joyfully, however, David again helps us out. "Praise be to the Lord, to God our Savior, who daily bears our burdens" (Psalm 68:19).

My new "one-day" friend perhaps experienced a brief lifting of her burden. I encourage you, God's everyday forever friend, to lift your burdens daily in prayer. We must acknowledge His presence. We must shift our cares from our hidden spot. We must trust His load-bearing ability, and then move forward, praising His love and care for us. We know He promised, "Come to me, all you who are weary and burdened, and I will give you rest. Take my yoke upon you and learn from me, for I am gentle and humble in heart, and you will find rest for your souls. For my yoke is easy and my burden is light" (Matthew 11:28–30).

Our challenge today . . .
Find that metaphorical, empty grocery cart and then,
Reach out! Help carry the burden of one other soul,
plus Trust and thrust your own burdens
onto the Great Burden Carrier — Christ!

CHAPTER SIXTY-SEVEN
Tiny Turtle and A Mouse

Relaxing one spring morning, following nine holes of golf, my eyes blinked twice. What was that tiny spot on the nearby chair? Refocusing, my brain clicked in. The dark, moving object was a wee turtle about half the size of a golf ball.

Movement was almost imperceptible, but slowly, slowly, oh so slowly, the tiny legs methodically plodded ahead. Its destination was unknown to me, but I'm certain it was on course. Perhaps our mini creature was hunting a bite to eat, or seeking a place to nap, or trying to find its mother.

Online research suggested this size of turtle could be less than a year old. Imagine being on your own, a mere infant, all alone, attempting to cross an area like a "white plastic desert," which we humans call a deck chair. Probably a large human placed him there originally. I'd be terrified, confused, and wondering, "Where are my parents?" Regardless, we spent several moments watching and enjoying the focus and tenacity displayed by one of God's creatures.

Competing for the smallest creature title is the Pacific pocket mouse. It weighs about as much as three pennies and received its name from fur-lined, external cheek pouches used to carry food and nesting materials. One of these scurrying creatures, Pat, received the Guinness World Record title for longevity for being the oldest, living mouse in human care at the ripe age of nine years and two hundred nine days. Pat lived at the San Diego Zoo, so I'm certain many people have enjoyed watching him perform.

Why, you ask, would I take time to write about this pair of tiny, four-legged creatures? After all, they are so small the average person would rarely even notice them. Give me a Galapagos tortoise, weighing in at about five hundred pounds, or even a hippo. The bigger the better, perhaps we think. Certainly, we grab our cameras more swiftly when viewing a herd of elephants around a muddy watering hole, or a lion carrying her cub in her mouth, than a furry mouse.

"Big" is good. "Big" seems most important. We select the largest watermelon in the pile. Ears enjoy the music star with the longest list of hit songs. Boards hire a chief executive with the best profit ratio from her previous jobs. We select a guard for the school safety position who looks like a member of the front line of a professional football squad.

Or is the biggest, brightest, most talented, or well-known just what we always need? In football, the tackle weighing in at 340 pounds was valuable, but the MVP award at the 2023 Super Bowl went to a lightweight, 210-pound quarterback. Hmm, maybe "big" isn't always the criteria for getting the job done.

My phone captured the image of the tiny turtle. He is now the subject of this article. He brought a smile to our faces as we watched the wee body creep forward. We know not his goal, but he was persistent, despite his small frame.

Pacific pocket mice are useful in dispersing the seeds of native plants, as their tiny feet dig for food. Humans benefit from their God-given digging skills. "Small" can be useful. Many other wildlife, and even humans, survive because of the new plant growth resulting from the spreading of these seeds. "Small" or "Insignificant" can also be productive.

Translate this message to humans. God created, and the little creatures diligently carried out the tasks given them. "But God chose the foolish things of the world to shame the wise; God chose the weak things of the world to shame the strong" (1 Corinthians 1:27). A friend modeled an example of the small, quiet actions with which people can demonstrate God's love. On an extremely cold, January day, she spotted a single mom and her son walking. Pulling over, she invited them to hop in the heated car and quickly took them home. No fanfare, no public announcements, just a simple act of caring about others.

Remember in John 6:1-15, the young kid who went to hear the Master speak near the Sea of Galilee? Knowing growing boys, he had a bag of food with him. Not much, just five small barley loaves and two tiny, dried fish, but what a surprise was in store! Jesus gave thanks, and the little snack sack fed five thousand men, plus women and children, with twelve baskets remaining to feed others.

Our mouse digs in the dirt for food, and as a result creates food for others. Matthew 13:32 reminds us that the mustard seed is the smallest of all seeds, yet when full grown, is larger than other garden plants. Single acts of kindness can warm the hearts of recipients. Two simple phone calls to a shut-in recently brought her joy and comfort. A small zip-lock bag of fruit and snacks fed a hungry guy one Sunday morning at church.

God can take the humble and create riches.
Can this simple story accomplish a bold outcome?
It's up to you, dear reader.
"Go into all the world and
preach the gospel to all creation."
(Mark 16:15)

CHAPTER SIXTY-EIGHT
The Lonely Road

Recently, while returning home, I found myself slowing the car to a crawl. Why? Marching down the center of the pavement was one, single swan.

Why was he/she there? Where would this beautiful bird exit the roadway? Did this creature of God not know that an impatient individual was waiting to proceed forward on the same stretch of asphalt? Ugh!

Of course, I finally had a clear path as my bird friend crept onto the grass. As I proceeded forward, however, my mind drifted. Why was there only a single creature? I thought swans mated for life and if so, where was the partner?

My mind drifted even further off-course. Does a bird feel lonely? Isolation is not a great feeling for humans, but what about birds?

There was nothing on the road for a short distance forward or backward, just empty space. For a human this is nothing, but for this small, two-legged creature, it must seem endless. The tiny, shuffling steps edged the bird forward only inches at a time. Would the swan's mind begin to feel exhausted and hopeless with no water, no food, nor any companions in sight? Silly questions sometimes drift through my head.

Facing this same dilemma, I might want to just sit down and shed tears, give up, or more likely, call for help. In fact, years ago, while traveling on a back road in Missouri, I had a flat tire. I changed it myself and continued on. But you guessed it, later that day, while still in a rural area, bump, bump. The second tire was flat as a waffle.

What would I do? No replacement tire was in my trunk. I waited. I waited, hoping someone would come along on this lonely road that Saturday afternoon. Then, wonders of wonders, a truck approached. I signaled him down, explained my dilemma, and I was invited to jump in with him. He would take me to the nearest service station. I experienced a moment of panic, as I realized he was the county worker designated to pick up dead animals and garbage on the road. Was it safe? I had no choice. Long story short, we arrived where help was available, and the kind driver went his way. Later my car was picked up and the tires repaired.

Who comes to your mind from the scriptures who "walked" a lonely road? God decided that Adam needed a companion to help him in the Garden, and He created Eve to share life with Adam.

The sick man by the Sheep Gate in Jerusalem was lying by the pool when Jesus walked by. The Master inquired, "Do you want to get well?" The response by the invalid was, "Sir, I have no one to help me into the pool when the water is stirred." Alone. No one, and then Jesus commanded him, "Get up! Pick up your mat and walk" (John 5:1-15). Once again, God came to the rescue.

Jonah in the fish's stomach must have been lonely on that ride in the water. Help came as God caused the fish to spit our fellow out and sent him on his original journey to Nineveh.

I remembered Matthew's reporting, in Matthew 27:46, of Jesus as He hung alone on that terrible cross. About three in the afternoon Jesus cried out in a loud voice, "Eli, Eli, lema sabachthani?", "My God, my God, why have you forsaken me?" Oh! He was lonely, and even as God's son, He acknowledged the temporary departure of His father. The Savior had to die for each of us. But He knows about loneliness, about walking the road so bare of others.

What lonely road have you walked recently? Was there a heavy decision facing you, and only you could decide the course of action? Who was there to help when you faced a serious health situation? Can you remember a time when a spiritual obstacle, decision, or choice needed to be made and you yearned for an understanding, listening ear? Every one of us has faced many lonely paths.

Sometimes the spiritual highway of life is long and lonely. You want to scream or crawl into a hole and cover up your head. There appears to be no end in sight. Then remember, "Have I not commanded you? Be strong and courageous. Do not be afraid; do not be discouraged, for the Lord your God will be with you wherever you go" (Joshua 1:9).

Only you and the Lord really know what your l — o — n — g road experience is, but take comfort. Pray. Seek out a friend with whom you may perhaps unburden. Take an extra two minutes each morning to lift up your heavy heart to the Lord. Keep your eyes and heart open.

WAIT and WATCH for the LORD'S HELPING HAND!

CHAPTER SIXTY-NINE
Noah and the Challenges of Life

What comes to your mind when you hear the name, "Noah?" Perhaps you immediately think of the words, "flood," "ark," or "animals." Some readers may remember that Noah took along his wife, three sons, and a trio of daughters-in-law. Our childhood memories focus on pictures of pairs of beasts walking up the plank, through the single door of the ark, and into their home for about the next year. Maybe we even envision pairs of birds and bugs flying into the interior.

My imagination extends to the sights, sounds, and smells resulting from this menagerie of humans and animals sharing the vessel for several months. I'm certain no gas masks were available for producing less toxic air. The noise from the various passengers, human and wildlife, would probably drive a professional musician crazy, as well as everyone else.

I even wonder how Noah encouraged or convinced Shem, Ham, Japheth, and especially their wives, to pack up, leave their homes and friends, and board the ark. Would they really believe their father-in-law was serious? What would they pack into a bag for a year long trip? Would an argument result as time drew near to raise the ramp, and for God to close the door? I have no idea, but it is interesting to wonder.

Stop the ship! We've forgotten something. F-O-O-D. Those guys, gals, gorillas, and guppies will need nourishment. McDonalds will not be found dispensing burgers from a barge as the flood waters rise. No farmers' market will exist, as the flood waters will have destroyed all farmers. Even an extra chubby elephant lady, wishing to lose weight, could not go without food for multiple fortnights. A malnourished array of animals would defeat God's desire to replenish the world following the flood.

Thank goodness God knows all. After providing the design and dimensions for the ark and explaining who would ride around in safety during the rain and rising waters, he added one last command.

"You are to take every kind of food that is to be eaten and store it away as food for you and for them" (Genesis 6:21). The "them" included our six-hundred-year-old leader, his family, and two of all living creatures, male and female. I guess God wanted to keep little ones coming right along behind their parents.

Where would one begin to acquire provisions for all diets? Meat-loving tigers, blood-sucking fleas, or happy hippos, all need something different. How do you find sufficient amounts of all types of food before boarding the boat? Will some food spoil, with no ice or refrigeration? Does all food need to be eaten raw, as starting a fire on the boat might be dangerous? Have plans been made for retrieving water for drinking as it rises below the ark?

The Internet suggests that the average male African elephant will eat about 200-300 pounds of vegetation per day. That does not fit into a grocery bag, not even one day's need. And this is just one of the many hundreds of animals on the ark! Minor thought, where do you store the seeds for the canary so as not to be eaten by the pair of mice?

These are but a few of the questions the boat captain must answer. He must predict, locate, load and then store all these edible tidbits for use by his passengers. Perhaps a garden could have existed, thus having fresh vegetables for at least the eight humans aboard. The Lord provided exact measurements for the ark, but no such details for food. He just told Noah to take every kind of food needed and store it away. It blows my mind, just thinking about it, let alone if I had to accomplish that shopping trip to acquire needed supplies.

Noah did exactly what each of us must do. He followed the directions provided, and then trusted God. I'm certain as the waters began to rise, Noah had some sleepless nights, especially as people and livestock alike complained after a month of "riding it out." But, just like the children of Israel in the wilderness, Paul in prison, Daniel staying overnight with a lion, or Peter trying to walk on the water, God provided safety. Prayers, trust, and faith helped.

Perhaps you have faced traumatic challenges, health issues, financial shortage, wandering children, or even just plain loneliness and discouragement. The task of moving forward is daunting. Noah followed directions and God helped him weather the storm. David wrote, "Praise the Lord, my soul, and forget not all his benefits—who forgives all your sins and heals all your diseases, who redeems your life from the pit and crowns you with love and compassion, who satisfies your desires with good things so that your youth is renewed like the eagle's" (Psalm 103:2-5).

Sometimes we don't fully understand God's total plan for us, just as Noah only had part of the directions for his year on the water experience. Yet he trusted and kept working, and God safely brought him back to dry land. Today, the road map of life is often hidden from us. We fail to know God's timeline, but He is faithful to the end. He promised Noah safety and it happened. He promises us eternal life if we remain faithful, seek forgiveness for our goof-ups, and trust that in the end, an eternal home full of joyful celebration with God awaits us. Yes, we have challenges and disappointments. Ask God for daily bread and needs, not dessert and treats.

Then Trust and Stay Faithful.
He is coming to get us someday.

CHAPTER SEVENTY
The Boats Keep Coming

Headlines following the horrendous fire on Lahaina, Hawaii on August 8, 2023

People watched in horror as the news reported deadly wildfires spreading rapidly across Maui, and especially in the small town of Lahaina. Wind gusts up to sixty-seven miles per hour fueled the flames. Many fled their homes with absolutely nothing but the clothes on their backs. Cars, attempting to escape, were burning in the streets. Some people fled into the ocean to escape the flames, and many spent hours helping each other fight the waves in order to survive.

Dozens were killed. Search dogs spent many hours sniffing as they attempted to locate the many missing residents. Citizens crowded a satellite Division of Motor Vehicles Office to apply for replacement of Hawaii State identification cards and driver's licenses.

Then I read the phrase, "The Boats Keep Coming." One by one, a brigade of cruisers, small motorboats, wave runners, and catamarans were sliding quietly into the harbor and beach areas. Each was loaded with supplies: generators, propane tanks, bags of clothing and ready-to-eat meals. As the vessels pulled toward shore, each was met by at least two dozen people. The first person would wade in waist-deep ocean water to retrieve provisions and pass them down the chain of eager hands, and eventually to shore. Others transported the gifts of love to distribution areas, as the water transportation vessels hurried back for their next load.

As I read and listened to news reports of huge losses and multiple deaths, my heart grew sad, thinking of missing families and ash heaps of personal belongings. Then a quick smile, mentally thanking the crowds of eager workers reaching out to help others.

Throughout the scriptures, we have umpteen examples of unexpected people helping others. The first that popped into my thoughts and fits this context, happened in Egypt. Remember, the

Pharaoh became worried that the Children of Israel, who were living there under extreme bondage and slavery, were growing in number. Fearing that they might rebel, he gave an order to kill all the Israelite male infants. One mother, Jochebed, had a new baby boy. Not wanting him to be killed, she devised a clever way to save him. She placed the three-month-old in a papyrus boat, coated it with tar and pitch, and placed it in the reeds along the bank of the Nile.

The baby's sister, Miriam, watched over him until the princess went down to the Nile to bathe. As the princess walked along the riverbank, she saw the basket. Calling her slaves, they heard the cries and rescued the cradle and baby. Big sister immediately stepped out and inquired of the Pharaoh's daughter if she would like for her to get one of the Hebrew women to nurse the baby. And then, you know the rest of the story. Moses lived with Mom during his nursing stage, and then was raised in the Egyptian court. His life was spared in order to later become the leader of God's people as they fled Egypt. We certainly can see God's hand in this boat rescue operation.

Another hero, Noah, also used a boat for safety and rescue, but in a much different manner. Short story — He built his own boat, based on God's blueprints. He loaded it up with a sampling of all animals, along with a giant snack pack of food for nearly a year on the water. He and his family then jumped aboard, and escaped the flood, which destroyed the entire world. That flood, was a flood to end all, allowing God to begin again with new life. Now, that is one rescue story for just one family. We even have a clever reminder of the success of that rescue operation. Remember? It is God's rainbow promise never to repeat that operation again.

I'd like to highlight one final example of rescue on the water. Matthew 14:14-36 shares the story of our impetuous Jesus-follower, Mr. Peter. The Master sent the disciples out in a boat one afternoon, following the wonderful miracle when He preached and then took a kid's sack lunch and fed five thousand men and their families.

Jesus stayed behind and dismissed the crowd. I wonder how long it took for that crowd to head back home. He probably did not sign autographs, but maybe prayed for some of them. Then, how would you feel after preaching and feeding the crowd? Yep! TIRED. What would you do? I would have taken a nap, but Christ went up on a mountain by himself, and prayed. By the time he finished praying, the disciples and their boat were some distance away. The waves were very rough. Things were a bit scary.

Jesus, wanting to join the guys, did not wait for a rescue boat. No, He just started walking — walking right ON the rough seas. Probably his robe got a bit damp.

The disciples spotted Jesus, with the waves buffeting his body, and became terrified, thinking it was a ghost. Jesus called out to them, encouraging them not to be afraid. Peter, calling out to Jesus, asked permission to come to Him. The Lord said, "Come." Peter started to walk, but with the wind and the waves, he was overcome with fear and yelled for help. Jesus grabbed his hand and added a phrase I'm certain Pete remembered for ever. Jesus said, "You of little faith, why did you doubt?" (Matthew 14:31).

Sometimes we each get into "water over our heads." Hopefully we, too, call out for help, with faith that the Master will grasp our outstretched hand. I'm certain many of the people in the Maui area who ran for the water to avoid the flames, were also terrified. As some waited as many as six hours for rescue, perhaps they uttered prayers for a loving arm of God to send the right rescue boats or humans before they perished.

I'd like to offer one last challenge. The rescue operation bringing supplies to the homeless and hungry was led by ordinary human volunteers. They saw a need and pitched in.

Today, in our communities and in the world, there are countless people who need rescue from a life not connected to the Lord. Professional pastors and staff are incredibly important, b-u-t teams of volunteers must also step forward and help in the rescue, bringing souls to the shore and into the hand of the Lord.

Our challenge today is this: Grab your rubber boots and your courage. Step into the troubled waters of life and stretch out your arms to help those in the deep water of sadness, sorrow, sin, or anger.

Everyone needs the peaceful shores of Christ's love.

Note: There is a plant, a native of Mexico, called Moses-in-the-Cradle or Moses-in-the-Bullrushes. It gets its common name from its boat-shaped purple bracts, which also look like cradles.

CHAPTER SEVENTY-ONE
The Empty Cup

Leaving our church campground one afternoon, I noticed a white spot on the grass. The curiosity of a cat caused me to grab my phone, hop out of the car, and investigate. No, it was not a gummy, glob of melted marshmallows. Snuggled between the weeds and grass was an empty Styrofoam cup. Never one to pass up an opportunity for a future Ransom Note subject, I quickly snapped a shot. The picture lay hidden in my phone for several days, and then an idea began to bloom.

How did this cylinder land there? Undoubtedly some camper finished her beverage, and not obsessed with tidiness, just dropped it. "What did that cup represent?" however, was the real question filling my thoughts as I drove home. Several phrases drifted slowly through my consciousness. Could there be a theme on wastefulness, a feeling of uselessness, a recycling challenge, or maybe even memories of a pleasant beverage on a ninety-two-degree afternoon? What would work?

Later, while reading the 2023 September/October issue of *Christian Standard*, a lightning bolt struck home. Alan Ahlgrim's article focused on the role that hope has in our lives. He started the article with an acute observation that our daily lives are filled with the word HOPE as well as its rhyming opposite, MOPE. Wow! That is powerful. Which of us has not experienced major ups and downs with our emotions and in our life? There are days when joy and anticipation of exciting opportunities cause me to leap forward, but other mornings my heart just wants to snuggle in the covers, forgetting about what the next ten or twelve hours require. Maybe I don't exactly mope, but certainly feelings of exhaustion or even discouragement and inadequacy creep into my thoughts.

The author enumerated fifteen examples of current reasons for moping. As I read number fourteen, my heart stopped for a moment as I read the startling statistics about pastors and their risk of BURNOUT. Nearly half of pastors in the report indicated that they were in the High-Risk category for burnout. Stop and think! That rate is too high for the "lead puppies" of our churches who are worn out, discouraged, experiencing sleepless nights, or perhaps even considering changing professions.

Now, let's return to my empty cup analogy. Psalm 23:5 finds the psalmist discussing the concept: "You (the Lord) prepare a table before me in the presence of my enemies. You anoint my head with oil; my cup overflows." David began with the idea that the Lord was his shepherd; that he lacked nothing. Imagine the huge number of church leaders whose cup does not run over but has "run out." They are drained from stress, challenges, decision-making, and attempts to feed the flock adequately during these post COVID-19 days.

My lonely, empty cup certainly brings home the concept of desertion, emptiness, and isolation. The challenge now for our Christian community is how to turn this exodus around, and refill the cups with joy, love, eagerness, and ministry for our spiritual leaders. Of course, prayer for and with our leaders is a starting point, but God depends on the earthly troops to carry out some of His wishes. When Jesus' audience on the hillside became hungry, the "chief" pastor sent the worker bees (disciples) out into the audience to solve the problem. Lo and behold, one wee lad gave up his lunch of a few fish and snacks of bread and the entire congregation was fed and blessed.

Certainly, there is no simple answer, but we — "We The People" — must step up. What if each of us occasionally dropped a note or email of encouragement, listing a very specific, positive comment? Have we checked to see if finances for the church, as well as staff compensation, are meeting goals and expectations? Could our eyes be opened to the needs of some of the congregation, resulting in members stepping up, without being asked, to help fill the need, thus relieving some staff stress? Is a quick two night holiday or a week in a borrowed vacation spot by the lake or in a mountain retreat something a group might pool their nickels and give unexpectedly to the staff member?

Would it be possible for our grumbling and mumbling to be minimized, and our words filled with encouragement, as we "water the withered leaders" with kindness? Remember each staff person. Most are stressed, just as we are.

**Are you ready to help save our leaders,
not just at your church,
but throughout the entire kingdom of God?
I pray for that.**

CHAPTER SEVENTY-TWO
Lessons from a Kid

Twin cuddly pygmy kid goats arrived at Concordia Village, pulled in a canvas baby wagon, bringing laughs, lessons, and joy to fifty ladies one morning.

Johnny and June allowed eager senior strangers an opportunity to touch, pet, and sometimes even hold them. Their caregiver Megan allowed us to experience the joys and challenges of raising these fluffy creatures with bleats like soft, tinkling bells.

Our speaker/goat owner shared that pygmy kids should always have at least one other goat with whom to play, romp, and socialize. They are rambunctious little fellows and they delight in having high energy socialization with a family member or friends. She suggested small goats are herd animals, and therefore truly need companionship, including a bit of roughhousing.

Is that not a lesson for followers of God? We are His children, and thus part of an adopted family. We are told to love one another (John 13:34-35), and certainly that includes loving, caring, and sharing. Go find friends in Christ and become a part of their friend list. Friends do things together. Tea and crumpets, fishing outings, baby-sitting, or crying over sadness within the family are part of what friends do. We adults may not be as rambunctious as a pygmy goat, but certainly young boys and girls need opportunities to jump, scream, splash in a pool, and yes, sometimes even have a bit of pushing and shoving.

Friends also invite new neighbors into the fold, just like the goat family welcomes newborns. At first there may be moments of silence, awkwardness, or shouting, but getting to know one another, through activities and conversation, builds bonds of friendship. Our twins found several other pygmy friends in their home pasture. Most of the four-legged, furry-ones developed goat-type friendships. Perhaps they even, when eager to escape, joined their new buddies as together they jumped over the three-and-one-half foot tall fence surrounding their play area.

Remember when Jesus and the disciples were in the Jericho area? A tax collector, Zacchaeus, wanted to see and maybe even meet Jesus. Being rather short in stature, he shimmied up a tree and waited for the famous one and his group of guys to pass. Mr. Z thought no one would see him, but you know the story. Jesus arrived at the sycamore fig tree, focused his eyes on the hidden one, and invited himself and the guys to go to Mr. Z's house.

How's that for inviting a stranger into the family? Of course, Jesus and all the men went to the house of the tax collector. They had a very serious conversation, resulting in Mr. Z repenting. Maybe they even time for a cup of tea and a sardine sandwich. Check out Luke 19 beginning with verse one for details. Our goat friends and Jesus and his disciples are wonderful models of the need for companionship and the value of inviting newcomers into your group. Just be a bit brave and maybe even somewhat bold and fearless.

Goat experts indicate that as these furry, bright-eyed, mini goats play and nibble grass and leaves together, often one of the goats is the guard or has eyes on the group, watching for danger. As members of the family of God, we too need to be on the lookout for trouble and be aware of the needs of others. We may need to lend a hand, offer advice, or spot danger and seek help, but at least to be on guard. God, of course, is also guarding over each of us, but He uses earthly helping hands every day, everywhere.

Another interesting fact about goats and their eyes surfaced during my research. Apparently, baby goats are born with rectangular-shaped pupils, providing them with amazing peripheral vision, and thus keeping them safer. A side benefit is that these oddly shaped pupils help their vision in the dark, as more light is allowed in. The final benefit of the rectangular pupils made me a bit envious. This strange shape permitted the baby goats to see in several directions at once. Teachers are said to have eyes in the back of their heads, but I never experienced that phenomenon while teaching. That would have been such a wonderful side-benefit for caring for my class of young people.

2 Chronicles 16:9 suggests that God's eyes are probably even better than the pygmy kids. "For the eyes of the Lord range throughout the earth to strengthen those whose hearts are fully committed to him." To have our Father watch over us is a true blessing, especially in times of danger, pain, or discouragement. It does, however, perhaps encourage us to restrain ourselves from kicking up our heels too much.

Megan sometimes finds that the goats need a bit of persuasion to come into the fold, meet visitors, or whatever else goats should do, but don't want to do. When questioned on how she gets these frisky fellows to obey, her answer made this author chuckle a bit. She replied, "I persuade them with food."

Sounds like a good excuse for a family, thinking of inviting newcomers and/or friends to get together, stack wood in a pile, find a match, grab those hotdogs, and go for it. Food and friendship help cement relationships. God's food basket is found in His word. "Then Jesus declared, 'I am the bread of life. Whoever comes to me will never go hungry, and whoever believes in me will never be thirsty'" (John 6:35).

A final lesson seems to spring from our goat exploration. One person shared that she had heard goats do not like rain. Was that true? Our guest responded that apparently goats are not good at regulating their own body temperature. Therefore, when it rains, the fluff gets wet and cold, and they often get chilled and sometimes develop pneumonia. A goat owner therefore must have an optional place for the goats to shelter in order to stay dry and warm. Also, as I did a bit of research, I found that mud makes goats more susceptible to foot rot, rain rot, or other fungal issues of the skin. Muddy, cold feet could make anyone dislike rain. All these factors increase the need for shelter in the time of storm (see Isaiah 4:6).

Humans, hopefully, are not in great danger if they get wet, at least under normal rains, but other events and activities can be very dangerous for a Christian's spiritual health. Just as the farmer needs to provide a shelter from the storm for his four-legged friends, so we need to provide shelters and care centers for humans when the storms of life assail them.

Worship services, pastors, church staff and leaders become some of the safe shelters for hurting, grieving, sinning people. Good friends can extend their figurative and literal arms around an injured follower of God. A listening ear, a sharing of the Word, or maybe even a strong voice suggesting new directions in the life of the person needing shelter, can help heal and protect.

> **Isaiah 41:10 reminds us that God
> provides the support we need.
> "So do not fear, for I am with you;
> do not be dismayed, for I am your God.
> I will strengthen you and help you;
> I will uphold you with my right hand.**

CHAPTER SEVENTY-THREE
Banquet With a Giant

Saturday morning found us entering the cozy Cook's Spice Rack and Chili Restaurant in Springfield, IL. The morning was pleasant, and it had been many months since we had partaken of their delicious meals. I confess, I weakened and enjoyed a half-order of biscuits and gravy. Shame on me, but oh, they were delicious!

As we entered, we realized some re-decorating had happened since our previous visit. The restaurant, formerly a home, is rather compact but warm and friendly. The walls were covered with a variety of interesting plaques and memorabilia, much of it antique. We chuckled and smiled as we selected our table.

Then my eyes glanced at the wall staring me in the face. Could it be real? Did a giant now own this eating hang-out or were the utensils on the wall there for a special guest with huge hands and mouth? There hanging before our eyes were a fork, spoon, and knife, each about eight feet in length. Certainly, no normal person would be able to sip soup or chop a carrot into pieces with utensils that size. Maybe Giant

Goliath, who David popped with his slingshot stone so many years ago, had left behind this trio of eating tools, uncovered by an archaeology team working in the Judean foothills. Well, I suppose these are more modern wall hangings, but it was fun sitting there, letting my imagination run wild. Perhaps there was a large banquet and these were decorations created for a joke.

My mind then made a detour. I thought of Isaiah's words as he shared the vision of God's return, when the Lord will wipe away the tears from all faces. Whether literal or figurative, the banquet is described in Isaiah 25:6. "On this mountain the Lord Almighty will prepare a feast of rich food for all peoples, a banquet of aged wine — the best of meats and the finest of wines."

Luke reports the words of Jesus, as the Master told the audience in Luke 12:35-37, "Be dressed ready for service and keep your lamps burning, like servants waiting for their master to return from a wedding banquet, so that when he comes and knocks they can immediately open the door for him. It will be good for those servants whose master finds them watching when he comes." I guess we'd better keep our eyes open and our hearts ready if we want to be seated at His banquet. I'll be willing to eat at His table, using my fingers, if necessary, but I certainly want to be at the banquet. I will attempt not only to keep my eyes open for His coming, but I'll faithfully wear my trifocals daily, even if they get a bit scratched or bent during my journey in life.

Invitations to a special dinner are fun to receive. One question that often pops up as you read the words is, "Who else will be at the gathering?" Luke again reports on some of Jesus' interesting comments about the guests. Hang on as you read the words He spoke to the host of the party, a prominent Pharisee, in Luke 14:12:

"When you give a luncheon or dinner, do NOT invite your friends, your brothers or sisters, your relatives, or your rich neighbors; if you do, they may invite you back and so you will be repaid." Hum! Who then should we invite to our gatherings? Verses thirteen and fourteen provide the answer. "But when you give a banquet, invite the poor, the crippled, the lame, the blind, and you will be blessed. Although they cannot repay you, you will be repaid at the resurrection of the righteous."

I wonder how often I remember to include others besides my close friends and family to things like church events, home BBQs, or a trip to an ice cream parlor? Certainly, there are times for a gathering of friends, but it is clear that God expects us to include those with challenges of poverty, neglect, health issues, or personality concerns. How else are they going to learn of the love of the Lord and become partners with Him? If no one shares the gospel with the "left-behind," they will be absent from the Lord's banquet table when He returns.

Jesus reminds us later in the fifteenth chapter of Luke, about the shepherd with a hundred wooly sheep. When one wanders away, the shepherd leaves the ninety-nine and goes scrambling all over the hillside searching for the lost one. When the lost is found, the guy with the staff calls his friends in for a "rejoicing" party. The Master Host welcomes all to His table, and we, too, are charged with the responsibility to invite and include all. We must celebrate the finding of the "lost," whether a sheep or a prodigal son.

One more observation from my breakfast experience. Hanging beside our giant silverware model was a banner. The words were a tad funny. "Mind your own BISCUITS and life will be GRAVY." There is an element of truth, of course, as we don't need to necessarily try to take care of everyone else's business or even nibble the biscuits on our neighbor's plate.

But, and this is a giant but, the scriptures are clear that we must be concerned about others who may need a warm arm of love or a silent prayer for healing and support. Jesus came to seek the lost and heal the sick. Our eyes must pay a bit of attention to people who are struggling. Then we can quietly reach out to encourage, support, provide a warm meal, care for their puppy who needs daily walks, or take junior to his soccer practice. Remember, our neighbor is not limited to the one whose yard connects with ours. The Good Samaritan story makes it very clear that we may even need to reach out of our comfort zone to help one in need, even if from a group we would normally ignore.

Let's put on our party clothes of love, peace, and long suffering, plus a few other attributes. We need to keep our eyes open, and be ready for His return. In Revelation 19:7-9, John shares a lovely closing for our little visit today.

"'Let us rejoice and be glad and give him glory! For the wedding of the Lamb has come, and his bride has made herself ready. Fine linen, bright and clean, was given her to wear.' (Fine linen stands for the righteous acts of God's holy people.) Then the angel said to me, [John] 'Write this: Blessed are those who are invited to the wedding supper of the Lamb!' And he added, 'These are the true words of God.'"

Keep your silverware polished,
and your party clothes ready
for we know not the hour
when He, our Giant Lord,
will return for His children.

CHAPTER SEVENTY-FOUR
Chlorine to the Rescue

*"How wonderful it is that nobody need wait
a single moment before starting to improve the world"*
- **Anne Frank**

As I read Anne Frank's words, my mind did a quick review of the young Jewish girl whose family moved from Germany to the Netherlands. Life was severe in Germany as Adolf Hitler and his party were gaining supporters. Anne's parents decided to move to Amsterdam where her father, Otto, founded a company. Although Anne quickly felt comfortable in her new home, Nazi Germany was on the move in 1939. As the Second World War began, the Jews found life quite difficult, and the Frank family decided to hide out in 1942.

Life then became terrible. The family stayed hidden in very cramped quarters. During that time, this thirteen-year-old girl began to write daily in her diary.

Leaping forward to August 1944, the police arrested the family and transported them to Auschwitz. Life was terrible for all the family members. Ultimately Anne and her sister were separated from their parents. Her new life in prison was even more horrible than life in hiding and by February 1945, both sisters died as a result of contracting typhus.

Remembering that Anne was only sixteen when she died, it is incredible that she was able to produce such powerful bits of wisdom. Anne certainly did not waste a single moment as she filled a diary with deep thoughts. Many have been blessed by her writings.

In 1846 Ignaz Semmelweis, a Hungarian doctor and assistant professor at John Hopkins School of Public Health, had a problem. He was a living example of Anne Frank's belief that anyone can hustle right now and make the world a safer place. Ignaz studied two maternity wards in the hospital. One was staffed with all male doctors and male med students. The other was staffed by female midwives. His findings shocked him. He discovered that women in the all-male staff clinic had a death rate five times higher than the mothers in the clinic staffed by all female midwives.

He modeled Anne's belief that one should not wait to improve the world, e.g., reduce the death rate of mothers in the maternity ward. He began investigating the reason for the discrepancy between the two clinics. Initially he observed that in the midwives' clinic, the women gave birth on their sides while in the doctors' clinic, women gave birth on their backs. Initiating the change in the doctors' clinic to having mothers give birth on their sides however, had no effect.

Ignaz then observed that whenever someone in the doctors' ward died of childbed fever, a priest would walk slowly through the area, past the women's beds with an attendant ringing a bell. Semmelweis theorized that the bell ringing so terrified the women after birth, that they developed a fever and died. So, you guessed it. The route of priest was changed, and the bell ditched. Still no positive results.

Our researcher tried one more theory. The doctors and interns were accustomed to performing autopsies just prior to entering the neonatal unit. He began to theorize that perhaps small cadaverous particles, or pieces of the corpse, were getting on the men's hands but the washing with soap was not sufficient cleansing.

How could he get rid of those germs? He ordered the medical staff to start cleaning their hands and instruments with not just soap but with a chlorine solution. Chlorine is about the best disinfectant there is, even in the twenty-first century. Actually, our doctor did not know much about germs at the time, but hoped that the chlorine would help get rid of any of the smell left from the tiny bits of corpse.

And yes, when this cleansing method was imposed, the rate of childbed fever fell dramatically in the doctors' clinic. Ignaz helped improve the health of the world, even without fully understanding the value of chlorine.

My mind switches to biblical examples of leaders, who upon receiving knowledge, moved forward to help improve the world of people around them. David, the shepherd boy, seeing the standoff with the giant, immediately grabbed his sling and changed the outcome of the war with Goliath and the Philistines. I often wonder if his soldier brothers and the rest of the Israelites were a bit embarrassed that the young kid appeared to trust God and be braver than any of the soldiers. I think Anne F. would have celebrated David's helping hand.

Saul/Paul certainly made a gigantic change in his life following his "wake-up" experience on the road to Damascus. The fellow that breathed out murderous threats against the Lord's disciples, had a dramatic wake-up call. Blinded for several days after hearing the voice of the Lord that day on his road trip, he must have been shaken up. Ananias arrived at the house where the newly blinded man was waiting and had a little chat with Saul. He laid his hands on him and Saul was filled with the Holy Spirit. The scales on his eyes fell off, and Saul arose and was baptized immediately.

Saul wasted no time changing his set of goal posts. The ends of the field flipped, and he immediately grabbed a bite to eat and began a short period of study with the disciples in Damascus. I doubt that they dumped chlorine on him, but his soul was cleansed. He then went on to be one of the greatest representatives for the Lord. No doubt about it — he helped change the world for good. Check out Acts 9 for a quick review of his "about-face" decision.

Just so we don't let ourselves off the hook from being a vessel for blessings and help for others, I share Paul's comments from Ephesians 4:22-24: "You were taught, with regard to your former way of life, to put off your old self, which is being corrupted by its deceitful desires; to be made new in the attitude of your minds; and to put on the new self, created to be like God in true righteousness and holiness." Our corruption was cleaned up because of Christ's blood that was shed for us. I'm glad, however, I didn't need to be doused in a bath of chlorine to have my sins washed away.

Our challenge is to begin each day with a goal to drape our lives with righteousness and holiness. Perhaps Paul was challenging the Ephesians to do a quick inventory of their attitude and thoughts. He prayed they would "hop-to," or "get with it," as they modeled Christ-likeness. Just like Anne Frank said, "Nobody need wait a single moment before starting to improve the world."

Join the Team of God with a Goal to Share His Word Throughout the World

CHAPTER SEVENTY-FIVE
Are You a Bug?

Sometimes people think I'm a bit buggy. Now, I am not exactly certain what they mean, but I'm confident it is not a compliment. Checking with my online search engine, a series of adjectives appear. I'll let you quietly decide which word below best describes this author.

My search engine selected this series of informal or slang terms when I typed in the word "buggy": fruity, haywire, kookie, loco, loony, loopy, nuts, round the bend, whacky, or insane. Probably with my own analysis but, "a bit kookie" or "nuts" could describe my idiosyncrasies. I really hope I'm not "loony", and definitely pray that people won't describe me as "insane."

A search of the scriptures uncovered at least five people for whom the word "buggy" might apply. I found each reference intriguing and we'll see if your life and habits match up with any of this quintet.

Moses had sent a team to explore the land of Canaan. The twelve were to sneak into the country and see what the land was like and whether the people were strong or weak. The advanced guard was instructed to pay attention to the houses and towns. See what the people are like. In other words, snoop around quietly.

He did not say to check out the pizza joints or the Chevrolet dealership, but Moses did want to know about the soil. I guess if you're going to take over an area from your enemy, you want to know if you are getting a rock heap or dark, fertile soil, good for growing wheat, barley, olives, and of course grapes. Perhaps Welch's grape juice company might have wanted to conduct some experimentation with that strain of grapes and then pay Moses big money for the opportunity.

The dozen men designated from each of the tribes explored this area for forty days. Reporting back to Moses, they brought a single cluster of grapes so large that two men were needed to carry the fruit. Their verbal report, however, was less than positive, at least from ten of the spies. They thought the land flowed with milk and honey, and even beautiful fruit on which to pour some of the milk. But, and they had a giant "but," they thought the people of Canaan were stronger than the Israelites. In fact, they were so giant, the spies said "we seemed like grasshoppers in our eyes" (Numbers 13:33b).

You probably remember that Caleb and Joshua were the two who disagreed. They felt that all should move forward. The story is found in Numbers thirteen and fourteen. We, however, have just met our first bug, the **grasshopper**. These grasshoppers were represented by a group of God's people who lost faith in God, and in His power to deliver.

David accused Saul, the king, of coming after him with his army, as if he were chasing a "**flea**." David had just saved the king from being killed with the king's own sword while he was sleeping. Instead of letting Abishai stab the king, David took the king's spear and water jug. He then crossed the river, and shouted back to the army, giving them a hard time for not watching over the king. David added to Abner, the leader of the soldiers, "Why didn't you guard your king?" Read First Samuel twenty-six for details, but in summary, Saul woke up and realized he had been spared death, because of David's care. I'm certain Saul was repentant of his desire to capture David, but I'm glad he did not capture this "flea", David, the future king of Israel.

Our third and fourth examples of a bug come from Job 25:4-6. Bildad, one of the three friends visiting Job as he suffered through so many losses, asks the question, "How then can a mortal be righteous before God? How can one born of woman be pure? If even the moon is not bright and the stars are not pure in his eyes, how much less a mortal, who is but a **maggot**— a human being, who is only a **worm**!" I guess that might apply to each of us. Since I am a human, maybe I am "buggy."

Psalm 58:8 identifies the fifth bug. This is a bug that is slimy and not my favorite. The Psalmist accuses the rulers of failing to speak and judge the wicked justly and with equity. The words the Psalmist used to describe the wicked are horrible, but these rulers are not sending down appropriate punishment.

The writer wants God to break the teeth of these charmers (sinners) and tear out the fangs of these lions. Yuck! Yuck! He wants these evil ones to vanish like water that flows away. And then we see the next bug reference. He wishes them to become like **slugs** and melt away.

Five bugs that I would rather not be are used to describe humans. Obviously, these people are not faithful followers of the Lord, but who would want to be a grasshopper, flea, maggot, worm, or least of all, a slug?

Let us pray that none of God's children behave in ways that are so evil, thus becoming a bug in the eyes of others and the Lord. Out with a can of Raid.

None of these five bugs for me.
Let's instead, become a butterfly for God
and beautify the world around us.

CHAPTER SEVENTY-SIX
Optic Challenges

The day was pleasant. A friend drove out to the lake to take a walk with me. I had been home from the hospital a few days following open heart surgery. Although gaining strength, I was still a bit unsteady on my feet. Having a companion join me was such a wonderful blessing.

Well, it was really a double blessing. We chatted, observed nature, and had just about reached the end of the lane when it happened. Somehow, I instantaneously found myself flat on my face on the road. She offered to assist me up, but my pride indicated that I would be fine.

As I slowly got up, I realized that blood was flowing down my cheek. Oh, me! We were about a mile from the house with no Kleenex, warm water, or band-aids. My friend found a Kleenex or something to hold over my eye.

I'm still wondering about the return home trip, when a neighbor on her way to work stopped, inspected the damage, and returned home for ice and paper towels. We got a ride back to the house, a trip to urgent care, several stitches, and the rest is history. Incidentally my glasses were also history, but fortunately an extra pair resided in my dresser drawer.

Looking back on that event much later, my brain attempted to make a connection between God and the eye. He made our eyes to be incredible camera-like image recorders, sending those images to our brain. When working up to par, the telescopic-like ability allows us to instantaneously view a tiny flea in front of our nose and then with a blink and a slight movement of the head we can view a canary sitting on a bush many yards away.

This image-maker takes long naps while reading the back of her eyelids, but her eyes snap open with the slightest noise. We can cry, let our eyes twinkle, or even squint like a hoot owl, leaving the observer wondering if we are upset with them. Our eyes are the windows for our soul and our mind.

But there are a number of challenges for eyes. Let's review a few of those, but in the context of our Christian life. For example, many people experience a common condition called dry eye syndrome. The eyes aren't able to provide adequate lubrication, thus making tears almost impossible. Sometimes in our Christian life, we find we are unable to cry tears for people who are lost and know not the Lord. Get out the spiritual, liquid drops and then shed a tear for people who do not know the Lord. It is great to have Christian friends who walk with you, but we must not forget to be aware of people who have not given their life to Christ.

Double vision is a very awkward eye challenge. Focusing on a single image or frame is almost impossible. Some must close one eye in an effort to view words or see clearly. As a Christian, we also have problems with double vision. We suddenly appear to focus on Satan, self, and sin, while at the same time attempting to bring into vision God, grace, and goodness. Our entire being - mind, soul, and body - can be focused on two paths in life. We need to medicate, refocus, and bring back single vision into our eyes. "The eye is the lamp of the body. If your eyes are healthy, your whole body will be full of light. But if your eyes are unhealthy, your whole body will be full of darkness, how great is that darkness" (Matthew 6:22-23).

Macular degeneration (m.d.) is a degenerative eye disease. Damage to the macula can cause central vision loss. Vision becomes blurry and eventually may lead to blindness. We, too, in our spiritual life may begin to lose our focus on the main goal in our lives. We need to follow our King and His commands, such as developing the fruit of the spirit including attributes like love, joy, long-suffering, or gentleness (Galatians 5:22-23). We may crank up our peripheral vision, looking out the side of our eyes, and begin to focus only on "me-first," careers, raking in hundred-dollar bills, or snacking and napping in our recliners. Early signs of m.d. can be subtle. Likewise, as Christians, we may skip the service project at church, or reduce our offering to the Lord. Then as the condition grows, we skip some Sunday worship, or forget to say our nightly, "Now I Lay Me Down to Sleep" prayers. Suddenly we realize God is no longer in our center focus. Even our peripheral view of the Lord can become limited to only remarking to your grandchildren, while driving by a church, that this is where you went each Sunday when you were younger.

People with very normal eyesight, if driving, have several blind spots. These are areas of the road that cannot be seen while looking forward or through the rear-view or side mirrors. In our spiritual lives we often have a blind spot. There are simply things we cannot see. Perhaps in your Bible study you have skipped or misunderstood some challenge, or principle God expects us to follow. Suddenly you turn your eyes (re-read a verse or three) and realize that a change in your life is called for. The Holy Spirit might catch hold of your heart and mind and redirect your mind to greater understanding. Often a friend will even help you understand and guide you. The blind spot is gone for the moment.

Eyes are absolutely important to existing in our world, both physical and spiritual. Certainly many people with blindness from birth would appreciate even limited vision.

Let's each of us, humbly attempt to make our spiritual eyes as healthy and possible.

CHAPTER SEVENTY-SEVEN
Are You Unique???

"There will never be another one like him," the reporter remarked, as he summed up headlines from 2018. "There will never be another senator like John McCain." Driving along, as I listened to the news, I thought, "You are so right. John McCain was truly unique. The mold was thrown away following his birth." Then my thoughts wandered on. "Could that not also really be said about Abraham Lincoln, Hitler, the apostle Paul, or Judas Iscariot?"

My mind reflected on the life of Senator McCain. His service for our country in the armed forces and then later in the US government, imprisonment, permanent injuries, and ability to speak tough when needed, made him one-of-a-kind man. Through all his trials, he remained loyal to our country. Yes, he was unique.

As I mentally reviewed Lincoln, Hitler, Paul, and Judas, I realized that each of them also had very unique personalities, abilities, dreams, and objectives. They, too, were unique in their own ways—some for good, others for evil.

Then my mind charged on. I believe that is true about each of God's human creations. Could that really be true? Did God create each of us as a unique individual? We each have strengths and weaknesses. Even twins are unique.

Visiting with a mother of triplets, she described her three sons as very different in their approach, even as toddlers. Let me illustrate. Pretend the boys have just seen cows in a pasture. Son #1, seeing the world through literal eyes, comments, "Mom, there are seventeen cows in the field." Son #2, Mr. Professor, begins to describe the anatomy of the cows, how they chew, and the number of stomachs each of the seventeen bovines has. Then, Son #3, the creative, artistic fellow, comments. "Hey, Mom, wouldn't it be great to imagine cows flying, or I wonder what type of costume we would need for a play about three cows on a journey to the moon." They are lookalikes but oh, so different.

We, as Christians, are to resemble our heavenly Father, but our talents, energy levels, goals, personalities, and even physical capabilities have no exact twin. "Thank goodness," you might mumble, "there is no one just like this author," or you might even add, no one else just like yourself. Even though we are made in God's own image (Genesis 1:26-28), we are each different.

Think of a mirror. The image one sees in the mirror is not the actual person. It is a reflection. We are to be the reflection of Christ. We are not Christ, but we must reflect His image. So often, however, we are like the distortions found when viewing a carnival mirror. The person, when standing in front of one of those mirrors, may become tall, short, fat, bent, or even crooked. It's the same when we appear in God's mirror. Sin transforms us into distorted images of our Savior. God still wants us, in spite of our pimples, bruises, and distortions. He can continue to help us transform our lives to more closely resemble His image, but we must exert effort and dedication for transformation to happen. As Paul states, "And we all, who with unveiled faces contemplate the Lord's glory, are being transformed into his image with ever-increasing glory, which comes from the Lord, who is the Spirit" (2 Corinthians 3:18).

Allow me to illustrate. Peter, Thomas, and Paul, all followers of Jesus, were different from each other and also imperfect. Peter became fearful and denied Christ. Thomas, with perhaps a tad of skepticism, doubted the truth of the resurrection. Paul persecuted Christians prior to his conversion. Yet, all members of this imperfect trio reflected the image of Christ to others, as they witnessed and shared God's love with everyone. They just accomplished their witnessing in unique ways, utilizing their individual talents, skills, and knowledge. Paul reminds us that we, however, must shed our former self and "… put on the new self, which is being renewed in knowledge in the image of its creator" (Colossians 3:10).

So, what about you? What message must you hear? You, my friend, are different from every other Christian but you are also commanded to be a reflection of Christ. What does that imply?

- Step One: Think of the characteristics of Christ—E.g., compassionate, loving, friend to saints and sinners, observant, a servant, respectful of others, yet tough when He needed to be, humble, forgiving, and committed.

- Step Two: Take inventory of your own behaviors and traits. Which of Christ's characteristics are you reflecting in your life? Where do you need to initiate a remediation plan? E.g., with whom have you shown compassion recently? Has your true self exhibited anger instead of love and forgiveness toward another human? (Ugh! That is stepping on my toes.)
- Step Three: Set at least two to three specific goals designed to improve your Christ like image. E.g., I will . . .
  - A. increase my study of His Word, in order to enhance my understanding of His way of life.
  - B. reach out, with increased fervor, to the lonely and hurting folk around me.
- Step Four: Now, the hard part. Think about your unique talents, skills, interests, and knowledge. How can you use those one-of-a-kind abilities to accomplish the goals you set for yourself in step three? E.g., you want to reach out to the lonely. You have great interest in fishing. What about finding a young lad who has few, if any friends, and needs attention? Could you combine your fishing skills with building a relationship with that teen?

You are unique. You are one of a kind. You have responsibilities for modeling and spreading the Word to others in a way that no one else can do exactly like you. Each of us must become like Peter, Thomas, and Paul and recognize the task God has given us that only we can do. We cannot just sit comfortably in our cozy homes, nibbling pumpkin pie, and completing jigsaw puzzles. Invite a hurting friend over for tea, sardines, and a game of Scrabble. Model love, friendship, and then invite them to join you in worship the following Sunday.

Don't waste a day.
Ignite your UNIQUE YOU
as a servant for the Savior.

CHAPTER SEVENTY-EIGHT
Pioneer or Settler: Which Are You?

During a recent trip to Lincoln, Illinois, a Guinness World Book of Records display was brought to my attention. A likeness of Abe Lincoln was seated on the "World's Largest Covered Wagon" on the grounds across from The Christian Village. Speaking to a group of seniors that afternoon, we shared creative experiences in our lives. One gentleman proudly announced that he had ridden in this huge, covered wagon during a celebration.

As I left the grounds of this Christian Horizons community, I steered car over to the parking area. I grabbed my phone and captured the image of the record-breaking wagon, just as the shadows were beginning to lengthen. Driving back to Springfield, I reflected on this hand-built, 40 x 12 x 24-foot, 10,000-pound wagon. A fiberglass, 350-pound, twelve-foot-tall Abe was seated, reading a "law book." Who and why would someone make such a replica? Well, nternet, here I come.

Yeah! This mammoth, hand-built structure of steel and oak, built by David Bentley, was featured as Lincoln, IL, prepared for the 75th anniversary of Route 66. No, these wheels did not bounce across the two-thousand-mile trail a century ago, carrying pioneers to Oregon. This replica carried no crying babies, weary mothers, or dads with hunting rifles who piled their worldly belongings under a canvass cover and set out to explore new lands. The Railsplitter Covered Wagon was transported from its original home in Pawnee, IL and parked along Route 66. A "Do Not Touch" sign prevented this writer from crawling up and sitting beside Abe. I was disappointed, but at least I didn't break a leg attempting to scramble up the side of the monster wagon.

Downloading the images from my phone, my mind wandered back in time. Who were these original 18th-19th century pioneers who left family and friends to explore the West? True courage was required to expose one's family to an environment filled with disease, violence, death, lack of sufficient food and water, and unpredictable weather – all without effective shelter. A spirit of adventure dominated their lives. A reliable team leader was crucial for survival as these pioneer caravans rolled through uncharted territory. Obviously, these people were ready to explore, to view lands few, if any, had seen. They were risk takers.

Contrasting these pioneers were the settlers of that generation. These families basically wanted to stake out a plot of land, plant their gardens, build a log cabin, and give birth to a new generation of tough folk. Although life was not easy for settlers, stability and safety were higher on their "want list." As their horses plowed the fields, and wells were dug for water, the families snuggled under warm comforters on winter evenings, versus huddling under a blanket, perhaps, in the wind-blown wagon bed, in a wilderness with howling wolves. Danger and a creative, adventuresome spirit filled the pioneer. Stability and safety were high priorities for the settler.

This brings us back to the original question in the title. Which are you today—a pioneer or a settler? Are you a risk taker for the Lord? Do you reach out to the needy, lonely, hurting, tough spots of your community, state or the world? Would you encourage a grandchild or son to forsake the hometown comforts and venture into the inner-city communities of modern society and spread God's word? Are you willing to visit the prisoners, volunteer at the homeless shelter, or speak boldly to a neighbor or clerk in the store about your life with Christ? Do you just cringe, thinking about praying aloud with a hurting friend or group? Is your outreach limited to settling yourself in a pew, dropping a few bucks in the collection plate, saying "Amen" to the pastor's sermon and then dashing off, with family in tow, to the newest pizzeria? Are you a pioneer or a settler?

Perhaps today's pioneers might be identified as those willing to cast their nets and follow Christ's command in Matthew 28:18-20, "Therefore go and make disciples of all nations." They would follow Paul's example, as described in Philippians 1:12-26, when he reminded the Philippians that his prison time, while in chains, provided him an opportunity to proclaim the gospel. Paul anticipated and hoped that he would have sufficient courage in all that happened to him, so that Christ would be exalted. Likewise, I must take a chance to share my belief in God. Onto the interstate and side roads, my light must shine boldly to folk around me in nursing homes, fishing boats, shopping malls, or the garden club—even a small German coffee house or tiny library in the Czech Republic. We each must be visionaries, seeking out new recruits for service where no one has gone before.

Settlers were much more safety conscious. Dangers were always around, but these great-grandparents of the eighteen-hundreds were looking for stability, protection for the family, and "normalcy." Pioneers, on the other hand, were willing to be risk-takers, even with the price of pain, discomfort, and death for themselves and/or their families.

Perhaps you are a settler. You quietly pray but seldom are with a stranger or teen in trouble or a heart-hurting, grief-stricken family from a neighboring country. Stepping out for Christ might seem to be a "no-no" for you. Christ, however, seems clear about making and helping disciples of all ethnic groups and countries, not just of our Sunday morning pew mates. Into what first step of adventuring for Christ could you tiptoe? Be brave and bold. Hint: Send an email or special card to a stranger whom you recognize needs a little hand-holding and love.

Christ today may want us to accept some danger and discomfort as we tell His story. Reaching out, versus privacy and silence, may bring pain and even embarrassment, but let's grow into "God's Risk-Takers."

Won't you join me as we each take that FIRST most difficult step? Be a Pioneer.

CHAPTER SEVENTY-NINE
Rescue of the Potbellied Pig

The alarm interrupted my dreams that Saturday morning. Rolling over, stretching, and shoving back the covers, I popped out of bed. The room was a tad dark. Flashing lightning peeked through the shades, and thunder, at low volume, replaced the usual quiet.

Nine and one-half hours of sleep, broken only with a couple of short, middle of the night jaunts to the bathroom, surprised me. God was good that evening. I was ready to tackle the day's challenges. Too often, my sleep was interrupted with thirty to sixty minutes of open eyes, as I squirmed around under the covers, trying to return to dreamland.

Glancing at the news reports on my phone, my eyes stopped and moved in reverse. What did I just read? "Potbellied pig rescued." Hog Haven Farm, located near Denver, Colorado, rescues these mini pigs which have been abandoned, abused, neglected, or are about to be slaughtered. They apparently rehabilitate them and then find new homes for these little porkers. In fact, Hog Haven staff even provide support and education for future mini pig owners.

Could that be possible? "Who in the world would want to save a pig?" I thought. Pigs are for pork chops, bacon, or perhaps for sloshing around in mud puddles. Certainly, there must be a mistake. Goodness! My grandfather used to raise pigs near Ellensburg, Washington. Who in the world would want to hug such an awkward, tubby, big-nosed, ugly beast?

Evidently many people are willing to adopt these animals, which are allegedly very intelligent and can be housebroken. Word has it that pigs are also able to express their fondness for their owners, much like a kitty or puppy might do. Somehow a stiff-haired pig cuddled on my lap or licking my face does not bring warm thoughts.

As I nibbled on breakfast that morning, I thought that perhaps I was being a bit doubtful about the true nature of this little creature. After all, God created this species, and it must have value in His eyes.

Proverbs 12:10 reminds us, "The righteous care for the needs of their animals . . ." All animals deserve compassion and kindness, but I guess I was a bit reluctant to open wide my front door, inviting Porky Pig onto my couch.

Reflecting over several days, I thought about homeless people. Do they not also need to be rescued and relocated to a place where they can receive food, care, and love? What about grumpy humans, or people of all ages who are unable to care for themselves because of illness, disease, or stress? Of course, there are also widows and orphans to whom warm, kindhearted adults need to reach out and help.

After a bit of online searching, I discovered umpteen scripture references to our responsibility for caring for widows, fatherless, or a brother in need. 1 John 3:17 is rather direct. "If anyone has material possessions and sees a brother or sister in need but has not pity on them, how can the love of God be in that person?"

Psalm 82:3-4 gives directions. "Defend the weak and the fatherless; uphold the cause of the poor and the oppressed. Rescue the weak and the needy; deliver them from the hand of the wicked." Humans may not need formal adoption, like these little pigs, but certainly God assumes we will care for others exhibiting a variety of needs.

John 14:15-21 adds another dimension to this little essay. God promises that to those who love him and keep his commands, he will give them support and be an advocate for all time. Christ left to be with His father, but the Holy Spirit is present always. "I will not leave you as orphans; I will come to you" (vs. 18). The Holy Spirit can work through many reading these thoughts today. Paul, in Acts 20:35, says it all. "In everything I (Paul) did, I showed you that by this kind of hard work we must help the weak, remembering the words the Lord Jesus himself said: 'It is more blessed to give than to receive.'"

We never adopted a potbellied pig, but several homeless kitties found their way into our home and hearts. Actually, I have two chairs in my bedroom that show evidence of their presence over the years. It is far more important, though, to ask if there will be evidence supporting the fact each of us cared for other people in tangible ways.

Consider one last thought. Matthew 6:1 has a strong warning. "Be careful not to practice your righteousness in front of others to be seen by them. If you do, you will have no reward from your Father in heaven." Probably, if I announce on social media that I've adopted another homeless cat, the Lord will not scold me, but helping others should be communicated only between the giver and our heavenly Father, who in turn will reward you.

**Perhaps you can both adopt a
Potbellied Pig AND be a servant,
helping people in need.
Go For It**

CHAPTER EIGHTY
Christ Follower + 'ing'

What in the world is Christ Follower + ing? The world is always creating new words for us to explore, and our youth pastor did just that recently.

The occasion was a gathering of senior adults and high school youth during a Sunday morning class. The goal was to help each age group develop a deeper appreciation for our counterparts. Following brunch, prepared by the youth, about fifty gathered at small tables with mixed ages sharing and talking together. As a conclusion for the experiment, Caitlin Billingsley helped us think about our responsibilities as Christians.

This delightful, young leader made my/our minds stumble over some "invented" words, as she challenged us to each become less invisible and more active in our daily lives. Although my adaptation will be different from Caitlin's, she is the creator of this new vocabulary.

As you first attempt to pronounce the words, your tongue will probably stumble. Be brave. Read, say the word, think of the implied meanings, and then incorporate the ideas into your daily life. Let's see what we can create, beginning with our title.

1. **Christ Follower + ing**: We are each to be a Christ Follower. Jesus began his ministry by inviting these early disciples to come follow and become "Fishers of men." It was not just a title. The Lord expected them to follow him daily. Peter, James, and John, for example, were to leave their homes and fishing boats behind. The invitation was to listen to his teaching and to help him as, together, they would lay the foundation for the beginning of the church. They were *Followering*. Christ expected daily action. We, too, must be more than words on a nameplate. We are Christ *Followerings* and working and witnessing daily.

2. **Faith + ing**: "Without faith it is impossible to please God..." (Hebrews 11:6). Christians must have faith and belief in God. That, however, is not the final word. James 2:26b reminds us that, "Faith without deeds is dead." We must practice *faithing*. An active, in-motion, working, *faithing* follower will constantly share his faith with others.
3. **Mature + ing**: Paul, in Romans, reminded the Christians that through baptism they died to sin and were raised from the dead to begin living a new life. New followers are babes in Christ, but they must mature. It is a continual, maturing process through study, and action. Thus, our new word, *matureing*. Consider checking your actions and thoughts to assure spiritual growth is continuing, just like your new plant sitting on the shelf. Continual watering is essential for life and growth for both plants and souls.
4. **Peace + ing**: "Blessed are the peacemakers, for they will be called children of God" (Matthew 5:9). Peace is more than being calm with yourself and your own thoughts. Peacemakers are active, always seeking the truth. These action-oriented humans help negotiate, mediate, arbitrate, and clarify misunderstandings and disagreements. Compromise may slip into that listing. They must be active listeners, able to calm and ease tensions of those experiencing conflict. *Peaceing* is more than just saying, "Peace be with you." *Peaceing* people are active, modeling the love of Christ, and striving to reduce tension rather than being troublemakers. In the process you may experience a few bruises. Then remember Christ. "But he was pierced for our transgressions, he was crushed for our iniquities; the punishment that bought us PEACE was on him, and by his wounds we are healed" (Isaiah 53:5). *Peaceing* is a daily challenge and opportunity to put your love of God to work.
5. **Ordinary + ing**: Christ *followering* people are humble. Their daily actions shun being top-dog, chief of the tribe, or headliners in the daily news. *Ordinarying* followers seek to connect with others, to lift each other up, to get their hands dirty as they scrub pots, visit nursing homes, assist in clearing storm damage, fly a plane searching for lost families,

or cook chili dogs for the basketball team. They get their hands dirty and don't require center stage action. When was the last time you participated in an *ordinarying* service on behalf of others?

6. **Encourage + ing**: Encouraging is a common word, but today we push it just a bit. This action should be part of our basic lifestyle. Our eyes should be alert for opportunities to quietly provide a pat on the back, silent note of appreciation, or a quick smile to the worker in the nursery or first-time youth sponsor. Even leaders need words of encouragement to balance the barrage of complaints and criticism they receive. Sometimes a new Christian stumbles and loses faith. The *encourageing*-oriented follower is present to lend a helping hand.

7. **Doubt + ing:** Today we are using the definition of doubting as more investigating, wondering, looking for understanding and clarification when a person just doesn't understand what the scripture means or the troubles they are experiencing in his life. Every follower should continue *doubting*, to search, query, verify, validate, and check accuracy of information. Satan, working through individuals, is delighted to mislead God's children. "Be alert and of sober mind. Your enemy the devil prowls around like a roaring lion looking for someone to devour. Resist him, standing firm in the faith, because you know that the family of believers throughout the world is undergoing the same kind of sufferings" (1 Peter 5:8-9). Join study groups, search the scriptures for depth of understanding, and pray for clarification. Then share your thoughts and renewal of wisdom with others.

Of course, sincere followers sometimes do experience true doubt or unbelief. Friends must immediately grab the hand of the "doubters." Prayers and gentle conversations can restore the prodigal to God's family.

Today, as you finish reading these thoughts, take a moment to identify which of the seven "plus" words are already a part of your life. Thank God for guiding you as you continue to implement those actions.

BUT also find at least one action that needs the cobwebs brushed off. For this author, *faithing* needs amplification and renewal. Yes, of course I believe and attempt to share my faith with others, but there are moments in my life when my tongue seems glued to the roof of my mouth as I let an opportunity of witnessing slip by.

That is my challenge. What is yours?

Acknowledgments

It is with great joy, that this author has a second opportunity to share thoughts and ideas that reflect her love of God in her life. The scriptures encourage believers to be bold in their expressions of thanks for the gift of hope and a future life with Him.

I am eternally thankful for the many words of support which friends have shared. Their kindness not only encouraged me, but also provided ideas which often sprouted into lessons of help and encouragement for others. I am reminded of Barnabas, who, when he arrived in Jerusalem, as recorded in Acts 11:23, immediately encouraged the new followers to "... remain true to the Lord with all their hearts." Encouragement is a vital part of living for Christ. Hopefully you will be blessed as you explore these bits of wisdom and humor.

Particular words of thanks come to mind, as several individuals provided thoughtful and creative material for the author. Dale Rogers, organist at Westminster Presbyterian Church, assembled a program of music that captured my heart one evening, resulting in the 'Unused, Yellow Safety Hat' essay.

One day Carolyn Crawford related a very touching moment in her life. I appreciate the courage it took that day to share her challenges and blessings.

My heart leaps with joy, as poet Richard Bilinsky, sent me one of his creative collections of words, that then became the heart of "You Have a Choice".

Caitlin Billingsley generously allowed me to include her ingenious use of words, which were part of her presentation to a group of youth and seniors. What a blessing to have a young leader catch my heart and ears that day. As a result, "Christ Follower + ing" ideas found their way into this epistle.

Special thanks to Kimberly Hughes for editing this book. Your ability to step into my head and make the changes sound like me is impressive. Your suggestions improved the readability of this book and I am forever grateful for all your hard work.

Long-time friend, Donna VanderKolk, spent many moments reviewing each essay and providing thoughtful suggestions. My heart sings happy notes, as I think of her helping spirit and gracious and caring comments.

In addition, Mary Lou Aulbert and Donna Hutcherson also willingly shared their editing skills in an effort to make this manuscript as error free and readable as possible. I am grateful for their parts in the team that created *More Ransom Notes*.

Although John Bailey will never see my note of appreciation, as he has since left this world, a story from his challenging life helped produce, "A Jar of Frozen Pears . . ." I know many of you will find a tiny tear forming in the corner of your eye as you reflect on this tough experience in the life of a young man.

Today, as I write this, I'm reminded of the wonderful few moments I had with Mrs. Gayle Boatman that afternoon in Joplin, Missouri. Her sight was minimal, but this eighty-four-year-old was so young at heart. Part of her story is found in "He is Risen". What a joy to visit with a friend from 1953 and re-connect.

A giant 'shout-out' goes to Roger VanderKolk, chief editor and publisher, who patiently guided me through some difficult changes necessary to meet publishing guidelines. He was so calm, kind, but steadfast with his helping hand, as together, we attempted to create a spirit filled collection of essays, that will hopefully brighten your day. Thank you Roger.

Finally, I'd like to mention a dear friend, and wordsmith, Lynn Poling, who continually offered assistance and support when I struggled with refinement of ideas and thoughts.

As you read and reflect on these various scenarios, my hope is your life will be blessed and recharged. The joy of being a follower of the King of Kings must shine forth brightly.

Join me as we "Walk With Joy."
Kathryn Ann Ransom

Bibliography / Notes / Resources

Chapter 10: Three Choices

The idea for this essay was an article in the winter 2021 edition of the Nature Conservancy Magazine. The survival instinct that is ingrained into animals certainly speaks to the presence of the Almighty Creator. How do animals sense the arrival of winter and then put their survival plans into motion? Simply amazing.

Chapter 72: The Empty Cup

The Barna report referenced in the essay was originally published in 2021 but since that time there have been numerous follow-on discussions regarding the condition of pastors in churches today. As the world continues to get crazier and crazier, it should be expected that the percentage of pastors in the High-Risk category for burnout will continue to increase. Research the latest figures on Barna's website and afterwards, pray for all of our pastors.

Chapter 74: Chlorine to the Rescue

The quote at the beginning of the chapter was taken from *"The Diary of Anne Frank"*. This is an must-read from the life of someone taken too soon from this world in 1945, in the midst of World War 2.

Printed in the USA
CPSIA information can be obtained
at www.ICGtesting.com
JSHW071508210124
55369JS00008B/14